MICROS[...]

Excel 2002

Introductory Course

Mastering and Using

H. Albert Napier
Philip J. Judd
Benjamin Rand

COURSE
TECHNOLOGY

THOMSON LEARNING™

Australia • Canada • Mexico • Singapore • Spain • United Kingdom • United States

**COURSE
TECHNOLOGY**

THOMSON LEARNING

**Mastering and Using Microsoft® Excel 2002
Introductory Course**

by H. Albert Napier, Ph.D. & Philip J. Judd, Benjamin Rand

Managing Editor:
Melissa Ramondetta

Development Editor:
Robin M. Romer, Pale Moon Productions

Product Marketing Manager:
Kim Wood

Product Manager:
Robert Gaggin

Editorial Assistant:
Jodi Dreissig

Production Services:
GEX Publishing Services

Copy Editor:
GEX Publishing Services

Cover Design:
Steve Deschene

Compositor:
GEX Publishing Services

Disclaimer

Course Technology reserves the right to revise this publication and make changes from time to time in its content without notice.

ISBN 0-619-05829-3

What's New in Excel 2002

Office XP

- ► Streamlined, flatter look
- ► Multiple task panes containing command shortcuts
- ► Ask A Question Box Help tool
- ► Smart Tags
- ► AutoCorrect Options
- ► Revised Office Clipboard
- ► Paste Options
- ► Route documents for review with tracked changes via e-mail
- ► Speech Recognition
- ► Improved "crash" recovery features
- ► Search task pane
- ► Digital signatures for documents routed over the Internet

Excel 2002

- ► Query data directly from Web pages and XML files
- ► Import data from a variety of sources, including databases, OLAP data sources, and SQL Server
- ► Function arguments displayed in ScreenTips as functions entered
- ► Function Wizard uses natural language query to help find best function available
- ► Cut-and-paste function examples from Help into a worksheet
- ► Expanded AutoSum functionality includes commonly used functions such as MIN, MAX, and AVERAGE
- ► Formula evaluator shows results of nested formulas
- ► Formula error checking
- ► Color-coded worksheet tabs
- ► Smart tags for paste, fill, insert, and formula checking
- ► Border drawing to create complex outline borders
- ► AutoRepublish Excel data to the Web
- ► Open and save XML files
- ► Speech playback of cell content
- ► Graphics can be inserted into headers and footers for printing
- ► Merge and unmerge cells with a Format toolbar button
- ► Links Management

Napier & Judd

In their over 50 years of combined experience, Al Napier and Phil Judd have developed a tested, realistic approach to mastering and using application software. As both academics and corporate trainers, Al and Phil have the unique ability to help students by teaching them the skills necessary to compete in today's complex business world.

H. Albert Napier, Ph.D. is the Director of the Center on the Management of Information Technology and Professor in the Jesse H. Jones Graduate School of Management at Rice University. In addition, Al is a principal of Napier & Judd, Inc., a consulting company and corporate trainer in Houston, Texas, that has trained more than 120,000 people in computer applications.

Philip J. Judd is a former instructor in the Management Department and the Director of the Research and Instructional Computing Service at the University of Houston. Phil now dedicates himself to consulting and corporate training as a principal of Napier & Judd, Inc.

Philip J. Judd

H. Albert Napier, Ph.D.

Preface

At Course Technology, we believe that technology will change the way people teach and learn. Today millions of people are using personal computers in their everyday lives—both as tools at work and for recreational activities. As a result, the personal computer has revolutionized the ways in which people interact with each other. The *Mastering and Using* series combines the following distinguishing features to allow people to do amazing things with their personal computers.

Distinguishing Features

All the textbooks in the *Mastering and Using* series share several key pedagogical features:

Case Project Approach. In their more than twenty years of business and corporate training and teaching experience, Napier & Judd have found that students are more enthusiastic about learning a software application if they can see its real-world relevance. The textbook provides bountiful business-based profiles, exercises, and projects. It also emphasizes the skills most in demand by employers.

Comprehensive and Easy to Use. There is thorough coverage of new features. The narrative is clear and concise. Each unit or chapter thoroughly explains the concepts that underlie the skills and procedures. We explain not just the *how*, but the *why*.

Step-by-Step Instructions and Screen Illustrations. All examples in this text include step-by-step instructions that explain how to complete the specific task. Full-color screen illustrations are used extensively to provide students with a realistic picture of the software application feature.

Extensive Tips and Tricks. The authors have placed informational boxes in the margin of the text. These boxes of information provide students with the following helpful tips:

▶ *Quick Tip.* Extra information provides shortcuts on how to perform common business-related functions.

▶ *Caution Tip.* This additional information explains how a mistake occurs and provides tips on how to avoid making similar mistakes in the future.

▶ *Menu Tip.* Additional explanation on how to use menu commands to perform application tasks.

▶ *Mouse Tip.* Further instructions on how to use the mouse to perform application tasks.

▶ *Task Pane Tip.* Additional information on using task pane shortcuts.

▶ *Internet Tip.* This information incorporates the power of the Internet to help students use the Internet as they progress through the text.

▶ *Design Tip.* Hints for better presentation designs (found in the PowerPoint chapters).

End-of-Chapter Materials. Each book in the *Mastering and Using* series places a heavy emphasis on providing students with the opportunity to practice and reinforce the skills they are learning through extensive exercises. Each chapter has a summary, commands review, concepts review, skills review, and case projects so that the students can master the material by doing. For more information on each of the end-of-chapter elements see page ix of the How to Use This Book section in this preface.

Appendices. Mastering and Using series contains three appendices to further help students prepare to be successful in the classroom or in the workplace. Appendix A teaches students to work with Windows 2000. Appendix B illustrates how to format letters; how to insert a mailing notation; how to format envelopes (referencing the U.S. Postal Service documents); how to format interoffice memorandums; and how to key a formal outline. It also lists popular style guides and describes proofreader's marks. Appendix C describes the new Office XP speech recognition features.

Microsoft Office User Specialist (MOUS) Certification.

What does this logo mean? It means this courseware has been approved by the Microsoft® Office User Specialist Program to be among the finest available for learning Microsoft

Office XP, Microsoft Word 2002, Microsoft Excel 2002, Microsoft PowerPoint® 2002, and Microsoft Access 2002. It also means that upon completion of this courseware, you may be prepared to become a Microsoft Office User Specialist.

What is a Microsoft Office User Specialist? A Microsoft Office User Specialist is an individual who has certified his or her skills in one or more of the Microsoft Office desktop applications of Microsoft Word, Microsoft Excel, Microsoft PowerPoint®, Microsoft Outlook® or Microsoft Access, or in Microsoft Project. The Microsoft Office User Specialist Program typically offers certification exams at the "Core" and "Expert" skill levels. The Microsoft Office User Specialist Program is the only Microsoft approved program in the world for certifying proficiency in Microsoft Office desktop applications and Microsoft Project. This certification can be a valuable asset in any job search or career advancement.

More Information: To learn more about becoming a Microsoft Office User Specialist, visit *www.mous.net*. To purchase a Microsoft Office User Specialist certification exam, visit *www.DesktopIQ.com*.

SCANS. In 1992, the U.S. Department of Labor and Education formed the Secretary's Commission on Achieving Necessary Skills, or SCANS, to study the kinds of competencies and skills that workers must have to succeed in today's marketplace. The results of the study were published in a document entitled *What Work Requires of Schools: A SCANS Report for America 2000.* The in-chapter and end-of-chapter exercises in this book are designed to meet the criteria outlined in the SCANS report and thus help prepare students to be successful in today's workplace.

Instructional Support

All books in the *Mastering and Using* series are supplemented with an **Instructor's Resource Kit.** This is a CD-ROM that contains lesson plans with teaching materials and preparation suggestions, along with tips for implementing instruction and assessment ideas; a suggested syllabus; and SCANS workplace know how. The CD also contains:

- ► Career Worksheets
- ► Evaluation Guidelines
- ► Hands-on Solutions
- ► Individual Learning Strategies
- ► Internet Behavior Contract
- ► Lesson Plans
- ► Portfolio Guidelines
- ► PowerPoint Presentations
- ► Solution Files
- ► Student Data Files
- ► Teacher Training Notes
- ► Test Questions
- ► Transparency Graphics Files

ExamView® This textbook is accompanied by ExamView, a powerful testing software package that allows instructors to create and administer printed, computer (LAN-based), and Internet exams. ExamView includes hundreds of questions that correspond to the topics covered in this text, enabling students to generate detailed study guides that include page references for further review. The computer-based and Internet testing components allow students to take exams at their computers, and also save the instructor time by grading each exam automatically.

MyCourse.com. MyCourse.com is an online syllabus builder and course-enhancement tool. Hosted by Course Technology, MyCourse.com is designed to reinforce what you already are teaching. It also adds value to your course by providing content that corresponds with your text. MyCourse.com is flexible: choose how you want to organize the material, by date or by class session; or don't do anything at all, and the material is automatically organized by chapter. Add your own materials, including hyperlinks, assignments, announcements, and course content. If you're using more than one textbook, you can even build a course that includes all your Course Technology texts—in one easy-to-use site! Start building your own course today…just go to *www.mycourse.com/instructor*

Student Support

Data Disk. To use this book, students must have the Data Disk. Data Files needed to complete exercises in the text are contained on the Review Pack CD-ROM. These files can be copied to a hard drive or posted to a network drive.

How to Use This Book

Learning Objectives — A quick reference of the major topics learned in the chapter

Case profile — Realistic scenarios that show the real-world application of the material being covered

Chapter Overview — A concise summary of what will be learned in the chapter

Clear step-by-step directions explain how to complete the specific task

Caution Tip — This additional information explains how a mistake occurs and provides tips on how to avoid making similar mistakes in the future

Task Pane Tip — Additional information about using task pane shortcuts

Quick Tip — Extra information provides shortcuts on how to perform common business-related functions

Internet Tip — Information to help students incorporate the power of the Internet as they progress through the text

Mouse Tip — Further instructions on how to use the mouse to perform application tasks

Design Tip — Hints for better presentation designs (found in only the PowerPoint chapters)

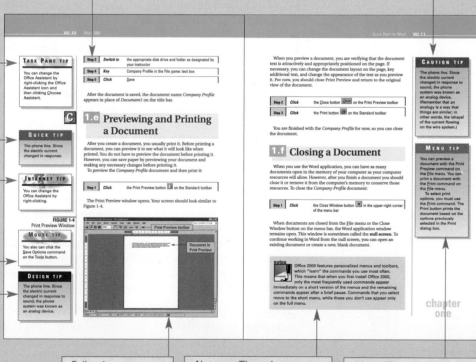

Full-color screen illustrations provide a realistic picture to the student

Notes — These boxes provide necessary information to assist you in completing the activities

Menu Tip — Additional explanation on how to use menu commands to perform application tasks

End-of-Chapter Material

Concepts Review — Multiple choice and true or false questions help assess how well the student has learned the chapter material

Summary — Reviews key topics discussed in the chapter

Commands Review — Provides a quick reference and reinforcement tool on multiple methods for performing actions discussed in the chapter

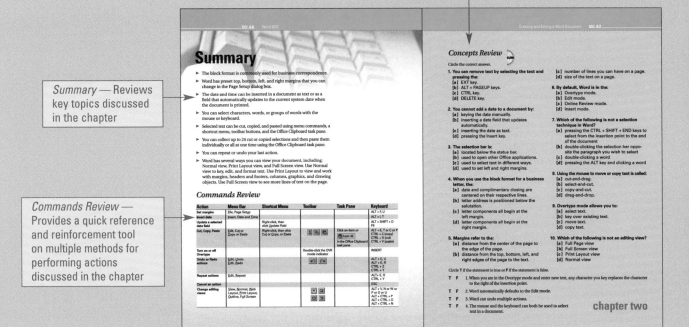

Skills Review — Hands-on exercises provide the ability to practice the skills just learned in the chapter

Case Projects — Asks the student to synthesize the material learned in the chapter and complete an office assignment

SCANS icon — Indicates that the exercise or project meets SCANS competencies and prepares the student to be successful in today's workplace

MOUS Certification icon — Indicates that the exercise or project meets Microsoft's certification objectives that prepare the student for the MOUS exam

Internet Case Projects — Allow the student to practice using the World Wide Web

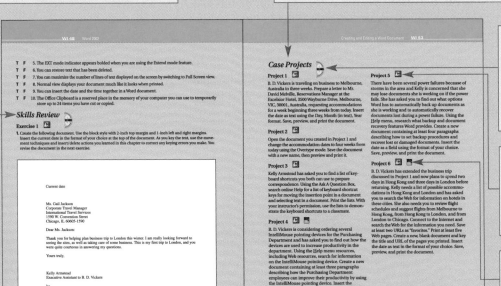

Acknowledgments

We would like to thank and express our appreciation to the many fine individuals who have contributed to the completion of this book. No book is possible without the motivation and support of an editorial staff. Therefore, we wish to acknowledge with great appreciation the project team at Course Technology: Melissa Ramondetta, managing editor; Robert Gaggin, product manager; and Jodi Dreissig, editorial assistant. Our appreciation also goes to Robin Romer for managing the developmental editing of this series. In addition, we want to acknowledge the team at GEX for their production work, especially Karla Russell, Kendra Neville, Michelle Olson, and Angel Lesiczka.

We are very appreciative of the personnel at Napier & Judd, Inc., who helped to prepare this book. We acknowledge, with great appreciation, the assistance provided by Ollie Rivers and Nancy Onarheim in preparing and checking the many drafts of the Office unit and the Appendixes of this book.

We gratefully acknowledge the work of Benjamin Rand for writing the Excel unit for this series.

H. Albert Napier
Philip J. Judd

Thanks go to my wife Erika, who was so supportive throughout the writing of this book (I think her exact words were, "Oh no, not again"). More thanks to my boys who had to wait too many times for Daddy to finish working. Thanks for being so patient—it's wrestle time!

I was extremely fortunate to be paired with Kitty again on this venture. Thanks for all your suggestions, input, help, and hard work. Thanks also to the team at Course Technology for having me back and for their support and encouragement.

Benjamin Rand

Contents

APPENDIX ——————————————————————————— AP 1

Microsoft Office XP

Getting Started with Microsoft Office XP

Chapter Overview

Microsoft Office XP provides the ability to enter, record, analyze, display, and present any type of business information. In this chapter, you learn about the capabilities of Microsoft Office XP, including its computer hardware and operating system requirements and elements common to all its applications. You also learn how to open and close those applications and get Help.

LEARNING OBJECTIVES

- ► Describe Microsoft Office XP
- ► Determine hardware and operating system requirements
- ► Identify common elements of Office applications
- ► Start Office applications
- ► Get Help in Office applications
- ► Close Office applications

chapter one

notes

This book assumes that you have little or no knowledge of Microsoft Office XP but that you have worked with personal computers and are familiar with Microsoft Windows 2000 or Windows 98 operating systems.

1.a What Is Microsoft Office XP?

Microsoft Office XP is a software suite (or package) that contains a combination of software applications you use to create text documents, analyze numbers, create presentations, manage large files of data, and create Web pages.

The **Word 2002** software application provides you with word processing capabilities. **Word processing** is the preparation and production of text documents such as letters, memorandums, and reports. **Excel 2002** is software you use to analyze numbers with worksheets (sometimes called spreadsheets) and charts and to perform other tasks such as sorting data. A **worksheet** is a grid of columns and rows in which you enter labels and data. A **chart** is a visual or graphical representation of worksheet data. With Excel, you can create financial budgets, reports, and a variety of other forms.

PowerPoint 2002 software is used to create a **presentation**, or collection of slides. A **slide** is the presentation output (actual 35mm slides, transparencies, computer screens, or printed pages) that can contain text, charts, graphics, audio, and video. You can use PowerPoint slides to create a slide show on a computer attached to a projector, to broadcast a presentation over the Internet or company intranet, and to create handout materials for a presentation.

Access 2002 provides database management capabilities, enabling you to store and retrieve a large amount of data. A **database** is a collection of related information. A phone book and an address book are common examples of databases you use every day. Other examples of databases include a price list, school registration information, or an inventory. You can query (or search) an Access database to answer specific questions about the stored data. For example, you can determine which customers in a particular state had sales in excess of a particular value during the month of June.

Outlook 2002 is a **personal information manager** that provides tools for sending and receiving e-mail as well as maintaining a calendar, contacts list, journal, electronic notes, and electronic "to do" list. The **FrontPage 2002** application is used to create and manage Web sites.

QUICK TIP

Office contains a variety of new features designed to minimize the impact of system crashes and freezes, such as one-click save in case of a system crash, timed recoveries, a new document recovery task pane, the Hang Manager, and a new corrupt document recovery feature.

chapter
one

notes

For the remainder of this book, Microsoft Office XP may be called Office. Rather than include the words *Microsoft* and *2002* each time the name of an application is used, the text refers to the respective software package as Word, Excel, PowerPoint, Access, or Outlook.

A major advantage of using the Office suite is the ability to share data between the applications. For example, you can include a portion of an Excel worksheet or chart in a Word document, use an outline created in a Word document as the starting point for a PowerPoint presentation, import an Excel worksheet into Access, and merge names and addresses from an Outlook Address Book with a Word letter.

1.b Hardware and Operating System Requirements

You can install Office applications on computers using the Windows 2000, Windows 98, or Windows NT Workstation 4.0 (with Service Pack 6a installed) operating systems. Office XP applications do not run in the Windows 95, Windows 3.x or the Windows NT Workstation 3.5 environments.

You can install Office on a "x86" computer with a Pentium processor, at least 32 MB of RAM for Windows 98 or 64 MB of RAM for Windows 2000, a CD-ROM drive, Super VGA, 256-color video, Microsoft Mouse, Microsoft IntelliMouse, or another pointing device, a 28,800 (or higher) baud modem, and 350 MB of hard disk space. To access certain features you should have a multimedia computer, e-mail software, and a Web browser. For detailed information on installing Office, see the documentation that comes with the software.

1.c Common Elements of Office Applications

Office applications share many technical features that make it easier for Information Technology (IT) Departments in organizations to manage their Office software installations. Additionally, the Office applications share many features that enable users to move seamlessly between applications and learn one way to perform common tasks, such as creating, saving, and printing documents or moving and copying data.

Office applications share many common elements, making it easier for you to work efficiently in any application. A **window** is a rectangular area on your screen in which you view a software application, such as Excel. All the Office application windows have a similar look and arrangement of shortcuts, menus, and toolbars. In addition, they share many features—such as a common dictionary to check spelling in your work, identical menu commands, toolbar buttons, shortcut menus, and keyboard shortcuts to perform tasks such as copying data from one location to another.

notes You learn more about the common elements of the Office applications in later chapters of this unit or in specific application units.

Figure 1-1 shows many of the common elements in the Office application windows.

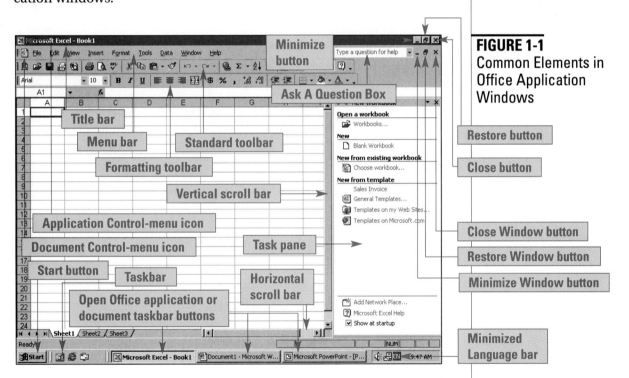

FIGURE 1-1
Common Elements in Office Application Windows

Title Bar

The application **title bar** at the top of the window includes the application Control-menu icon, the application name, the filename of the active document, and the Minimize, Restore (or Maximize), and Close buttons.

The **application Control-menu** icon, located in the upper-left corner of the title bar, displays the Control menu. The Control menu commands manage the application window, and typically include commands such

chapter
one

as Restore, Move, Size, Minimize, Maximize, and Close. Commands that are currently available appear in a dark color. You can view the Control menu by clicking the Control-menu icon or by holding down the ALT key and then pressing the SPACEBAR key.

The **Minimize** button, near the right corner of the title bar reduces the application window to a taskbar button. The **Maximize** button, to the right of the Minimize button, enlarges the application window to fill the entire screen viewing area above the taskbar. If the window is already maximized, the Restore button appears in its place. The **Restore** button reduces the application window to a smaller size on your screen. The **Close** button, located in the right corner of the title bar, closes the application and removes it from the computer's memory.

Menu Bar

The **menu bar** is a special toolbar located at the top of the window below the title bar and contains the menus for the application. A **menu** is list of commands. The menus common to Office applications are File, Edit, View, Insert, Format, Tools, Window, and Help. Other menus vary between applications.

The **document Control-menu** icon, located below the application Control-menu icon, contains the Restore, Move, Size, Minimize, Maximize, and Close menu commands for the document window. You can view the document Control menu by clicking the Control-menu icon or by holding down the ALT key and pressing the HYPHEN (-) key.

The **Minimize Window** button reduces the document window to a title-bar icon inside the document area. It appears on the menu bar below the Minimize button in Excel and PowerPoint. (Word documents open in their own application window and use the Minimize button on the title bar.)

The **Maximize Window** button enlarges the size of the document window to cover the entire application display area and share the application title bar. It appears on the title-bar icon of a minimized Excel workbook or PowerPoint presentation. (Word documents automatically open in their own application window and use the Maximize button on the title bar.) If the window is already maximized, the Restore Window button appears in its place.

The **Restore Window** button changes the size of the document window to a smaller sized window inside the application window. It appears in the menu bar to the right of the Minimize Window button in Excel and PowerPoint. (Word documents automatically open in their own application Window and use the Restore button on the title bar.)

The **Close Window** button closes the document and removes it from the memory of the computer. It appears in the menu bar to the right of the Restore Window or Maximize Window button.

Default Toolbars

The **Standard** and **Formatting toolbars**, located one row below the menu bar, contain a set of icons called buttons. The toolbar buttons represent commonly used commands and are mouse shortcuts that enable you to perform tasks quickly. In addition to the Standard and Formatting toolbars, each application has several other toolbars available. You can customize toolbars by adding or removing buttons and commands.

When the mouse pointer rests on a toolbar button, a **ScreenTip** appears, identifying the name of the button. ScreenTips are also provided as part of online Help to describe a toolbar button, a dialog box option, or a menu command.

Scroll Bars

The vertical scroll bar appears on the right side of the document area. The **vertical scroll bar** is used to view various parts of the document by moving or scrolling the document up or down. It includes scroll arrows and a scroll box. The horizontal scroll bar appears near the bottom of the document area. The **horizontal scroll bar** is used to view various parts of the document by moving or scrolling the document left or right. It includes scroll arrows and a scroll box.

Ask A Question Box

The **Ask A Question Box** is a help tool alternative to the Office Assistant that appears on the menu bar of every Office application. The Ask A Question Box is used to quickly key a help question in plain English and then view a list of relevant Help topics.

Task Pane

Office XP includes a **task pane** feature, a pane of shortcuts, which opens on the right side of the application window. The contents of the task pane vary with the application and the activities being performed. For example, task pane shortcuts can be used to create new Office documents, format Word documents or PowerPoint presentations, or perform a Word mail merge. The task pane can be displayed or hidden as desired.

Taskbar

The **taskbar,** located across the bottom of the Windows desktop, includes the Start button and buttons for each open Office document. The **Start button,** located at the left end of the taskbar, displays the Start menu or list of tasks you can perform and applications you can use.

You can switch between documents, close documents and applications, and view other items, such as the system time and printer status, with buttons or icons on the taskbar. If you are using Windows 2000 or Windows 98, other toolbars, such as the Quick Launch toolbar, may also appear on the taskbar.

QUICK TIP

The **Office Assistant** is an interactive, animated graphic that appears in the Office application windows. When you activate the Office Assistant, a balloon-style dialog box opens to display options for searching online Help by topic. The Office Assistant may also automatically offer suggestions when you begin certain tasks. You can customize the Office Assistant by changing the animated graphic image or turning on or off various options. Any customization is shared by all Office applications.

chapter
one

1.d Starting Office Applications

You access the Office applications through the Windows desktop. The Windows operating system software is automatically loaded into the memory of your computer when you turn on your computer. After turning on your computer, the Windows desktop appears.

You begin by using the Start button on the taskbar to view the Start menu and open the Excel application. To use the Start button to open the Excel application:

Step 1	*Click*	the Start button 🏁Start on the taskbar
Step 2	*Point to*	Programs
Step 3	*Click*	Microsoft Excel on the Programs menu

The Excel software is placed into the memory of your computer and the Excel window opens. Your screen should look similar to Figure 1-1.

notes You may sometimes use the keyboard to use Office application features. This book lists all keys, such as the TAB key, in uppercase letters. When the keyboard is used to issue a command, this book lists keystrokes as: Press the ENTER key. When you are to press one key and, while holding down that key, to press another key, this book lists the keystrokes as: Press the SHIFT + F7 keys.

You can open and work in more than one Office application at a time. When Office is installed, two additional commands appear on the Start menu: the Open Office Document command and the New Office Document command. You can use these commands to select the type of document on which you want to work rather than first selecting an Office application. To create a new Word document without first opening the application:

Step 1	*Click*	the Start button 🏁Start on the taskbar
Step 2	*Click*	New Office Document
Step 3	*Click*	the General tab, if necessary

The New Office Document dialog box on your screen should look similar to Figure 1-2. A **dialog box** is a window that contains options for performing specific tasks.

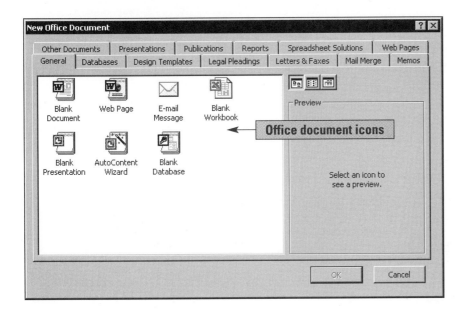

FIGURE 1-2
General Tab in the
New Office Document
Dialog Box

This dialog box provides options for creating different Office documents. **Icons** (or pictures) represent the Office document options; the number of icons available depends on the Office suite applications you have installed. The icons shown here create a blank Word document, a blank Web page (in Word), an e-mail message (using Outlook or Outlook Express), a blank Excel workbook, a blank PowerPoint presentation, a PowerPoint presentation using the AutoContent Wizard, and a blank Access database. You want to create a blank Word document.

Step 4	*Click*	the Blank Document icon to select it, if necessary

Step 5	*Click*	OK

The Word software is placed in the memory of your computer, the Word application window opens with a blank document. Your screen should look similar to Figure 1-3.

MOUSE TIP

Double-clicking an icon is the same as clicking the icon once to select it and then clicking the OK button.

chapter
one

FIGURE 1-3
Word Application Window

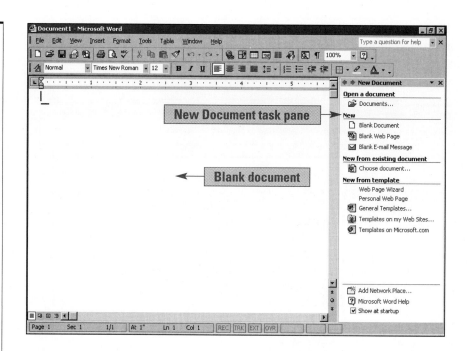

MENU TIP

The task pane containing shortcuts to create new documents or open existing documents opens by default when you launch a Word, Excel, or PowerPoint application. However, if you create or open another document in the same application, the task pane automatically hides. To display it again, click the Task Pane command on the View menu.

Next you open a blank presentation. To open the PowerPoint application:

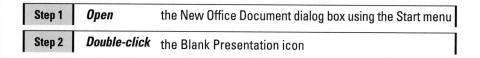

| Step 1 | *Open* | the New Office Document dialog box using the Start menu |
| Step 2 | *Double-click* | the Blank Presentation icon |

Your screen should look similar to Figure 1-4.

FIGURE 1-4
Blank PowerPoint
Presentation

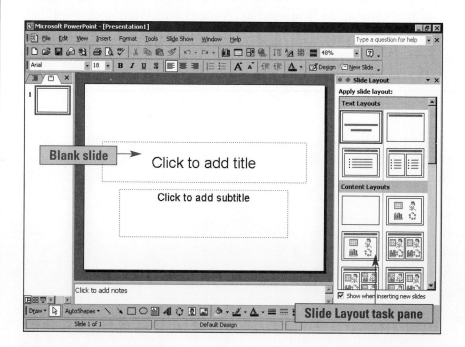

You can also open an Office application by opening an existing Office document from the Start menu. To open an existing Access database:

Step 1	*Click*	the Start button [Start] on the taskbar
Step 2	*Click*	Open Office Document
Step 3	*Click*	the Look in: list arrow in the Open Office Document dialog box
Step 4	*Switch to*	the disk drive and folder where the Data Files are stored
Step 5	*Double-click*	*International Sales*

The Access application window and Database window that open on your screen should look similar to Figure 1-5.

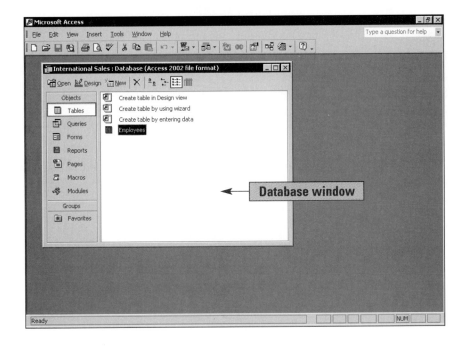

FIGURE 1-5
International Sales
Database in Access
Window

QUICK TIP

You can have multiple Excel workbooks, PowerPoint presentations, and Word documents open at one time. The number of documents, workbooks, and presentations you can have open at one time is determined by your computer's resources. You can open only one Access database at a time.

You can switch between open Office documents by clicking the appropriate taskbar button. If multiple windows are open, the **active window** has a dark blue title bar. All inactive windows have a gray title bar. To switch to the Excel workbook and then the Word document:

Step 1	*Click*	the Excel button on the taskbar
Step 2	*Observe*	that the Excel application window and workbook are now visible
Step 3	*Click*	the Word Document1 button on the taskbar
Step 4	*Observe*	that the Word application window and document are now visible

chapter
one

1.e Getting Help in Office Applications

You can get help when working in any Office application in several ways. You can use the Help menu, the Help toolbar button, or the F1 key to display the Office Assistant; get context-sensitive help with the What's This command or the SHIFT + F1 keys; or launch your Web browser and get Web-based help from Microsoft. You can also key a help question in the Ask A Question Box on the menu bar.

Using the Ask A Question Box

Suppose you want to find out how to use keyboard shortcuts in Word. To get help for keyboard shortcuts using the Ask A Question Box:

Step 1	*Verify*	that the Word document is the active window
Step 2	*Click*	in the Ask A Question Box
Step 3	*Key*	keyboard shortcuts
Step 4	*Press*	the ENTER key

A list of help topics related to keyboard shortcut keys appears. Your list should look similar to the one shown in Figure 1-6.

FIGURE 1-6
List of Help Topics

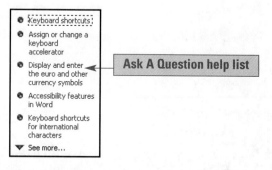

If you want to view the detailed help for any topic, simply click that topic in the list.

| Step 5 | *Press* | the ESC key |
| Step 6 | *Click* | in the document area to deselect the Ask A Question Box |

Using the Help Menu

The Help menu provides commands you can use to view the Office Assistant or Help window, show or hide the Office Assistant, connect to the Microsoft Web site, get context-sensitive help for a menu command or toolbar button, detect and repair font and template files, and view licensing information for the Office application. To review the Help menu commands:

Step 1	Click	Help on the menu bar

The Help menu on your screen should look similar to Figure 1-7.

FIGURE 1-7
Help Menu

Step 2	Observe	the menu commands
Step 3	Click	in the document area outside the menu to close the Help menu

Using What's This?

You can get context-sensitive help for a menu command or toolbar button using the What's This? command on the Help menu. This command changes the mouse pointer to a help pointer, a white mouse pointer with a large black question mark. When you click a toolbar button or menu command with the help pointer, a brief ScreenTip help message appears, describing the command or toolbar button. You can quickly change the mouse pointer to a help pointer by pressing the SHIFT + F1 keys.

To view the help pointer and view a ScreenTip help message for a toolbar button:

Step 1	Press	the SHIFT + F1 keys
Step 2	Observe	the help mouse pointer with the attached question mark
Step 3	Click	the Save button 🖫 on the Standard toolbar
Step 4	Observe	the ScreenTip help message describing the Save button

QUICK TIP

You can click the Help button on the title bar in any dialog box to convert the mouse pointer to a What's This help pointer.

chapter
one

| Step 5 | *Press* | the ESC key to close the ScreenTip help message |

1.f Closing Office Applications

There are many ways to close the Access, Excel, and PowerPoint applications (or the Word application with a single document open) and return to the Windows desktop. You can:

- double-click the application Control-menu icon on the title bar.
- click the application Close button on the title bar.
- right-click the application button on the taskbar to display a short-cut menu and then click the Close command.
- press the ALT + F4 keys.
- click the Exit command on the File menu to close Office applications (no matter how many Word documents are open).

To close the Excel application from the taskbar:

| Step 1 | *Right-click* | the Excel button on the taskbar |
| Step 2 | *Click* | Close |

You can close multiple applications at one time from the taskbar by selecting the application buttons using the CTRL key and then using the shortcut menu. To close the PowerPoint and Access applications at one time:

Step 1	*Press & hold*	the CTRL key
Step 2	*Click*	the PowerPoint button and then the Access button on the taskbar
Step 3	*Release*	the CTRL key and observe that both buttons are selected (pressed in)
Step 4	*Right-click*	the PowerPoint or Access button
Step 5	*Click*	Close

Both applications close, leaving only the Word document open. To close the Word document using the menu:

Step 1	*Verify*	that the Word application window is maximized
Step 2	*Click*	File
Step 3	*Click*	Exit

Summary

► The Word application provides word processing capabilities for the preparation of text documents, such as letters, memorandums, and reports.

► The Excel application provides the ability to analyze numbers in worksheets and for creating financial budgets, reports, charts, and forms.

► The PowerPoint application is used to create presentation slides and audience handouts.

► You use the Access databases to store and retrieve collections of data.

► The Outlook application helps you send and receive e-mail and maintain a calendar, "to do" lists, and the names and addresses of contacts—and perform other information management tasks.

► One major advantage of using the Office suite applications is the ability to integrate the applications by sharing information between them.

► Another advantage of the Office suite applications is that they share a number of common elements such as window features, shortcuts, toolbars, and menu commands.

► You can start the Office suite applications from the Programs submenu on the Start menu and from the Open Office Document or New Office Document commands on the Start menu.

► To close the Office applications, you can double-click the application Control-menu icon, single-click the application Close button on the title bar, right-click the application button on the taskbar, press the ALT + F4 keys, or click the Exit command on the File menu.

► To get help in an Office application, you can click commands on the Help menu, press the F1 key or the SHIFT + F1 keys, or click the Microsoft Help button on the Standard toolbar.

chapter one

Concepts Review

Circle the correct answer.

1. **ScreenTips do not provide:**
   [a] the name of a button on a toolbar.
   [b] help for options in a dialog box.
   [c] context-sensitive help for menu commands or toolbar buttons.
   [d] access to the Office Assistant.

2. **To manage a Web site, you can use:**
   [a] Outlook.
   [b] FrontPage.
   [c] Excel.
   [d] Publisher.

3. **The title bar contains the:**
   [a] document Control-menu icon.
   [b] Close Window button.
   [c] Standard toolbar.
   [d] application and document name.

4. **The Excel application is best used to:**
   [a] prepare financial reports.
   [b] maintain a list of tasks to accomplish.
   [c] prepare text documents.
   [d] manage Web sites.

5. **A major advantage of using Office applications is the ability to:**
   [a] store mailing lists.
   [b] analyze numbers.

   [c] share information between applications.
   [d] sort data.

6. **Word processing is used primarily to:**
   [a] create presentation slides.
   [b] analyze numbers.
   [c] prepare text documents.
   [d] maintain a calendar and "to do" lists.

7. **Right-click means to:**
   [a] press the left mouse button twice rapidly.
   [b] place the mouse pointer on a command or item.
   [c] press and hold down the right mouse button and then move the mouse.
   [d] press the right mouse button and then release it.

8. **You cannot close Office XP applications by:**
   [a] clicking the Exit command on the File menu.
   [b] clicking the Close button on the title bar.
   [c] right-clicking the application button on the taskbar and clicking Close.
   [d] pressing the SHIFT + F4 keys.

Circle **T** if the statement is true or **F** if the statement is false.

T   F   1. You use Excel to create newsletters and brochures.

T   F   2. Word is used to create presentation slides.

T   F   3. The Office Assistant is an interactive graphic used to get online help in Office applications.

T   F   4. Access is used to create and format text.

T   F   5. You can open and work in only one Office application at a time.

T   F   6. When you open multiple documents in an Office application, each document has its own button on the taskbar.

Skills Review

Exercise 1

1. Identify each of the numbered elements of Office application windows in the following figure.

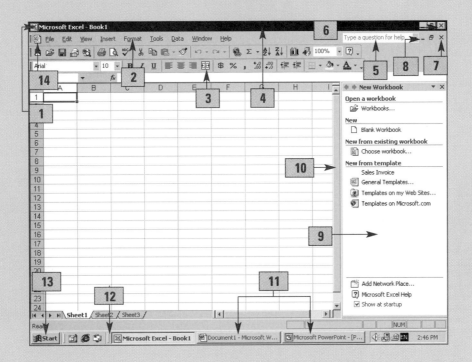

Exercise 2

1. Open the Word application using the Programs command on the Start menu.

2. Close the Word application using the taskbar.

Exercise 3

1. Open the Excel application using the Programs command on the Start menu.

2. Open the PowerPoint application using the Programs command on the Start menu.

3. Open the Access application and the *International Sales* database using the Open Office Document command on the Start menu.

4. Switch to the PowerPoint application using the taskbar button and close it using the Close button on the title bar.

5. Close the Excel and Access applications at the same time using the taskbar.

Exercise 4

1. Create a new, blank Word document using the New Office Document command on the Start menu.

2. Create a new, blank Excel workbook using the New Office Document command on the Start menu.

3. Switch to the Word document using the taskbar and close it using the Close button on the title bar.

4. Close the Excel workbook using the taskbar button.

chapter one

Exercise 5

1. Open the Word application using the Start menu.

2. Show the Office Assistant, if necessary, with a command on the Help menu.

3. Hide the Office Assistant with a shortcut menu.

4. Show the Office Assistant with the Microsoft Word Help button on the Standard toolbar.

5. Search online Help using the search phrase "key text."

6. Click the "Change typing and editing options" link.

7. Review the Help text and then close the Help window.

8. Show the Office Assistant, and then click the Options command on the Office Assistant shortcut menu.

9. Click the Use the Office Assistant check box to remove the check mark and turn off the Office Assistant.

Exercise 6

1. Write a paragraph that describes the different ways to close the Word application.

Exercise 7

1. Open any Office application and use the Ask A Question Box and the keyword "Office Assistant" to search for online Help for information on using the Office Assistant.

2. Write down the instructions for selecting a different Office Assistant graphic image.

Case Projects

Project 1

You are the secretary to the marketing manager of High Risk Insurance, an insurance brokerage firm. The marketing manager wants to know how to open and close the Excel application. Write at least two paragraphs describing different ways to open and close the Excel application. With your instructor's permission, use your written description to show a classmate several ways to open and close the Excel application.

Project 2

You work in the administrative offices of Alma Public Relations and the information management department just installed Office XP on your computer. Your supervisor asks you to write down and describe some of the Office Assistant options. Display the Office Assistant. Right-click the Office Assistant graphic, click the Options command, and view the Options tab in the Office Assistant dialog box. Click the What's This? or Help button on the dialog box title bar and review each option. Write at least three paragraphs describing five Office Assistant options.

Project 3

As the new office manager at Hot Wheels Messenger Service, you are learning to use the Word 2002 application and want to learn more about some of the buttons on the Word toolbars. Open Word and use the What's This? command on the Help menu to review the ScreenTip help for five toolbar buttons. Write a brief paragraph for each button describing how it is used.

Project 4

You are the administrative assistant to the vice president of operations for Extreme Sports, Inc., a sports equipment retailer with stores in several cities in your state. The vice president wants to save time and money by performing business tasks more efficiently. She asks you to think of different ways to perform common business tasks by sharing information between the Office XP applications. Write at least three paragraphs describing how the company can use Word, Excel, PowerPoint, Access, and Outlook to improve efficiency by combining information.

Working with Menus, Toolbars, and Task Panes

Chapter Overview

Office tries to make your work life easier by learning how you work. The personalized menus and toolbars in each application remember which commands and buttons you use and add and remove them as needed. Office has two new tools—task panes and Smart Tags—that provide shortcuts for performing different activities. In this chapter, you learn how to work with the personalized menus and toolbars and how to use task panes and Smart Tags.

LEARNING OBJECTIVES

- ▶ Work with personalized menus and toolbars
- ▶ View, hide, dock, and float toolbars
- ▶ Work with task panes
- ▶ Review Smart Tags

chapter
two

2.a Working with Personalized Menus and Toolbars

A **menu** is a list of commands you use to perform tasks in the Office applications. Some of the commands also have an associated image, or icon, which appears to the left of each command in the menu. Most menus are found on the menu bar located below the title bar in the Office applications. A **toolbar** contains a set of icons (the same icons you see on the menus) called "buttons" that you click with the mouse pointer to quickly execute a menu command.

notes

The activities in this chapter assume the personalized menus and toolbars are reset to their default settings. As you learn about menus and toolbars, task panes, and Smart Tags you are asked to select menu commands and toolbar buttons by clicking them with the mouse pointer. You do not learn how to use the menu command or toolbar button, task pane, or Smart Tags to perform detailed tasks in this chapter. Using these features to perform detailed tasks is covered in the individual application chapters.

When you first install Office and then open an Office application, the menus on the menu bar initially show only a basic set of commands and the Standard and Formatting toolbars contain only a basic set of buttons. These short versions of the menus and toolbars are called **personalized menus and toolbars**. As you work in the application, the commands and buttons you use most frequently are stored in the personalized settings. The first time you select a menu command or toolbar button that is not part of the basic set, that command or button is automatically added to your personalized settings and appears on the menu or toolbar. If you do not use a command for a while, it is removed from your personalized settings and no longer appears on the menu or toolbar. To view the personalized menus and toolbars in PowerPoint:

Step 1	*Click*	the New Office Document command on the Start menu
Step 2	*Click*	the General tab in the New Office Document dialog box, if necessary
Step 3	*Double-click*	the Blank Presentation icon
Step 4	*Click*	Tools on the menu bar
Step 5	*Observe*	the short personalized menu containing only the basic commands

The Tools menu on your screen should look similar to Figure 2-1.

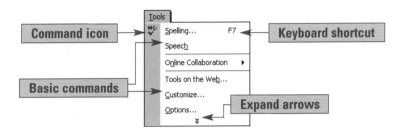

FIGURE 2-1
Personalized Tools Menu

If the command you want to use does not appear on the short personalized menu, you can expand the menu. The fastest way to expand a personalized menu is to double-click the menu command on the menu bar. For example, to quickly expand the Insert menu, you can double-click the Insert command on the menu bar. Another way to expand a menu is to click the Expand arrows that appear at the bottom of the personalized menu when it opens. Finally, after opening a menu, you can pause for a few seconds until the menu automatically expands. To expand the Tools menu:

| Step 1 | *Pause* | until the menu automatically expands *or* click the Expand arrows at the bottom of the menu to expand the menu |

The expanded Tools menu on your screen should look similar to Figure 2-2.

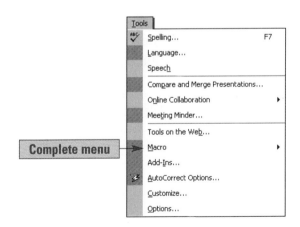

FIGURE 2-2
Expanded Tools Menu

You move a menu command from the expanded menu to the personalized menu simply by selecting it. To add the AutoCorrect Options command to the short personalized Tools menu:

| Step 1 | *Click* | AutoCorrect Options |

Step 2	*Click*	Cancel in the AutoCorrect dialog box to close the dialog box without making any changes
Step 3	*Click*	Tools on the menu bar
Step 4	*Observe*	the updated personalized Tools menu contains the AutoCorrect Options command

The Tools menu on your screen should look similar to Figure 2-3.

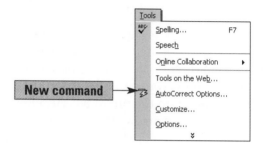

| Step 5 | *Press* | the ESC key twice to close the menu |

The first time you launch most Office applications, the Standard and Formatting toolbars appear on one row below the title bar. In this position, you cannot see all their default buttons. If a toolbar button is not visible, you can resize or reposition one of the toolbars. When the mouse pointer is positioned on a toolbar **move handle** (the gray vertical bar at the left edge of the toolbar), the mouse pointer changes from a white arrow pointer to a **move pointer**, a four-headed black arrow. You can drag the move handle with the move pointer to resize or reposition toolbar. To resize the Formatting toolbar:

| Step 1 | *Move* | the mouse pointer to the move handle on the Formatting toolbar |
| Step 2 | *Observe* | that the mouse pointer becomes a move pointer |

The move pointer on your screen should look similar to Figure 2-4.

FIGURE 2-4
Move Pointer on the
Formatting Toolbar Handle

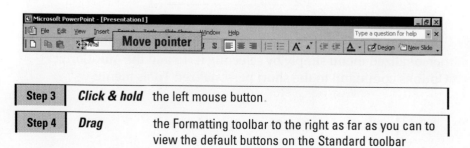

| Step 3 | *Click & hold* | the left mouse button |
| Step 4 | *Drag* | the Formatting toolbar to the right as far as you can to view the default buttons on the Standard toolbar |

Step 5	*Drag*	the Formatting toolbar to the left as far as you can to view the default buttons on the Formatting toolbar
Step 6	*Release*	the mouse button
Step 7	*Observe*	that you now see three buttons on the Standard toolbar

The buttons that don't fit on the displayed area of a toolbar are collected in a Toolbar Options list. The last button on any toolbar, the Toolbar Options button, is used to display the Toolbar Options list. To view the Toolbar Options list:

| Step 1 | *Click* | the Toolbar Options button list arrow ⟩⟩ on the Standard toolbar |
| Step 2 | *Observe* | the default buttons that are not visible on the toolbar |

The Toolbar Options list on your screen should look similar to Figure 2-5.

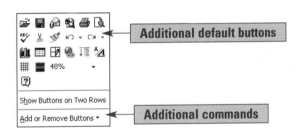

FIGURE 2-5
Toolbar Options List

If you want to display one of the default buttons on a personalized toolbar, you can select it from the Toolbar Options list. To add the Search button to the personalized Standard toolbar:

| Step 1 | *Click* | the Search button 🔍 |
| Step 2 | *Observe* | that the Search button is added to the personalized Standard toolbar |

When you add another button to the personalized Standard toolbar, one of the other buttons might move out of view. This is because of the limited viewing area of the Standard toolbar in its current position. If you want to view all the menu commands instead of a short personalized menu and all the default toolbar buttons on the Standard and Formatting toolbars, you can change options in the Customize dialog box. To view the Customize dialog box:

| Step 1 | *Click* | Tools on the menu bar |

chapter
two

Step 2	*Click*	<u>C</u>ustomize

Step 3	*Click*	the <u>O</u>ptions tab, if necessary

The Customize dialog box on your screen should look similar to Figure 2-6.

FIGURE 2-6
Options Tab in the
Customize Dialog Box

Personalized menus and toolbars options

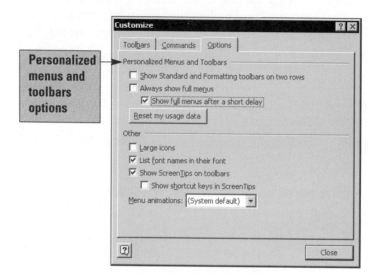

If you reposition the Formatting toolbar below the Standard toolbar, you can view all the default buttons on both toolbars. You can do this by inserting a check mark in the <u>S</u>how Standard and Formatting toolbars on two rows check box. You can insert a check mark in the Always show full me<u>n</u>us check box to view the entire set of menu commands for each menu instead of the short personalized menus. If you do not want the short personalized menus to expand automatically when you pause, you can remove the check mark from the Show f<u>u</u>ll menus after a short delay check box. Then, to show the full menu, you have to double-click the menu or click the expand arrows at the bottom of the menu.

You want to show all the Standard and Formatting toolbar buttons and menu commands.

Step 4	*Click*	the <u>S</u>how Standard and Formatting toolbars on two rows check box to insert a check mark

Step 5	*Click*	the Always show full me<u>n</u>us check box to insert a check mark

Step 6	*Click*	Close to close the dialog box

Step 7	*Observe*	the repositioned and expanded Standard and Formatting toolbars

| Step 8 | Click | Tools to view the entire set of Tools menu commands |
| Step 9 | Press | the ESC key to close the Tools menu |

You can return the menus and toolbars to their initial (or **default**) settings in the Customize dialog box. To open the Customize dialog box and reset the default menus and toolbars:

Step 1	Click	Tools
Step 2	Click	Customize
Step 3	Click	the Options tab, if necessary
Step 4	Remove	the two check marks you just inserted
Step 5	Click	Reset my usage data
Step 6	Click	Yes to confirm you want to reset the menus and toolbars to their default settings
Step 7	Close	the Customize dialog box
Step 8	Observe	that the Tools menu and Standard toolbar are reset to their default settings

2.b Viewing, Hiding, Docking, and Floating Toolbars

Office applications have additional toolbars that you can view when you need them. You can also hide toolbars when you are not using them. You can view or hide toolbars by pointing to the Toolbars command on the View menu and clicking a toolbar name or by using a shortcut menu. A **shortcut menu** is a short list of frequently used menu commands. You view a shortcut menu by pointing to an item on the screen and clicking the right mouse button. This is called right-clicking the item. The commands on shortcut menus vary depending on where you right-click, so that you view only the most frequently used commands for a particular task. An easy way to view or hide toolbars is with a shortcut menu.

 notes Although the PowerPoint application is used to illustrate how to customize toolbars, the same techniques are used to customize toolbars and menus in the Word, Excel, and Access applications.

chapter two

To view the shortcut menu for toolbars:

| Step 1 | *Right-click* | the menu bar, the Standard toolbar, or the Formatting toolbar |
| Step 2 | *Observe* | the shortcut menu and the check marks next to the names of displayed toolbars |

Your shortcut menu should look similar to Figure 2-7.

FIGURE 2-7
Toolbars Shortcut Menu

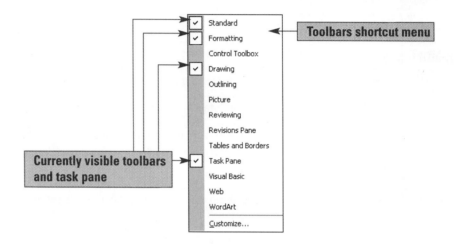

| Step 3 | *Click* | Tables and Borders in the shortcut menu |
| Step 4 | *Observe* | that the Tables and Borders toolbar appears on your screen |

The Tables and Borders toolbar, unless a previous user repositioned it, is visible in its own window near the middle of your screen. When a toolbar is visible in its own window, it is called a **floating toolbar** and you can move and size it with the mouse pointer similar to any window. When a toolbar appears fixed at the screen boundaries, it is called a **docked toolbar**. The menu bar and Standard and Formatting toolbars are examples of docked toolbars because they are fixed below the title bar at the top of the screen. In PowerPoint, the Drawing toolbar is docked at the bottom of the screen above the status bar. You can dock a floating toolbar by dragging its title bar with the mouse pointer to a docking position below the title bar, above the status bar, or at the left and right boundaries of your screen.

To dock the Tables and Borders toolbar below the Standard and Formatting toolbars, if necessary:

| Step 1 | *Click & hold* | the title bar in the Tables and Borders toolbar window |

QUICK TIP

Some of the toolbars that appear on the toolbars shortcut menu vary from one Office application to another.

Step 2	*Observe*	that the mouse pointer becomes a move pointer
Step 3	*Drag*	the toolbar window up slowly until it docks below the Standard and Formatting toolbars
Step 4	*Release*	the mouse button

Similarly, you float a docked toolbar by dragging it away from its docked position toward the middle of the screen. To float the Tables and Borders toolbar, if necessary:

| Step 1 | *Position* | the mouse pointer on the Tables and Borders toolbar move handle until it becomes a move pointer |
| Step 2 | *Drag* | the Tables and Borders toolbar down toward the middle of the screen until it appears in its own window |

When you finish using a toolbar, you can hide it with a shortcut menu. To hide the Tables and Borders toolbar:

| Step 1 | *Right-click* | the Tables and Borders toolbar |
| Step 2 | *Click* | Tables and Borders to remove the check mark and hide the toolbar |

2.c Working with Task Panes

The task pane is a tool with many uses in the Office applications. For example, when you launch Word, Excel, PowerPoint, or Access a new file task pane appears on the right side of the application window. This task pane allows you to create new documents in a variety of ways or open existing documents and replaces the New dialog box found in earlier versions of the Office applications. For example, in the Word application, this task pane is called the New Document task pane and contains hyperlink shortcuts for creating a new document or opening an existing document, creating a blank Web page, sending an e-mail message, choosing an existing document to use as the basis for a new document, and other options. A **hyperlink** is text or a graphic image that you can click to view another page or item. The hyperlink shortcuts in the task pane are colored blue. When you place your mouse pointer on a blue hyperlink shortcut, the mouse pointer changes to a hand with a pointing finger. You can then click the hyperlink shortcut to view the page or option to which the shortcut is linked.

Another way to use a task pane in each of the Office applications is to display the Search task pane and use it to search your local computer

chapter
two

system and network for files based on specific criteria such as keywords in the file text, the file's location, the file type, and the file's name. You can also search for Outlook items using the Search task pane.

To view a blank Word document and the Search task pane:

Step 1	*Start*	the Word application using the Start menu
Step 2	*Click*	<u>F</u>ile on the menu bar
Step 3	*Click*	Search

The Basic Search task pane is now visible. Your screen should look similar to Figure 2-8.

FIGURE 2-8
Basic Search Task
Pane in Word

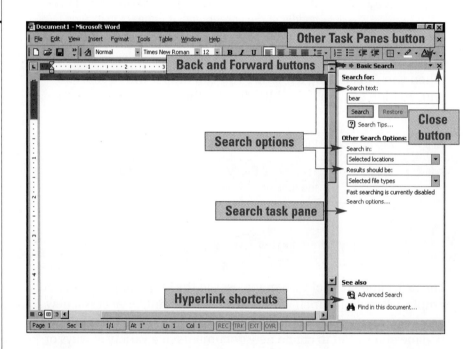

When you have multiple task panes open, you can use the Back and Forward buttons on the task pane title bar to switch between the task panes. To switch from the Basic Search task pane to the New Document task pane:

MOUSE **TIP**

You also can view the Search task pane by clicking the Search button on the Standard toolbar.

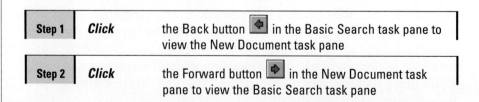

Step 1	*Click*	the Back button ⬅ in the Basic Search task pane to view the New Document task pane
Step 2	*Click*	the Forward button ➡ in the New Document task pane to view the Basic Search task pane

You can key text in the Search text: text box to look for files containing specific text. You can use the Search in: list to select the locations in which to search, and use the Results should be: list to select the file types to search for. If your search criteria are more complex, you can click the Advanced Search link to view the Advanced Search task pane, where you can set additional search criteria such as file attributes called **properties**, or use operators such as "and" to set multiple criteria or "or" to set exclusive criteria.

A task pane appears docked on the right side of the application window by default. You can "float" the task pane in the application window or dock it on the left side of the application window, as you prefer. Like docking a floating toolbar, when you double-click a task pane title bar, it returns to its last docked or floating position. To float the docked task pane:

Step 1	*Double-click* the Basic Search task pane title bar

Step 2	*Observe*	the task pane's new position, floating in the application window

Your screen should look similar to Figure 2-9.

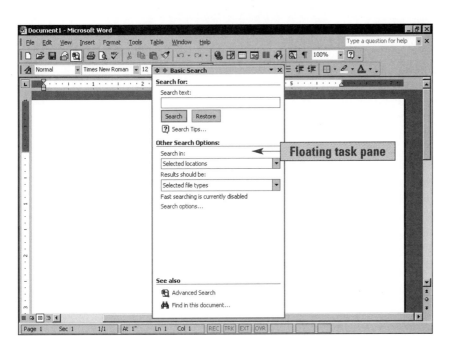

Step 3	*Double-click* the Basic Search task pane title bar

Step 4	*Observe*	that the Basic Search task pane returns to its previous docked position

FIGURE 2-9
Floating Task Pane

chapter
two

You can close the current task pane by clicking the Close button on the task pane title bar. When you close the current task pane, all open task panes are also closed. For example, you currently have the New Document task pane and the Basic Search task pane open. When you close the Basic Search task pane, both task panes are closed. You can view the New Document task pane again with a menu command or toolbar button. To close the Basic Search and New Document task panes and then reopen the New Document task pane:

Step 1	*Click*	the Close button ⊠ on the Basic Search task pane title bar
Step 2	*Observe*	that neither the Basic Search nor the New Document task pane is visible
Step 3	*Click*	File on the menu bar
Step 4	*Click*	New

The New Document task pane opens at the right side of the application window.

2.d Reviewing Smart Tags

Smart Tags are labels used to identify data as a specific type of data. You can use Smart Tags to perform an action in an open Office application instead of opening another application to perform that task. For example, a person's name is one kind of data that can be recognized and labeled with a Smart Tag. Suppose you key a person's name in a Word document and then want to create a contact item for that person in your Outlook Contacts folder. You can use a Smart Tag to create the contact item from Word without opening Outlook.

Smart Tags are represented by an action button and a purple dotted line underneath the text. The Smart Tag options are found in the AutoCorrect dialog box. To view the Smart Tag options in the Word application:

Step 1	*Click*	Tools on the menu bar
Step 2	*Click*	AutoCorrect Options
Step 3	*Click*	the Smart Tags tab in the AutoCorrect dialog box

The AutoCorrect dialog box on your screen should look similar to Figure 2-10.

QUICK TIP

The **Office Shortcut Bar** is a toolbar that you can open and position on your Windows desktop to provide shortcuts to Office applications and tasks. The Office Shortcut Bar can contain buttons for the New Office Document and Open Office Document commands you see on the Start menu, shortcut buttons to create various Outlook items, and buttons to open Office applications installed on your computer. You can access the Office Shortcut Bar with the Microsoft Office Tools command on the Programs menu.

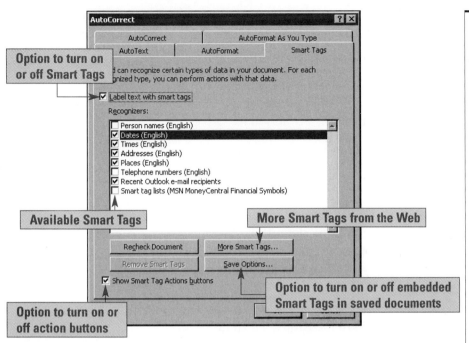

Option to turn on or off Smart Tags

Available Smart Tags

More Smart Tags from the Web

Option to turn on or off embedded Smart Tags in saved documents

Option to turn on or off action buttons

You can turn on or off the Smart Tag feature with the Label text with smart tags check box. You can use the Show Smart Tag Actions buttons check box to turn on or off the Smart Tag action buttons. By default, Smart Tags are embedded in a document when it is saved. You can turn off this feature with the Save Options button. You can also remove the Smart Tags or recheck the document using the Remove Smart Tags or Recheck Document buttons. The use of specific Smart Tags and action buttons is covered in more detail in later chapters.

Step 4	*Click*	the Cancel button to close the AutoCorrect dialog box without making any changes
Step 5	*Click*	the Close button ☒ on the title bar to close Word
Step 6	*Close*	the PowerPoint application

Q U I C K   T I P

A limited number of Smart Tags are installed with the Office applications. You can access more Smart Tags from the Microsoft Web site by clicking the More Smart Tags button in the Smart Tags tab of the AutoCorrect dialog box.

chapter
two

Summary

▶ The first time you launch an Office application after installing Office, you see personalized menus that contain basic commands. As you use different commands, they are automatically added to the personalized menu. Commands that are not used for some time are removed from the personalized menus.

▶ The first time you launch an Office application after installing Office, the Standard and Formatting toolbars share a single row below the menu bar. You can reposition the Formatting toolbar to view more or fewer toolbar buttons. The remaining default toolbar buttons that are not visible on the toolbars can be added from the Toolbar Options list. You can turn off or reset the personalized menus and toolbars in the Options tab of the Customize dialog box.

▶ You can hide or view toolbars as you need them by using a shortcut menu. Toolbars can be docked at the top, bottom, or side of the screen, or they can be floating on screen in their own window.

▶ You can open task panes that contain shortcuts to perform various activities; these task panes can be docked at the left or right side of the application window, or they can be floating in the application window. Two examples of a task pane are the New Document and Basic Search task panes.

▶ Smart Tags are labels that identify text or data as a certain type and provide shortcuts to taking certain actions with the text or data.

Commands Review

Action	Menu Bar	Shortcut Menu	Toolbar	Task Pane	Keyboard
Display or hide toolbars	View, Toolbars	Right-click a toolbar, click the desired toolbar to add or remove the check mark	☒ on the toolbar title bar		ALT + V, T
View the New Document task pane	File, New				ALT + F, N
View the Search task pane	File, Search		🔍		ALT + F, H
View the last visible task pane	View, Task Pane	Right-click a toolbar, click Task Pane			ALT + V, K
View the available Smart Tag options	Tools, AutoCorrect Options, Smart Tags tab				ALT + T, A

Concepts Review

Circle the correct answer.

1. A menu is:
[a] a set of icons.
[b] a list of commands.
[c] impossible to customize.
[d] never personalized.

2. A toolbar is:
[a] a list of commands.
[b] always floating on your screen.
[c] a set of icons.
[d] never docked on your screen.

3. Which of the following is not an option in the Options tab in the Customize dialog box?
[a] turning on or off ScreenTips for toolbar buttons
[b] turning on or off Large icons for toolbar buttons
[c] adding animation to menus
[d] docking all toolbars

4. Right-clicking an item on screen displays:
[a] the Right-Click toolbar.
[b] animated menus.
[c] expanded menus.
[d] a shortcut menu.

5. Double-clicking the menu name on the menu bar:
[a] resets your usage data.
[b] floats the menu bar.
[c] turns off the personalized menus.
[d] expands a personalized menu.

6. A Smart Tag is:
[a] a personalized menu.
[b] displayed by double-clicking an item on your screen.
[c] automatically expanded when you pause briefly.
[d] a label used to identify text or data items for shortcut actions.

7. To view all the default buttons on both the Standard and Formatting toolbars at once, you should:
[a] view the toolbar with a shortcut menu.
[b] add the View All button to the toolbar.
[c] reposition the Formatting toolbar on another row below the Standard toolbar.
[d] drag the Formatting toolbar to the left.

8. The Advanced Search task pane cannot be viewed by clicking a:
[a] command on a shortcut menu.
[b] command on the File menu.
[c] button on the Standard toolbar.
[d] link on the Basic Search task pane.

Circle **T** if the statement is true or **F** if the statement is false.

T   F   1. The Standard and Formatting toolbars must remain on the same row.

T   F   2. When updating docked personalized toolbars, some buttons may be automatically removed from view to make room for the new buttons.

T   F   3. One way to use a Smart Tag is to create an Outlook contact from a name in a Word document.

T   F   4. You cannot add animation to menus.

T   F   5. A floating toolbar window can be resized and repositioned using techniques that are similar to those used for any other window.

chapter two

T   F   6. When you open an Office application, the Search task pane is docked at the right side of the application window.

T   F   7. You cannot use keyboard shortcuts to run commands in Office applications.

T   F   8. You cannot turn off the personalized menus and toolbars options.

Skills Review

Exercise 1

1. Open the Word application.

2. Open the Options tab in the Customize dialog box and reset the usage data; show the Standard and Formatting toolbars on one row, and show full menus after a short delay.

3. If necessary, drag the Formatting toolbar to the right until you can see approximately half of the Standard and half of the Formatting toolbar.

4. Add the Show/Hide button to the personalized Standard toolbar using the Toolbar Options list.

5. Add the Font Color button to the personalized Formatting toolbar using the Toolbar Options list.

6. Open the Customize dialog box and reset your usage data in the Options tab.

7. Close the Word application and click No if asked whether you want to save changes to the blank Word document.

Exercise 2   C

1. Open the Excel application.

2. Open the Options tab in the Customize dialog box and reset the usage data; show the Standard and Formatting toolbars on one row, and show full menus after a short delay.

3. View the personalized Tools menu.

4. Add the AutoCorrect Options command to the personalized Tools menu.

5. Reset your usage data.

6. Close the Excel application.

Exercise 3

1. Open the PowerPoint application.

2. Display the Basic Search task pane using a menu command.

3. Display the advanced search options.

4. Close the Advanced Search task pane.

5. Close the PowerPoint application.

Exercise 4

1. Open an Office application and verify that the New Document, New Presentation, or New Workbook task pane is docked at the right side of the application window.

2. Float the task pane by dragging it to the center of the application window.

3. Drag the left border of the floating task pane to resize it.

4. Double-click the task pane title bar to dock it in its previous position.

5. Close the task pane.

6. Open the Basic Search task pane using the Search button on the Standard toolbar.

7. Open the New Document task pane using the File menu.

8. Switch between task panes using the Back and Forward buttons on the task pane title bar.

9. Close the task pane.

10. Close the application.

Exercise 5

1. Open the Excel application.

2. View the Drawing, Picture, and WordArt toolbars using a shortcut menu.

3. Dock the Picture toolbar below the Standard and Formatting toolbars.

4. Dock the WordArt toolbar at the left boundary of the screen.

5. Close the Excel application from the taskbar.

6. Open the Excel with the New Office Document on the Start menu. (*Hint:* Use the Blank Workbook icon.)

7. Float the WordArt toolbar.

8. Float the Picture toolbar.

9. Hide the WordArt, Picture, and Drawing toolbars using a shortcut menu.

10. Close the Excel application.

Exercise 6

1. Open the Word application.

2. Turn off the personalized menus and toolbars.

3. Open the Options tab in the Customize dialog box and change the toolbar buttons to large icons and add random animation to the menus.

4. Observe the toolbar buttons and the menu animation.

5. Turn off the large buttons and remove the menu animation.

6. Turn on the personalized menus and toolbars and reset your usage data.

7. Close the Word application.

chapter two

Case Projects

SCANS

Project 1

As secretary to the placement director for the XYZ Employment Agency, you have been using an earlier version of Word—Word 97. After you install Office XP, you decide you want the Word menus and toolbars to appear on two rows the way they did in the Word 97 application. Use the Ask A Question Box to search for help on "personalized menus." Review the Help topics and write down all the ways to make the personalized menus and toolbars appear on two rows.

Project 2

You are the administrative assistant to the controller of the Plush Pets, Inc., a stuffed toy manufacturing company. The controller recently installed Excel 2002. She is confused about how to use the task panes and asks for your help. Use the Ask A Question Box to search for help on "task panes." Review the topics and write down an explanation of how task panes are used. Give at least three examples of task panes.

Project 3

As administrative assistant to the art director of MediaWiz Advertising, Inc. you just installed PowerPoint 2002. Now you decide you would rather view the complete Standard and Formatting toolbars rather than the personalized toolbars and want to learn a quick way to do this. Use the Ask A Question Box to search for help on "show all buttons." Review the topic and write down the instructions for showing all buttons using the mouse pointer. Open an Office application and use the mouse method to show the complete Standard and Formatting toolbars. Turn the personalized toolbars back on from the Customize dialog box.

Introduction to the Internet and the World Wide Web

Chapter Overview

Millions of people use the Internet to shop for goods and services, listen to music, view artwork, conduct research, get stock quotes, keep up to date with current events, and send e-mail. More and more people are using the Internet at work and at home to view and download multimedia computer files that contain graphics, sound, video, and text. In this chapter, you learn about the Internet, how to connect to the Internet, how to use the Internet Explorer Web browser, and how to access pages on the World Wide Web.

LEARNING OBJECTIVES

- ▶ Describe the Internet
- ▶ Connect to the Internet
- ▶ Use Internet Explorer
- ▶ Use directories and search engines

**chapter
three**

3.a What Is the Internet?

To understand the Internet, you must understand networks. A **network** is simply a group of two or more computers linked by cable or telephone lines. The linked computers also include a special computer called a **server** that is used to store files and programs that everyone on the network can use. In addition to the shared files and programs, networks enable users to share equipment, such as a common network printer.

The **Internet** is a worldwide public network of private networks, where users view and transfer information between computers. For example, an Internet user in California can retrieve (or **download**) files from a computer in Canada quickly and easily. In the same way, an Internet user in Australia can send (or **upload**) files to another Internet user in England. The Internet is not a single organization, but rather a cooperative effort by multiple organizations managing a variety of different kinds of computers.

You find a wide variety of services on the Internet. You can communicate with others via e-mail, electronic bulletin boards called newsgroups, real-time online chat, and online telephony. You can also download files from servers to your computer and search the World Wide Web for information. In this chapter, you learn about using a Web browser and accessing pages on the World Wide Web. Your instructor may provide additional information on other Internet services.

3.b Connecting to the Internet

To connect to the Internet you need some physical communication medium connected to your computer, such as network cable or a modem. You also need a special communication program called a Web browser program (such as Microsoft Internet Explorer) that allows your computer to communicate with computers on the Internet. The Web browser allows you to access Internet resources such as Web pages.

After setting up your computer hardware (the network cable or modem) and installing the Internet Explorer Web browser, you must make arrangements to connect to a computer on the Internet. The computer you connect to is called a **host**. Usually, you connect to a host computer via a commercial Internet Service Provider, such as America Online or another company who sells access to the Internet. An **Internet Service Provider (ISP)** maintains the host computer, provides a gateway or entrance to the Internet, and provides an electronic "mail box" with facilities for sending and receiving e-mail. Commercial ISPs usually charge a flat monthly fee for unlimited access to the Internet and e-mail services.

3.c Using Internet Explorer

A **Web browser** is a software application that helps you access Internet resources, including Web pages stored on computers called Web servers. A **Web page** is a document that contains hyperlinks (often called links) to other pages; it can also contain audio and video clips.

notes The activities in this chapter assume you are using the Internet Explorer Web browser version 5.0 or higher. If you are using an earlier version of Internet Explorer or a different Web browser, your instructor may modify the following activities.

To open the Internet Explorer Web browser:

Step 1	**Connect**	to your ISP, if necessary
Step 2	**Double-click**	the Internet Explorer icon 🌐 on the desktop to open the Web browser

When the Web browser opens, a Web page, called a **start page** or **home page**, loads automatically. The start page used by the Internet Explorer Web browser can be the Microsoft default start page, a blank page, or any designated Web page. Figure 3-1 shows the home page for the publisher of this book as the start page.

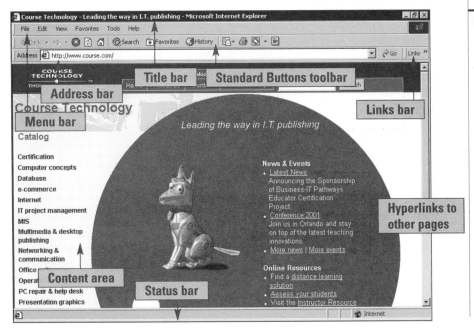

FIGURE 3-1
Internet Explorer Web Browser

chapter
three

MENU TIP

You can create a favorite by clicking the Favorites command on the menu bar and then clicking Add to Favorites, by right-clicking the background (not a link) on the current Web page and clicking Add to Favorites, or by right-clicking a link on the current Web page and clicking Add to Favorites.

MOUSE TIP

You can click the Stop button on the Standard Buttons toolbar to stop downloading a Web page.

QUICK TIP

Another way to load a favorite is to use the Favorites button on the toolbar to open the Favorites list in the Explorer bar. The **Explorer bar** is a pane that opens at the left side of the Web browser screen.

The **title bar** contains the Internet Explorer Web browser Control-menu icon and application name, the title of the current Web page, and the Internet Explorer Web browser Minimize, Restore, and Close buttons. The **menu bar** contains the menu commands you can use to perform specific tasks when viewing the Internet Explorer Web browser window—such as opening a file from your hard disk or printing the current Web page. The **Standard toolbar** contains buttons that provide shortcuts to frequently performed tasks. The **Address bar** contains a text box in which you key the path and filename of the Web page you want to load and a drop-down list of recently loaded Web pages and files. You can click the Go button to load the Web page after keying the page's address in the Address Bar. The **Links bar** is a customizable bar to which you can add shortcuts Web pages you load frequently. The **status bar** displays information about the current Web page. The security zone indicator on the right side of the status bar identifies the security zone you have assigned to the current Web page.

As a Web page loads, the progress bar illustrates the progress of the downloading process. When you place the mouse pointer on a link in the current Web page, its URL appears in the left side of the status bar. The **content area** contains the current Web page. Vertical and horizontal scroll bars appear as necessary so that you can scroll to view the entire Web page after it is loaded.

Loading a Web Page

Loading a Web page means that the Web browser sends a message requesting a copy of the Web page to the Web server where the Web page is stored. The Web server responds by sending a copy of the Web page to your computer. In order to load a Web page, you must either know or find the page's **URL** (Uniform Resource Locator)—the path and filename of the page that is the Web page's address. One way to find the URL for a Web page is to use a search engine or directory. If you are looking for a particular company's Web page, you might find its URL in one of the company's advertisements or on its letterhead and business card. Examples of URLs based on an organization's name are:

Course Technology	*www.course.com*
National Public Radio	*www.npr.org*
The White House	*www.whitehouse.gov*

You can try to "guess" the URL based on the organization's name and top-level domain. For example, a good guess for the U.S. House of Representatives Web page is *www.house.gov*.

You can key a URL directly in the Address bar by first selecting all or part of the current URL and keying the new URL to replace the selection. Internet Explorer adds the "http://" portion of the URL for you. To select the contents of the Address bar and key the URL for the U.S. House of Representatives:

Step 1	*Click*	the contents of the Address bar
Step 2	*Key*	www.house.gov
Step 3	*Click*	the Go button ⌐Go or press the ENTER key
Step 4	*Observe*	that the home page of the U.S. House of Representatives' Web site opens in your Web browser

Creating Favorites

Web pages are constantly being updated with new information. If you like a certain Web page or find a Web page contains useful information and plan to revisit it, you may want to save a shortcut to the page's URL in the Favorites folder. Such shortcuts are simply called **favorites**. Suppose you want to load the U.S. House of Representatives home page frequently. You can create a favorite that saves the URL in a file on your hard disk. Then at any time, you can quickly load this Web page by clicking it in a list of favorites maintained on the Favorites menu.

The URLs you choose to save as favorites are stored in the Favorites folder on your hard disk. You can specify a new or different subfolder within the Favorites folder and you can change the name of the Web page as it appears in your list of favorites in the Add Favorite dialog box. To create a favorite for the U.S. House of Representatives Web page:

Step 1	*Click*	F̲avorites
Step 2	*Click*	A̲dd to Favorites
Step 3	*Click*	OK
Step 4	*Click*	the Home button 🏠 to return to the default start page

One way to load a Web page from a favorite is to click the name of the favorite in the list of favorites on the Favorites menu. To load the U.S. House of Representatives home page from the Favorites menu:

Step 1	*Click*	F̲avorites
Step 2	*Click*	the United States House of Representatives favorite to load the page

chapter
three

| Step 3 | *Click* | the Home button 🏠 to return to the default start page |

The Back and Forward buttons allow you to review recently loaded Web pages without keying the URL or using the Favorites list. To reload the U.S. House of Representatives home page from the Back button list:

| Step 1 | *Click* | the Back button list arrow ⬅▾ on the toolbar |
| Step 2 | *Click* | United States House of Representatives |

3.d Using Directories and Search Engines

Because the Web is so large, you often need to take advantage of special search tools, called search engines and directories, to find the information you need. To use some of the Web's numerous search engines and directories, you can click the Search button on the Standard toolbar to open the Search list in the Explorer bar. To view the Search list:

| Step 1 | *Click* | the Search button 🔍Search on the Standard toolbar |
| Step 2 | *Observe* | the search list options |

Search engines maintain an index of keywords used in Web pages that you can search. Search engine indexes are updated automatically by software called **spiders** (or **robots**). Spiders follow links between pages throughout the entire Web, adding any new Web pages to the search engine's index. You should use a search engine when you want to find specific Web pages. Some of the most popular search engines include AltaVista, HotBot, and Northern Light.

Directories use a subject-type format similar to a library card catalog. A directory provides a list of links to broad general categories of Web sites such as "Entertainment" or "Business." When you click these links, a subcategory list of links appears. For example, if you click the Entertainment link, you might then see "Movies," "Television," and "Video Games" links. To find links to Web sites containing information about "Movies," you would click the "Movies" link. Unlike a search engine, whose index is updated automatically, Web sites are added to directories only when an individual or a company asks that a particular Web site be included. Some directories also provide review comments and ratings for the Web sites in their index. Most directories also provide an internal search engine that can only be used to search the directory's index, not the entire Web. You use a directory when you are looking for information on broad general topics. Popular directories include Yahoo and Magellan Internet Guide.

To search for Web pages containing "movie guides":

Step 1	*Key*	movie guides in the Find a Web page containing text box
Step 2	*Click*	the Search button or press the ENTER key
Step 3	*Observe*	the search results (a list of Web pages in the search list)

The search results list consists of Web page titles displayed as hyperlinks. You can click any hyperlink to load that page from the list. To close the Explorer bar and search list:

| Step 1 | *Click* | the Search button [Search] on the Standard toolbar |
| Step 2 | *Close* | Internet Explorer |

The Web's many search tools are all constructed differently. That means you get varying results when using several search engines or directories to search for information on the same topic. Also, search tools operate according to varying rules. For example, some search engines allow only a simple search on one keyword. Others allow you to refine your search by finding phrases keyed within quotation marks, by indicating proper names, or by using special operators such as "and," "or," and "not" to include or exclude search words. To save time, always begin by clicking the search tool's online Help link. Study the directions for using that particular search engine or directory, and then proceed with your search.

QUICK TIP

You can reload pages from the History folder, which stores the Web pages you load for a specific period of time. You set the number of days to store pages on the General tab in the Options dialog box. The default number of days to store pages in the History folder is 20 days. Click the History button on the toolbar to open the History list in the Explorer bar.

CAUTION TIP

After you find the desired information, "let the user beware!" Because the Web is largely unregulated, anyone can put anything on a Web page. Evaluate carefully the credibility of all the information you find. Try to find out something about the author and his or her credentials. Many college or university library Web sites have good tips on how to evaluate online information.

chapter
three

Summary

▶ A network is a group of two or more computers linked by cable or telephone lines, and the Internet is a worldwide "network of networks."

▶ The World Wide Web is a subset of the Internet from which you can download files and search for information.

▶ Other external networks related to the Internet are large commercial networks like America Online, CompuServe, Prodigy, the Microsoft Network and USENET.

▶ To access the Internet, your computer must have some physical communication medium such as cable or dial-up modem, and a special communication program such as Internet Explorer.

▶ An Internet Service Provider (or ISP) maintains a host computer on the Internet. In order to connect to the Internet, you need to connect to the host computer.

▶ You use a Web browser, such as Internet Explorer, to load Web pages. Web pages are connected by hyperlinks that are text or pictures associated with the path to another page.

▶ Directories and search engines are tools to help you find files and Web sites on the Internet.

Commands Review

Action	Menu Bar	Shortcut Menu	Toolbar	Task Pane	Keyboard
Load a Web page	File, Open		Go		ALT + F, O Key URL in the Address bar and press the ENTER key
Save a favorite	Favorites, Add to Favorites	Right-click hyperlink, click Add to Favorites	Drag URL icon to Links bar or Favorites command		ALT + A, A Ctrl + D
Manage the Standard toolbar, Address bar, and Links bar	View, Toolbars	Right-click the Standard toolbar, click desired command	Drag the Standard toolbar, Address bar, or Links bar to the new location		ALT + V, T
Load the search, history, or favorites list in the Explorer bar	View, Explorer Bar		Search Favorites History		ALT + V, E

Concepts Review

Circle the correct answer.

1. A network is:
[a] the Internet.
[b] two or more computers linked by cable or telephone wire.
[c] two or more computer networks linked by cable or telephone lines.
[d] a computer that stores Web pages.

2. Which of the following is not a challenge to using the Internet?
[a] light usage
[b] dynamic environment
[c] volume of information
[d] security and privacy

3. The Address bar:
[a] is a customizable shortcut bar.
[b] contains the search list.
[c] contains your personal list of favorite URLs.
[d] contains the URL of the Web page in the content area.

4. The content area contains the:
[a] Standard toolbar.
[b] status bar.
[c] list of favorites.
[d] current Web page.

5. You can view a list of recently loaded Web pages in the:
[a] Channel bar.
[b] Explorer bar.
[c] Address bar.
[d] Links bar.

6. Search engines update their indexes of keywords by using software called:
[a] Webcrawler.
[b] HTTP.
[c] HotBot.
[d] spiders.

Circle **T** if the statement is true or **F** if the statement is false.

T   F   1. Commercial networks that provide specially formatted features are the same as the Internet.

T   F   2. USENET is the name of the military Internet.

T   F   3. All search engines use the same rules for locating Web pages.

T   F   4. Internet users in Boston or New York can access computer files on computers located in the United States only.

T   F   5. Spiders are programs that help you locate pages on the Web.

T   F   6. A Web page URL identifies its location (path and filename).

chapter three

Skills Review

Exercise 1

1. Open the Internet Explorer Web browser.

2. Open the Internet Options dialog box by clicking the Internet Options command on the Tools menu.

3. Review the options on the General tab in the dialog box.

4. Write down the steps to change the default start page to a blank page.

5. Close the dialog box and close the Web browser.

Exercise 2

1. Connect to the Internet and open the Internet Explorer Web browser.

2. Open the search list in the Explorer bar.

3. Search for Web pages about "dog shows."

4. Load one of the Web pages in the search results list.

5. Close the Explorer bar.

6. Print the Web page by clicking the Print command on the File menu and close the Web browser.

Exercise 3

1. Connect to the Internet and open the Internet Explorer Web browser.

2. Load the National Public radio Web page by keying the URL, *www.npr.org*, in the Address bar.

3. Print the Web page by clicking the Print command on the File menu and close the Web browser.

Exercise 4

1. Connect to the Internet and open the Internet Explorer Web browser.

2. Load the AltaVista search engine by keying the URL, *www.altavista.com*, in the Address bar.

3. Save the Web page as a favorite.

4. Search for Web pages about your city.

5. Print at least two Web pages by clicking the Print command on the File menu and close your Web browser.

Exercise 5

1. Connect to the Internet and open the Internet Explorer Web browser.

2. Load the HotBot search engine by keying the URL, *www.hotbot.com*, in the Address bar.

3. Save the Web page as a favorite.

4. Locate the hyperlink text or picture that loads the online Help page. Review the search rules for using HotBot.

5. Print the HotBot Help page by clicking the Print command on the File menu and close your Web browser.

Exercise 6

1. Connect to the Internet and open the Internet Explorer Web browser.

2. Load the Yahoo directory by keying the URL, *www.yahoo.com*, in the Address bar.

3. Save the Web page as a favorite.

4. Search for Web sites that contain information about restaurants in your city.

5. Print at least two Web pages by clicking the Print command on the File menu and close your Web browser.

Exercise 7

1. Connect to the Internet and open the Internet Explorer Web browser.

2. View the Links bar by dragging the bar to the left using the mouse pointer.

3. Click each shortcut on the Links bar and review the Web page that loads.

4. Drag the Links bar back to its original position with the mouse pointer.

Exercise 8

1. Connect to the Internet and open the Internet Explorer Web browser.

2. Click the History button on the Standard toolbar to load the History list in the Explorer bar.

3. Review the History list and click a hyperlink to a page loaded yesterday.

4. Print the page by clicking the Print command on the File menu, close the Explorer bar, and close the Web browser.

Case Projects

Project 1

Your organization recently started browsing the Web with the Internet Explorer Web browser and everyone wants to know how to use the toolbar buttons in the browser. Your supervisor asks you to prepare a fifteen-minute presentation, to be delivered at the next staff meeting, that describes the Internet Explorer Standard Buttons toolbar buttons. Review the Standard Buttons toolbar buttons and practice using them. Write an outline for your presentation that lists each button and describes how it is used.

Project 2

You are working for a book publisher who is creating a series of books about popular movie actors and actresses from the 1940s and 1950s, including Humphrey Bogart and Tyrone Power. The research director asks you to use the Web to locate a list of movies that the actors starred in. Use the Explorer bar search list and the Yahoo directory search tool to find links to "Entertainment." Click the Entertainment link and close the Explorer bar. Working from the Yahoo Web page, click the Actors and Actresses link. Search for Humphrey Bogart in

chapter three

the Actors and Actresses portion of the database. Link to the Web page that shows the filmography for Humphrey Bogart. Print the Web page that shows all the movies he acted in. Use the History list to return to the Actors and Actresses search page. Search for Tyrone Power, then link to and print his filmography. Close the Internet Explorer Web browser.

Project 3

You are the new secretary for the Business Women's Forum, a professional association. The association's president asked you to compile a list of Internet resources, which she will distribute at next month's lunch meeting. Connect to the Internet, open Internet Explorer, and search for Web pages containing the keywords "women in business" (including the quotation marks) using the AltaVista search engine. To load the AltaVista search engine key the URL, *www.altavista.com*, in the Address bar. From the search results, click the Web page title link of your choice to load the Web page. Review the new Web page and its links. Create a favorite for that page. Use the Back button list to reload the AltaVista home page and click a different Web page title from the list. Review the Web page and its links. Create a favorite for the Web page. Continue loading and reviewing pages until you have loaded and reviewed at least five pages. Return to the default home page. Use the Go To command on the View menu and the History bar to reload at least three of the pages. Print two of the pages. Delete all the favorites you added in this chapter, and then close Internet Explorer.

Microsoft
Excel 2002
Introductory

Quick Start for Excel

Chapter Overview

Spreadsheet applications, such as Excel, help you organize and analyze information, especially information involving numbers. In this chapter, you learn about the components of the Excel window, and you perform simple tasks to become more familiar with how Excel works. You open a workbook file, navigate a workbook, select cells, work with worksheets, save your work, preview and print a workbook, and create a new workbook based on a predesigned template.

LEARNING OBJECTIVES

- ▶ Identify the components of the Excel window
- ▶ Locate and open an existing workbook
- ▶ Navigate a worksheet
- ▶ Select cells, columns, and rows
- ▶ Insert, reposition, and delete worksheets
- ▶ Save a workbook
- ▶ Preview and print a worksheet
- ▶ Close a workbook
- ▶ Create a new workbook from a template
- ▶ Exit Excel

Case profile

Luis Alvarez owns a computer store called Super Power Computers. His business has grown from a single location to a medium-sized chain of outlets spread out over several states. Luis employs several hundred people, and his business is divided into several departments to handle sales, inventory, delivery, technical support, accounting, and personnel. As an administrative assistant, you use Excel to organize and prepare a sales report for Luis.

chapter one

notes This text assumes that you have little or no knowledge of the Excel application. However, it is assumed that you have read Office Chapters 1–3 of this book and that you are familiar with Windows 98 or Windows 2000 concepts.

The illustrations in this unit were created using Windows 2000. If you are using the Excel application installed in Windows 98, you may notice a few minor differences in some figures. These differences do not affect your work in this unit.

1.a Identifying the Components of the Excel Window

A **spreadsheet** is a computer file specifically designed to organize data by using special containers, called **cells**. Cells are organized into rows and columns to create a **worksheet**. A collection of worksheets is called a **workbook** and is saved as an Excel file.

Before you can begin to work with Excel, you must open the application. When you open the application, a new, blank workbook opens as well. To open Excel and a new, blank workbook:

Step 1	*Click*	the Start button ⊞Start on the taskbar
Step 2	*Point to*	Programs
Step 3	*Click*	Microsoft Excel

Within a few seconds, Excel starts. Your screen should look similar to Figure 1-1.

chapter
one

FIGURE 1-1
Excel Application Window

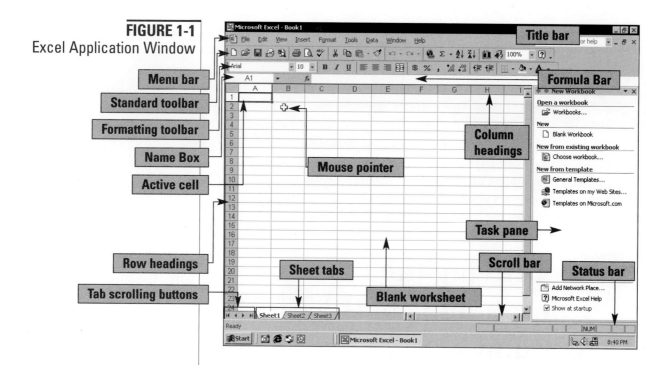

Menu bar
Standard toolbar
Formatting toolbar
Name Box
Active cell
Row headings
Tab scrolling buttons
Mouse pointer
Sheet tabs
Blank worksheet
Column headings
Task pane
Scroll bar
Status bar
Title bar
Formula Bar

Worksheets

Each new workbook contains three worksheets, similar to pages in a notebook. You switch between worksheets by clicking the **sheet tabs** near the bottom of the Excel window. Each worksheet can be named and color-coded individually. When you click a sheet tab, you make that worksheet the **active worksheet**, and any values you key are entered on that worksheet. The active sheet tab appears to be in front of the other tabs, with the sheet tab name in bold.

Worksheets are divided into columns and rows. **Columns** run vertically up and down a worksheet. **Rows** run horizontally from left to right across a worksheet. Across the top of each worksheet you see **column headings**, which are lettered from A to Z, AA to AZ, and so on to column IV (256 columns in total). On the left side of each worksheet are **row headings**, which are numbered from 1 to 65,536 (the maximum number of rows in a worksheet).

Cells are the containers where values are stored. **Values** include numbers, text, hyperlinks, formulas, and functions. A **cell reference** is the column letter and row number that identifies a cell; for example, cell A1 refers to the cell at the intersection of column A and row 1. Each cell can contain up to 32,000 characters. When you click a cell, it becomes the **active cell**, and a thick border surrounds it. Any values you enter are stored in the active cell.

When you move your mouse pointer over a worksheet, it changes to a large, white cross. This mouse pointer changes shape depending on what you are doing.

Task Pane

The **New Workbook task pane** helps you work faster by providing helpful shortcuts. Using the New Workbook task pane, you can quickly open recently used workbooks, create new workbooks from templates, or search for templates on the Microsoft Web site, *Microsoft.com*. There are other task panes to help you complete specific types of tasks, such as when you need to paste information from the Clipboard or when you need to search your computer for a certain file.

Top of the Window

The **title bar** displays the application name as well as the current workbook name. The default name for the blank workbook that appears when you start Excel is "Book1." On the right side of the title bar are the Minimize, Maximize/Restore, and Close buttons. The **menu bar**, located below the title bar, features drop-down menu commands that contain groups of additional, related commands. The activities in this book instruct you to select menu bar commands with the mouse; if you prefer, however, you can press the ALT key plus the underlined letter in the menu command to open the menu, then press the underlined letter in the command on the menu. In addition, many menu commands have an associated keyboard shortcut. For example, to open a file, you could click the File menu, then click Open; you could press the ALT + F keys, then press the O key; or you could press the CTRL + O keys. The Commands Review section at the end of each chapter summarizes both the mouse and keyboard techniques used to select a menu command.

The **Standard toolbar**, located beneath the menu bar, provides easy access to commonly used commands, such as Save, Open, Print, Copy, and Paste, as well as to many other useful commands. The **Formatting toolbar**, shown below the Standard toolbar in Figure 1-1, provides easy access to commonly used formatting commands, such as Style, Font, Font Size, Alignment, Fill Color, and Font Color. The **Name Box**, located beneath the Formatting toolbar, displays the current cell or cells. Use the **Formula Bar**, to the right of the Name Box, to create and edit values. The Formula Bar becomes active whenever you begin keying data into a cell. When the Formula Bar is active, the Enter, Cancel, and Edit Formula buttons appear.

chapter
one

notes Office XP features personalized menus and toolbars, which "learn" the commands you use most often. This means that when you first install Office XP, only the most frequently used commands appear immediately on a short version of the menus, and the remaining commands appear after a brief pause. Commands that you select move to the short menu, while those you don't use appear only on the full menu.

The Standard and Formatting toolbars appear on the same row when you first install Office XP. When they appear in this position, only the most commonly used buttons of each toolbar are visible. All the other default buttons appear on the Toolbar Options drop-down lists. As you use buttons from the Toolbar Options list, they move to the visible buttons on the toolbar, while the buttons you don't use move into the Toolbar Options list. If you arrange the Formatting toolbar below the Standard toolbar, all buttons are visible. Unless otherwise noted, the illustrations in this book show the full menus and the Formatting toolbar on its own row below the Standard toolbar.

Bottom of the Window

The **tab scrolling buttons** allow you to navigate through the sheet tabs, or worksheets, contained in your workbook. The right- and left-pointing triangles scroll one tab to the right or left, respectively. The right- and left-pointing triangles with the vertical line jump to the first and last sheet tabs in the workbook, respectively. Scrolling the sheet tabs does not change your active worksheet. The **status bar** at the bottom of the Excel window indicates various items of information, such as whether the NUM LOCK or CAPS LOCK feature is active. If you select a range of cells containing numbers, the sum of the selected cells is displayed on the status bar.

Luis, the company president, would like you to review the workbook he has been using to track regional sales.

C **1.b** # Locating and Opening an Existing Workbook

When you want to edit an existing workbook, you need to open it from the disk where it is stored. You can open several workbooks at a time. Luis asks you to review the *Super Power Computers – Q1 Sales* workbook he has created.

MOUSE TIP

Click the Open button on the Standard toolbar to open the Open dialog box.

notes If you do not know where your Data Files are stored, check with your instructor to find out the location.

To open an existing workbook:

| Step 1 | *Click* | the Workbooks or More workbooks link in the Open a workbook section of the New Workbook task pane |

The Open dialog box on your screen should look similar to Figure 1-2, although your file list might differ.

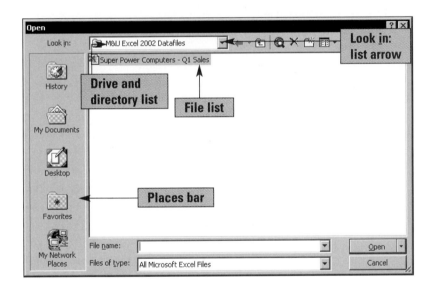

FIGURE 1-2
Open Dialog Box

Step 2	*Click*	the Look in: list arrow
Step 3	*Switch to*	the disk drive and folder where your Data Files are stored
Step 4	*Double-click*	*Super Power Computers – Q1 Sales* in the file list

The *Super Power Computers – Q1 Sales* workbook opens, and the New Workbook task pane closes until you need to use it again. Luis created this workbook to keep track of sales for the first quarter of 2003.

chapter
one

1.c Navigating a Worksheet

In Excel, data you enter is placed in the active cell. Recall that the active cell is the cell with the thick black border around it. When you want to make a cell active, position the mouse pointer over the cell you want to activate, and then click the cell. To activate a cell using the mouse:

Step 1	*Point to*	cell B6
Step 2	*Click*	cell B6
Step 3	*Verify*	that cell B6 is active by looking in the Name Box

You can use the ARROW keys and other keyboard shortcuts to move the active cell. Table 1-1 summarizes some of the keyboard shortcuts for moving around in Excel.

TABLE 1-1
Using the Keyboard to
Navigate a Workbook

To Move	Press
Up one cell	the UP ARROW key
Down one cell	the DOWN ARROW key
Right one cell	the TAB key or the RIGHT ARROW key
Left one cell	the SHIFT + TAB keys or the LEFT ARROW key
To first active cell of the current row	the HOME key
To last active cell of the current row	the END key and then the ENTER key
Down one page	the PAGE DOWN key
Up one page	the PAGE UP key
To cell A1	the CTRL + HOME keys
To last cell containing data in a worksheet	the CTRL + END keys or the END key and then the HOME key
To edge of the last cell containing a value or to the edges of a worksheet	the CTRL + ARROW keys

MOUSE TIP

You can scroll through a worksheet by clicking the scroll arrows to scroll one row or column at a time; drag the scroll boxes to scroll several rows or columns.

You also can move around a workbook using the keyboard. To navigate a workbook using the keyboard:

Step 1	*Press*	the CTRL + HOME keys to move to cell A1
Step 2	*Press*	the CTRL + END keys to move to the last cell containing data in the worksheet
Step 3	*Press*	the HOME key to move to the first cell in the current row

| Step 4 | *Press* | the CTRL + PAGE DOWN keys to move to Sheet2 |
| Step 5 | *Press* | the CTRL + PAGE UP keys to return to the Sales Report Data worksheet |

You also can switch to another worksheet by using the mouse. To switch to another worksheet by using the mouse:

| Step 1 | *Click* | the Sheet2 sheet tab |
| Step 2 | *Click* | the Sales Report Data sheet tab |

Throughout the remainder of this book, you are instructed to activate a particular cell or worksheet. Use your mouse to click the cell or sheet tab, or use your favorite keyboard shortcut, whichever you prefer.

1.d Selecting Cells, Columns, and Rows

Selecting cells is a fundamental skill used when working in Excel. You select cells for editing, for moving, for copying, for formatting, or as references in formulas. To select cells by using the mouse:

Step 1	*Click*	cell B3, *but do not release* the mouse button
Step 2	*Drag*	the pointer to cell D5
Step 3	*Release*	the mouse button

You have selected a range of cells. A **range** is any group of contiguous cells. To refer to a range, you specify the cells in the upper-left and lower-right corners. In this step, you selected the range B3:D5. As you select the range, the status bar displays the sum of all cells in the selected range containing numerical values, and the Name Box displays a running count of rows and columns in your selected range. In this example, the Name Box indicated 3R x 3C, indicating that three rows and three columns were being selected. As soon as you release the mouse button to close your selection, the Name Box displays the group's active cell reference. The first selected cell, B3, remains unshaded to indicate that it is the active cell in the group. Your screen should look similar to Figure 1-3.

chapter
one

FIGURE 1-3
Selected Range

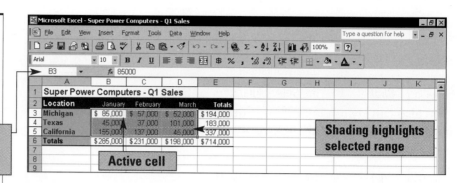

Name Box
indicates
active cell

Active cell

Shading highlights
selected range

QUICK TIP

While working in a
selection, press the
ENTER key to move the
active cell down one
cell. Press the TAB key
to move the active cell
to the right. Press the
SHIFT + TAB keys to
move the active cell to
the left.

You also can use keys to select cells. Holding down the SHIFT key
allows you to select cells by pressing only the ARROW keys. Pressing
the CTRL key in combination with the ARROW keys causes the
selection to jump to the last cell containing data. If the cells in the
direction you specify are blank, the selection moves to the limits of the
worksheet. To select cells using keys:

Step 1	*Activate*	cell B4
Step 2	*Press & hold*	the SHIFT key
Step 3	*Press*	the RIGHT ARROW key twice to select cells C4 and D4
Step 4	*Release*	the SHIFT key
Step 5	*Press & hold*	the SHIFT + CTRL keys
Step 6	*Press*	the UP ARROW key
Step 7	*Release*	the SHIFT + CTRL keys to select the range B2:D4
Step 8	*Click*	any cell in the worksheet to deselect the range

You often want to apply formatting to an entire column or row, or
several columns or rows at once. You can drag to select multiple
columns or rows with the mouse, or you click while pressing the
SHIFT or CTRL keys. To select an entire row or column, or to select
several rows or columns:

MOUSE TIP

Many situations require
the use of multiple,
nonadjacent ranges. For
example, to select cells
in columns A and C,
select the cells in column
A, press and hold the
CTRL key, then select the
cells in column C.

Step 1	*Click*	the number 3 in the row 3 heading at the left of the worksheet to select row 3
Step 2	*Drag*	across the column headings for columns B, C, and D to select columns B, C, and D
Step 3	*Click*	the column E heading
Step 4	*Press & hold*	the SHIFT key
Step 5	*Click*	the column B heading to select columns B through E

You can also quickly select an entire worksheet at once. To select an entire worksheet:

| Step 1 | **Click** | the Select All button located to the left of column A and above row 1 |
| Step 2 | **Activate** | cell A1 to deselect the worksheet |

QUICK TIP

Press the CTRL+ A keys to select an entire worksheet.

Now that you can easily select cells and navigate a worksheet, you are ready to organize a workbook.

1.e Inserting, Repositioning, and Deleting Worksheets

C

By default, Excel creates new workbooks that contain three worksheets. You can add or delete worksheets from your workbook at any time. You also can change the order of worksheets as you further refine your workbook design.

MENU TIP

You can insert a new worksheet by clicking the Worksheet command on the Insert menu.

Inserting a Worksheet

You need to add a new worksheet to the workbook. To add a new worksheet to a workbook:

Step 1	**Right-click**	the Sales Report Data sheet tab
Step 2	**Click**	Insert
Step 3	**Verify**	that the Worksheet icon in the Insert dialog box is selected
Step 4	**Click**	OK

A new worksheet is inserted to the left of the active worksheet.

Copying and Moving a Worksheet

You need to create a second copy of the Sales Report Data worksheet for second quarter data. To copy a worksheet:

| Step 1 | **Right-click** | the Sales Report Data sheet tab |
| Step 2 | **Click** | Move or Copy |

QUICK TIP

To have Excel insert more or fewer than three worksheets in each new workbook, click the Options command on the Tools menu to open the Options dialog box. On the General tab, enter the number of worksheets in the Sheets in new workbook: text box.

chapter one

The Move or Copy dialog box on your screen should look similar to Figure 1-4.

FIGURE 1-4
Move or Copy Dialog Box

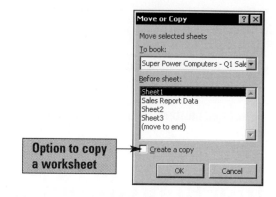

Option to copy a worksheet

| Step 3 | *Click* | the Create a copy check box to insert a check mark |
| Step 4 | *Click* | OK |

The active worksheet is copied and a new worksheet, called Sales Report Data (2) appears to the left of Sheet1.

You can reorganize your worksheets by dragging sheet tabs to a new location. In your workbook, the Sales Report Data worksheet should appear first, followed by the Sales Report Data (2) worksheet. To move a worksheet:

| Step 1 | *Point to* | the Sheet1 sheet tab |
| Step 2 | *Press & hold* | the left mouse button |

The pointer changes to an arrow with a small rectangle attached to it to indicate that you are moving a sheet tab, and a small black triangle appears at the left of the sheet tab to indicate the tab's position.

| Step 3 | *Drag* | the Sheet1 sheet tab to the right of the Sales Report Data sheet tab |

As you drag, the small black triangle moves with the pointer to indicate the worksheet's new position, and the sheet tabs scroll left. Your screen should look similar to Figure 1-5.

FIGURE 1-5
Moving a Sheet Tab

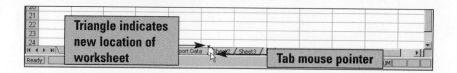

Triangle indicates new location of worksheet

Tab mouse pointer

QUICK TIP

To copy a worksheet, press and hold the CTRL key while you drag the sheet tab.

MOUSE TIP

Right-click a tab scroll button to display a menu of sheet tabs. Click any of the listed worksheets to scroll to and activate that worksheet.

| Step 4 | *Release* | the mouse button |

The sheet tab moves to the new location.

| Step 5 | *Follow* | Steps 1 through 4 to position the Sales Report Data (2) sheet tab to the right of the Sales Report Data sheet tab |

Deleting a Worksheet

You can also delete worksheets that you no longer need. To delete a worksheet:

Step 1	*Right-click*	the Sheet1 sheet tab
Step 2	*Click*	Delete
Step 3	*Click*	the Sales Report Data sheet tab

1.f Saving a Workbook

The first rule of computing is: Save Your Work Often! The second rule of computing is: Follow the first rule of computing. There are two distinct saving operations: Save and Save As.

Managing Files and Folders

To keep your work more organized, you decide to create a new folder. You can do this from the Open or Save As dialog box. To create a new folder:

Step 1	*Click*	File
Step 2	*Click*	Save As
Step 3	*Click*	the Save in: list arrow
Step 4	*Switch to*	the appropriate disk drive and folder, as designated by your instructor
Step 5	*Click*	the Create New Folder button in the Save As dialog box
Step 6	*Key*	your name as the name of the folder (Example: Kylie)
Step 7	*Click*	OK

C

chapter
one

The folder is created in the current location and listed in the Save in: list box.

Using the Save As Command

When you use the Save As command, you provide a filename and specify the disk drive and folder location where the workbook should be saved. A filename can have as many as 255 characters, including the disk drive reference and path, and can contain letters, numbers, spaces, and some special characters in any combination. If you use the Save As command on a previously saved workbook, you actually create a new copy of the workbook, and any changes you made appear only in the new copy.

You also can use the Save As command to save a workbook file in another format, such as HTML for the Internet, or for use in another spreadsheet or accounting application. First, you save the workbook to a different format to send to someone using a different spreadsheet application. To save a workbook in a different file format:

Step 1	*Verify*	that the Save As dialog box is still open
Step 2	*Click*	the Save as type: list arrow
Step 3	*Scroll*	the list to find WK4 (1-2-3)
Step 4	*Click*	WK4 (1-2-3)

This is the format for Lotus 1-2-3 workbooks.

Step 5	*Select*	All of the text in the File name: text box
Step 6	*Key*	Super Power Computers - Q1 Sales WK4 Format
Step 7	*Click*	Save

A warning message appears telling you that some of the workbook's features may not save correctly in the new format. Although Excel does its best to translate the workbook into another format, not everything transfers correctly. For more information about a specific format's limitations, click Help.

Step 8	*Click*	Yes

CAUTION TIP

Filenames cannot include the following special characters: the forward slash (/), the backward slash (\), the colon (:), the semicolon (;), the pipe symbol (|), the question mark (?), the less than symbol (<), the greater than symbol (>), the asterisk (*), and the quotation mark (").

INTERNET TIP

To distribute a workbook without personal information (such as your user name): Click the Options command on the Tools menu. On the Security tab, click the Remove personal information from this file on save check box, then click the OK button. The next time you save your document, the personal information will be removed.

You have now created a copy of your Excel formatted workbook. Next, you want to save the workbook back to Excel format. To save the workbook with a new filename in Excel format:

Step 1	*Open*	the Save As dialog box
Step 2	*Key*	Super Power Computers – Q1 Sales Revised in the File name: text box
Step 3	*Click*	Microsoft Excel Workbook in the Save as type: list box

The Save As dialog box on your screen should look similar to Figure 1-6.

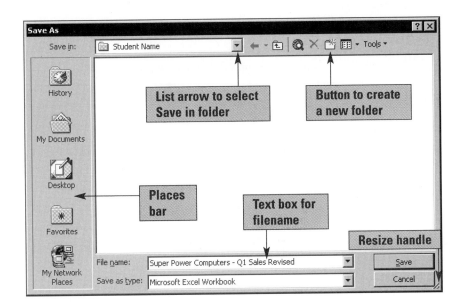

FIGURE 1-6
Save As Dialog Box

Step 4	*Click*	<u>S</u>ave

The workbook is saved to your folder as *Super Power Computer – Q1 Sales Revised*. Notice that the title bar includes the new filename.

Using the Save Command

When you want to save changes to a previously named workbook without creating a copy, you use the <u>S</u>ave command. No dialog box opens, but the changes are saved to your workbook, and you go back to work. To modify your workbook and save the changes:

Step 1	*Delete*	the Sheet2 and Sheet3 sheet tabs

chapter one

CAUTION TIP

Once you have completed a Save or Save As operation, you cannot undo it. To avoid inadvertently saving a workbook that you planned to copy, perform the Save As command as soon as you open the file you are going to edit. You can then save frequently without worrying about overwriting your original file.

Step 2	*Click*	the Save button 🖬 on the Standard toolbar

No dialog box opens because you have already named the workbook.

1.g Previewing and Printing a Worksheet

Luis asks you to print a copy of the Q1 Sales figures. Before you print a worksheet, preview it to ensure that you are printing the right information. To preview the worksheet:

Step 1	*Click*	the Sales Report Data sheet tab, if necessary
Step 2	*Click*	the Print Preview button 🔍 on the Standard toolbar

Your Print Preview might appear in color or in black and white. The Print Preview toolbar appears at the top of the window. The status bar indicates the number of pages that print. Your screen should look similar to Figure 1-7.

FIGURE 1-7
Print Preview Window

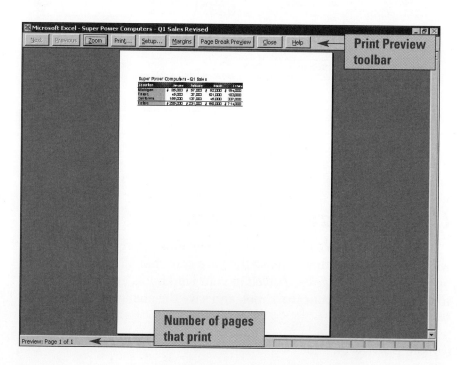

MENU TIP

Click Print Preview on the File menu to preview a document.

| Step 3 | *Click* | the Print button on the Print Preview toolbar |
| Step 4 | *Click* | OK to send the worksheet to the default printer |

1.h   Closing a Workbook

When you finish working with a workbook, you can close it without closing the Excel application. If you have modified the workbook you are closing, Excel prompts you to save your work. To close the *Super Power Computers – Q1 Sales Revised* workbook:

| Step 1 | *Click* | the Close Window button ⊠ on the right side of the menu bar |
| Step 2 | *Click* | Yes to save any changes, if prompted |

Excel displays the next open workbook, if there is one. If no workbooks are open, you see a blank workspace. You can quickly reopen a saved workbook from a folder that you created. To open a workbook from a folder:

Step 1	*Click*	the Open button 🗁 on the Standard toolbar
Step 2	*Click*	the Look in: list arrow
Step 3	*Click*	the folder with your name (the folder you created in the previous section)
Step 4	*Double-click*	*Super Power Computers – Q1 Sales Revised*

The workbook opens. Next you create a new workbook from a template.

1.i   Creating a New Workbook from a Template

A **template** is a workbook into which formatting, settings, and formulas are already inserted. When you create a new workbook, you are actually creating a new workbook based on Excel's default workbook template, which contains three blank worksheets. You can create a new workbook based on another template. You can choose from additional templates provided with Excel, or you can create your own.

CAUTION TIP

Be careful when clicking the Print button on the Standard toolbar. It immediately sends the file to the printer using the current page setup options. You may not be aware of the current print area or even which printer will print the file.

TASK PANE TIP

You can open a workbook by clicking the More workbooks link in the Open a workbook section in the New Workbook task pane.

MENU TIP

Click the Close command on the File menu to close the workbook.

chapter
one

You need to create a blank invoice to bill customers of Super Power Computers. To create a new workbook based on the Invoice template:

Step 1	*Click*	<u>F</u>ile

Step 2	*Click*	<u>N</u>ew

The New Workbook task pane opens.

Step 3	*Click*	the General Templates link in the New from template section in the New Workbook task pane

The Templates dialog box opens.

Step 4	*Click*	the Spreadsheet Solutions tab

Step 5	*Click*	the Sales Invoice template icon

You should see a preview of the template in the Preview box. Your dialog box should look similar to Figure 1-8.

FIGURE 1-8
Creating a New Workbook from a Template

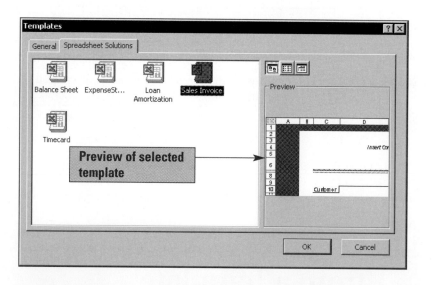

notes If you do not see a preview in the Preview box, but instead see instructions on how to install additional templates, insert the Office XP CD-ROM in your CD-ROM drive, click OK, and then skip Step 6 and continue reading.

| Step 6 | *Click* | OK |

A new workbook, based on the Sales Invoice template, opens. The title bar identifies this workbook as "Sales Invoice1." Changes you make to this workbook do not affect the template itself. Your screen should look similar to Figure 1-9.

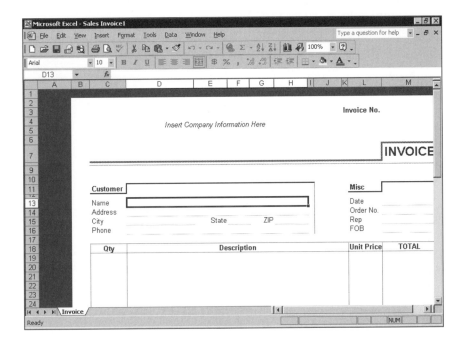

FIGURE 1-9
New Invoice Workbook

The new workbook looks very different from the workbooks you have seen thus far. Gridlines and column and row headings are turned off to reduce the amount of distracting elements in the template.

| Step 7 | *Scroll* | the worksheet to familiarize yourself with it |

Super Power Computers generates many invoices every day. By using this template, you save yourself a lot of time and effort.

1.j Exiting Excel

When you finish working in Excel, you should exit the application. You are prompted to save any modified workbooks that remain open. If you change your mind about exiting, click the Cancel button. To exit Excel:

| Step 1 | *Click* | the Close button ☒ on the Excel title bar |
| Step 2 | *Click* | No if prompted to save any changes to open workbooks |

CAUTION TIP

Some templates and workbooks contain macros that have been written by other users to automate certain routine tasks in the workbook. Unfortunately, some macros, known as macro viruses, are programmed to do malicious things. Whenever you open a workbook containing macros, you will receive a warning about the possibility of macro viruses. Excel cannot tell you whether the macros will do anything harmful; rather, it simply alerts you to the fact that the workbook contains macros. If you have downloaded a workbook from the Internet and are not sure of its origin, you should take a cautious approach and disable the workbook macros. The data will remain intact, even though the macros are disabled.

chapter
one

Summary

▶ A worksheet is an electronic spreadsheet. A workbook is a collection of worksheets.

▶ Cells are containers in worksheets for text, numerical values, and formulas that calculate data. Cells are organized into rows and columns. A cell reference identifies a particular cell through a combination of the column letter and the row number.

▶ You can open multiple workbooks in Excel.

▶ By default, new workbooks are created with three worksheets.

▶ You can use keyboard shortcuts such as the HOME key, the CTRL + HOME keys, the TAB key, and the SHIFT + TAB keys to navigate around a worksheet. You can also use the mouse to activate a cell or to scroll to other cells.

▶ You can select cells with the mouse by pressing and holding the left mouse button as you drag across cells. Select cells with the keyboard by pressing and holding the SHIFT key plus the ARROW keys, and other shortcut keys, such as the CTRL, HOME, and END keys. Select columns and rows by clicking the column and row headers.

▶ You can organize worksheets by inserting, moving, copying, or deleting worksheets.

▶ You can create new folders to organize your work from within the Open and Save As dialog boxes.

▶ You can use the Save As command when you want to make a copy of an existing workbook or save a workbook in a different file format.

▶ You can use the Save command to save a new workbook or to save changes to a previously named workbook.

▶ You should preview worksheets before you print them.

▶ Templates are used to start a new workbook with preset formatting, data, and formulas.

▶ When you close a new or modified workbook, Excel reminds you to save your work.

▶ When you close the Excel application, Excel reminds you to save any unsaved workbooks.

Commands Review

Action	Menu Bar	Shortcut Menu	Toolbar	Task Pane	Keyboard
Open a workbook	File, Open	Right-click empty Excel workspace, click Open	📂	More workbooks link in New Workbook task pane	CTRL + O ALT + F, O
Create a new workbook	File, New	Right-click empty Excel workspace, click New	🗋	Blank workbook link in New Workbook task pane	CTRL + N ALT + F, N
Insert a worksheet	Insert, Worksheet	Right-click sheet tab, click Insert			ALT + I, W
Move or copy a worksheet	Edit, Move or Copy Sheet	Right-click sheet tab, click Move or Copy			ALT + E, M
Delete a worksheet	Edit, Delete Sheet	Right-click sheet tab, click Delete			ALT + E, L
Save a workbook	File, Save		💾		CTRL + S CTRL + F12 ALT + F, S
Save As	File, Save As				ALT + F, A F12
Create a new folder from Open or Save As dialog box		Right-click blank area in dialog box, point to New, click Folder	📁		
Preview a worksheet	File, Print Preview		🔍		ALT + F, V
Print a worksheet	File, Print		🖨		ALT + F, P CTRL + P CTRL + Shift + F12
Close a workbook	File, Close		✖		CTRL + F4 ALT + F, C CTRL + W
Close multiple workbooks	Press and hold the SHIFT key, then File, Close All				SHIFT + ALT + F, C
Create a new workbook based on a template	File, New	Right-click empty Excel workspace, click New		General Templates link in New Workbook task pane	ALT + F, N
Exit Excel	File, Exit	Right-click application icon, click Close	✖		ALT + F4 ALT + F, X

Concepts Review

Circle the correct answer.

1. **Excel worksheets contain:**
   [a] 30 rows.
   [b] 256 rows.
   [c] 20,000 rows.
   [d] 65,536 rows.

2. **Excel worksheets contain:**
   [a] 30 columns.
   [b] 256 columns.
   [c] 20,000 columns.
   [d] 65,536 columns.

3. **Excel workbooks use the three-letter filename extension:**
   [a] doc.
   [b] txt.
   [c] htm.
   [d] xls.

chapter one

4. The status bar displays:
[a] text and formulas you are entering.
[b] results of the formula you are entering.
[c] important worksheet and system information.
[d] the filename of your workbook.

5. The active cell is identified by a:
[a] thick black border.
[b] change in the font color.
[c] shaded cell background.
[d] thin dashed border.

6. To save changes to a workbook without creating a new copy, use the:
[a] Save As command.
[b] Open command.
[c] More workbooks command.
[d] Save command.

7. To change the active worksheet:
[a] click the title bar.
[b] click the sheet tab.
[c] press the RIGHT ARROW key.
[d] click and drag the scroll bar at the bottom of the worksheet window.

8. To select nonadjacent ranges, you drag across the second range while you press and hold the:
[a] CTRL key.
[b] SHIFT key.
[c] CAPS LOCK key.
[d] ALT key.

9. To select adjacent cells using only the keyboard, you would use the ARROW keys as you press and hold the:
[a] CTRL key.
[b] SHIFT key.
[c] TAB key.
[d] ALT key.

10. To select an entire column or row:
[a] key the column letter or row number.
[b] press and hold the CTRL key, then key the column letter or row number.
[c] click the column or row header.
[d] key the column letter or row number in the Name Box.

Circle **T** if the statement is true or **F** if the statement is false.

T F   1. Excel can open many workbooks at once.

T F   2. Cells can contain numbers, text, or formulas.

T F   3. Rows run vertically down the worksheet.

T F   4. You can select menu items using only keyboard shortcuts.

T F   5. The Formula Bar displays the row and column number of the active cell.

T F   6. Columns run vertically down the worksheet.

T F   7. Clicking a tab scroll button changes the active worksheet.

T F   8. Pressing the CTRL + HOME keys closes the Excel application and saves any open workbooks.

T F   9. You cannot open a file unless it is saved on your computer.

T F   10. The Save and Save As commands do exactly the same thing.

Skills Review

Exercise 1

1. Start Excel.

2. Open the *Sweet Tooth Q1 2003 Sales* workbook located on the Data Disk.

3. Copy Sheet1 to a new worksheet.

4. Save the workbook as *Sweet Tooth Q1 2003 Sales Revised*, and print it.

5. Close the workbook.

Exercise 2

1. Open the *Region Sales Summary* workbook located on the Data Disk.

2. Save the workbook as *Region Sales Summary Revised*.

3. Change the worksheet order to: East, West, North, South.

4. Activate the East sheet tab.

5. Activate cell A1, if necessary.

6. Save your changes, and print the worksheet.

7. Close the workbook.

Exercise 3

1. Create a new workbook using the *ExpenseStatement* template.

2. Use Print Preview to preview the printed worksheet.

3. Print the worksheet.

4. Save the workbook as *My Expense Statement*, and print it.

5. Close the workbook.

Exercise 4 ⓒ

1. Open the *2003 Sales Projections* workbook located on the Data Disk.

2. Delete all the sheet tabs for the year 2002.

3. Switch between worksheets to locate the store whose projected sales total will be the greatest.

4. Select the cells containing data for that store.

5. Save the workbook as *2003 Sales Projections Revised*, and print it.

6. Close the workbook.

chapter one

Exercise 5   C

1. Open the *Half Marathon Mile Splits* workbook located on the Data Disk.

2. Select cells B3:B9 and D3:D9.

3. Delete the Sheet2 and Sheet3 worksheets from the workbook.

4. Save the workbook as *Half Marathon Mile Splits Revised*, and print it.

5. Close the workbook.

Exercise 6   C

1. Create a new, blank workbook.

2. Insert a new worksheet.

3. Move the new worksheet so it is the last worksheet in the workbook.

4. Save the workbook as *4 Blank Sheets* in a new folder named "Practice."

5. Close the workbook.

6. Open the workbook *4 Blank Sheets* located in the Practice folder.

7. Reorganize the worksheets in the following order: Sheet4, Sheet3, Sheet2, Sheet1.

8. Save the workbook as *4 Blank Sheets Revised* in the Practice folder.

9. Close the workbook.

Exercise 7   C

1. Open the *State Capitals* workbook located on the Data Disk.

2. Use Print Preview to preview the printed worksheet.

3. Print the worksheet.

4. Save the workbook as *State Capitals WK4 Format* in Lotus 1-2-3 format.

5. Close the workbook without saving any additional changes.

Exercise 8   C

1. Open the *2002 Sales Report* workbook located on the Data Disk.

2. On the Southwest Division 2002 sheet tab, select all of the data except the two title lines by using the mouse or keyboard.

3. On the Southeast Division 2002 sheet tab, select column C.

4. On the Northwest Division 2002 sheet tab, select row 9.

5. On the Northeast Division 2002 sheet tab, select cells B8:C8.

6. Save the workbook as *2002 Sales Report Revised*, and print it.

7. Close the workbook.

8. Exit Excel.

Case Projects

Project 1

You work for a large company with many offices spread throughout the United States and Canada. To facilitate information sharing between offices, your company stores many files on an FTP server. Your job is to train new employees how to open files on the company's FTP server. Using the Ask A Question Box, research how to open workbooks on an FTP server, then create a Word document and write at least two paragraphs explaining how to do this. Save your document as *Open an Excel Workbook on an FTP Server* and print it. Close the document and exit Word.

Project 2

You work as an office manager. You decide to reorganize the company's workbook files by date. To do this, you need to create folders for the last five years. Use the Open or Save As dialog box in Excel to create a new folder called "Project 2." Inside that folder, create a new folder for each of the last five years.

Project 3

You would like to find out more about Excel's keyboard shortcuts, particularly as they apply to navigating worksheets. Use online Help to search for keyboard shortcuts, then look for a topic "Move and scroll within worksheets." Copy and paste this list into a Word document and save the document as *Excel Worksheet Navigation Shortcuts*. Print the document, then close it.

Project 4

You work for a mortgage company, and it is your job to calculate amortization tables for clients. You'd like to use a template, but aren't sure how to start. You notice a Templates on Microsoft.com link in the New Workbook task pane, and decide to investigate. Click the link, locate a *Loan Calculator* template for Excel, and download it. Open the template in Excel, then preview and print a copy of the template. Save the workbook as *Loan Calculator*.

chapter one

Entering and Editing Data in a Worksheet

Chapter Overview

With Excel, you can store numerical data in a variety of formats. You can also store text data such as names and Social Security numbers. In this chapter, you learn how to enter and edit data in a worksheet. You also learn to use the Undo and Redo commands to help you when you make the inevitable mistake, how to zoom in on a worksheet, and how to name and color sheet tabs.

LEARNING OBJECTIVES

- ▶ Create new workbooks
- ▶ Enter text and numbers in cells
- ▶ Edit cell contents
- ▶ Use Undo and Redo
- ▶ Change the Zoom setting
- ▶ Rename a sheet tab
- ▶ Change a sheet tab color

Case profile

To keep track of employees at Super Power Computers, each store uses an employee name list workbook. This workbook stores important information such as the name, hourly wage, and phone number of each employee. A new store has just opened in Kansas City, and you need to provide them with this workbook.

chapter
two

2.a   Creating New Workbooks

In Chapter 1, you learned how to create a new workbook based on a template, a special type of Excel file. You also learned that Excel automatically creates a new, blank workbook when you start the application. In this section, you learn to create new, blank workbooks and to create new workbooks from existing workbooks, similar to using a template file.

Creating a New, Blank Workbook

When you start Excel, a new workbook is created for you automatically. However, you may need to create additional workbooks while you are working in Excel. To create a new blank workbook:

Step 1	*Start*	Excel
Step 2	*Click*	the Blank Workbook link in the New Workbook task pane

A new workbook is created in Excel.

| Step 3 | *Close* | both of the blank workbooks |

Creating a Workbook Based on an Existing Workbook

Instead of starting a new workbook, you decide to create the new workbook from an existing workbook file, and then add the data you need to change. The New Workbook task pane provides a quick shortcut for this task. To create a new workbook from an existing workbook file:

Step 1	*Click*	File
Step 2	*Click*	New
Step 3	*Click*	the Choose workbook link in the New Workbook task pane
Step 4	*Select*	*Super Power Computers – Blank Employee List* from the Data Disk
Step 5	*Click*	Create New

A new file is created from the existing workbook. Excel assigns the new workbook the same filename as the original workbook with a "1" at the end of the filename, as you can see in the title bar.

chapter
two

Step 6	*Save*	the workbook as *Super Power Computers – Kansas City Employee List*

2.b Entering Text and Numbers in Cells

You can enter numbers, letters, and symbols into the active cell. When you enter data in a cell, Excel recognizes the type of data you are entering. For example, if you enter your name in a cell, Excel knows that this is a text value and therefore cannot be used in numerical calculations. Date and time values are special cases of numerical data. When you enter this type of data, Excel automatically converts the value you key into a special numerical value, which makes it easier for Excel to use in calculations.

When you've finished entering data in a cell, you need to accept the entry by pressing the ENTER key, the TAB key, or any of the ARROW keys, or by clicking the Enter button next to the Formula Bar or another cell in the worksheet. Before accepting the entry in a cell, you can change your mind by pressing the ESC key, and the cell's content reverts to the way it was before you began entering or editing the data.

Entering Text

You receive the employee information from the new Kansas City store, as shown in Table 2-1. The first row of data has already been entered in the workbook you opened. These values are **column labels**, identifying the data stored in each column.

TABLE 2-1
Super Power Computers
Employee Data

Name	Wage	Phone
Jared Wright	$9.00	(816) 555-3456
Kaili Muafala	$9.00	(816) 555-9254
Jenna McGregor	$16.00	(816) 555-0012
Monica Chambers	$11.50	(816) 555-1827
Baka Hakamin	$12.75	(816) 555-4637
Homer Hansen	$14.00	(816) 555-8822

To enter text in a worksheet:

Step 1	*Activate*	cell A2

Step 2	*Key*	Jared Wright

Your screen should look similar to Figure 2-1.

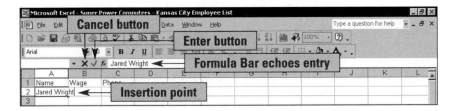

FIGURE 2-1
Entering Data

As you enter data, the status bar displays the word "Enter." The Formula Bar displays the contents of the active cell, while the cell itself shows the results of any formula entered in the cell. In the case of numbers or text, no calculation takes place, so you see exactly what you enter. As you enter or edit data in a cell, the Cancel and Enter buttons appear next to the Formula Bar, the mouse pointer changes to an I-beam pointer to indicate that you are entering a value in a cell, and a blinking **insertion point** appears in the cell to indicate where the next character that you key will go.

| Step 3 | Press | the ENTER key |

When you press the ENTER key, the entry is accepted, and the active cell moves down one row by default.

| Step 4 | Follow | Steps 2 and 3 to add each name listed in Table 2-1 to column A of your worksheet |

You can use any of the navigation keys to complete data entry in one cell and then move to another.

Entering Numbers

You enter number values directly into the active cell, the same way you enter text values, or date and time values. To enter numerical values:

Step 1	Activate	cell B2
Step 2	Key	$9.00
Step 3	Click	the Enter button ☑ on the Formula Bar

Excel recognizes the number you entered as currency. It shows the number in the cell with a dollar sign, but in the Formula Bar, the number is displayed without the dollar sign and the trailing zeros.

chapter
two

You can no longer see the full value in cell A2. The data (Jared's name) is still there; it is just hidden. You learn how to adjust column widths to display more characters in Chapter 4.

| Step 4 | *Enter* | the rest of the data in the Wage column in Table 2-1 |

Some types of data, although numeric in appearance, aren't really intended to be used in mathematical calculations. Examples of these special types of numbers include phone numbers and Social Security numbers. When you enter numbers mixed with other characters, such as parentheses, dashes, and so on, Excel automatically treats the cell value as a text value.

Step 5	*Key*	(816) 555-3456 in cell C2
Step 6	*Press*	the ENTER key
Step 7	*Enter*	the rest of the data in the Phone column in Table 2-1

Your worksheet should look similar to Figure 2-2.

FIGURE 2-2
Super Power Computers
Employee Data

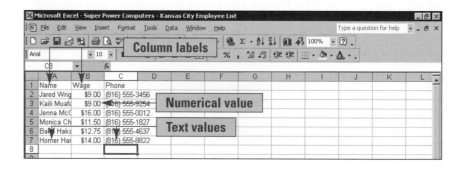

In general, entering data into cells is a simple process: activate the cell, enter the data, and accept the entry.

2.c Editing Cell Contents

Excel provides many ways to edit the contents of a cell. You receive updated information from the Kansas City store, and you need to modify your worksheet. To completely replace a cell's value:

| Step 1 | *Activate* | cell A7 |
| Step 2 | *Key* | Ross Phillips |

Step 3	*Press*	the TAB key
Step 4	*Key*	$13.00 in cell B7
Step 5	*Press*	the ENTER key

Editing in the Active Cell

Often, you need to revise only part of an entry. To edit in the active cell:

| Step 1 | *Double-click* | cell B4 |

The entry in cell B4 changes to display only the number 16 without the dollar sign and trailing zeros, and the blinking insertion point appears in the cell.

| Step 2 | *Drag* | the I-beam pointer ⌶ over the 6 to select it |

Your screen should look similar to Figure 2-3. The 6 in cell B11 is **selected**. Anything you key replaces the selected text.

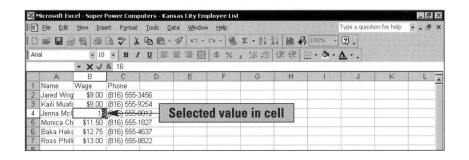

FIGURE 2-3
Editing in the Active Cell

| Step 3 | *Key* | 7.25 |
| Step 4 | *Press* | the ENTER key |

The wage for Jenna should be $17.25.

Editing in the Formula Bar

An alternative to editing directly in the cell is to use the Formula Bar. You can edit the contents of the active cell in the Formula Bar by either moving the insertion point to where you want to make changes or highlighting the text you want to change and then keying new text.

CAUTION TIP

Although the rekeying method is the fastest way to edit a cell, be careful when taking this approach. The previous contents of the cell are replaced with any new data you enter.

QUICK TIP

Sometimes it is difficult to select text precisely with the mouse. Try this: Click to position the insertion point at the start of your selection, then press and hold the SHIFT key while you press the right ARROW key to move across the text.

chapter
two

To edit in the Formula Bar:

Step 1	*Activate*	cell C3
Step 2	*Click*	to the left of 4 in the Formula Bar
Step 3	*Press*	the DELETE key

Pressing the DELETE key deletes the character to the right of the insertion point. Pressing the BACKSPACE key deletes the character to the left of the insertion point.

Step 4	*Key*	8
Step 5	*Click*	the Enter button ☑ on the Formula Bar

Your worksheet should look similar to Figure 2-4.

FIGURE 2-4
Modified Worksheet

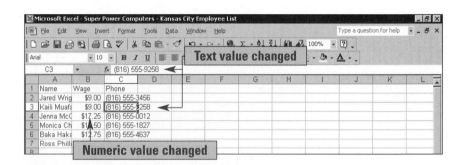

Clearing Cell Content

Sometimes you need to delete all of the contents in a cell. To clear cell content:

Step 1	*Drag*	to select cells A7:C7
Step 2	*Press*	the DELETE key

The contents of cell A7:C7 are deleted. In the next section you learn to use the Undo and Redo tools. Do *not* save your workbook at this point.

2.d Using Undo and Redo

The **Undo** command reverses your previous action or actions. The **Redo** command reinstates the action or actions you undid. You can Undo and Redo one action at a time, or you can select a number of actions to Undo and Redo from a list of up to 16 previous actions. To undo the last action, click the Undo button on the Standard toolbar. The Redo button is not active until you have used Undo. Click the Redo button to undo the last Undo command.

You realize that you changed the value in cell C3 by mistake. Rather than reentering the data, you can use Undo. To use the Undo and Redo commands:

| Step 1 | *Click* | the Undo button  on the Standard toolbar |

The contents of cells A7:C7 return.

| Step 2 | *Click* | the Redo button 🗘 to change the value back again |
| Step 3 | *Click* | the Undo button ↶ on the Standard toolbar to restore the contents again |

You can use the Undo list to quickly Undo several commands at once. To use the Undo list:

| Step 1 | *Change* | the value in cell C4 to (816) 555-1200 |
| Step 2 | *Change* | the value in cell A4 to Lori Jones |

You have performed two actions, both data entry. The Undo list allows you to select multiple actions to Undo.

Step 3	*Click*	the Undo button list arrow ↶▾ on the Standard toolbar
Step 4	*Move*	the pointer down the list, selecting the top two "Typing" actions
Step 5	*Click*	the second "Typing" action

Cells A4 and C4 return to their previous values. The Redo list functions in the same way as the Undo list.

CAUTION TIP

When you save a workbook, the Undo/Redo list starts over. You cannot reverse any action performed prior to the file save.

QUICK TIP

Press the CTRL + Z keys to Undo the last action. Press the CTRL + Y keys to Redo the last Undo action.

MENU TIP

Click the Undo command on the Edit menu to reverse your last action. Click the Redo or Repeat command on the Edit menu to reverse the previous Undo action.

chapter two

| Step 6 | *Save* | the workbook |

2.e Changing the Zoom Setting

If you use a small monitor or worksheets containing a lot of data, it may be hard to read or see the data you want to see. The Zoom setting allows you to **zoom**, to increase or decrease, the viewable area of your worksheet. Zooming in magnifies cells, making them appear much larger. Zooming out makes cells appear smaller, allowing you to see more of the worksheet. You can zoom in to 400% or out to 10%. To zoom in on the worksheet:

| Step 1 | *Click* | the Zoom button list arrow `100%` on the Standard toolbar |
| Step 2 | *Click* | 200% |

Your worksheet zooms in to 200%, or twice the default size. You can select any of the preset Zoom options, or key a custom Zoom setting.

Step 3	*Click*	in the Zoom button text box `200%` on the Standard toolbar
Step 4	*Key*	125
Step 5	*Press*	the ENTER key
Step 6	*Save*	the workbook

C 2.f Renaming a Sheet Tab

An organized workbook is one in which information is logically grouped and easy to find. Each store's staff comprises sales representatives and technicians. By separating employee data for each group onto different sheet tabs, your workbook will be more organized. Naming each sheet tab makes it much easier to find the data. To name a sheet tab:

| Step 1 | *Double-click* | the Sheet1 sheet tab |
| Step 2 | *Key* | Sales Reps |

Step 3	*Press*	the ENTER key
Step 4	*Rename*	Sheet2 as Technicians

2.g Changing a Sheet Tab Color

To make it even easier to identify sheet tabs, you can color-code the tabs to make them stand out. To change a sheet tab color:

Step 1	*Right-click*	the Sales Reps sheet tab
Step 2	*Click*	Tab Color

The Format Tab Color dialog box on your screen should look similar to Figure 2-5.

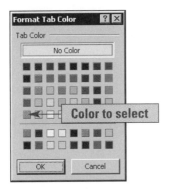

FIGURE 2-5
Format Color Tab

Step 3	*Click*	the pink color
Step 4	*Click*	OK
Step 5	*Change*	the Technicians sheet tab to light orange

Your screen should look similar to Figure 2-6.

FIGURE 2-6
Workbook with Colored Sheet Tabs

Step 6	*Save*	the workbook and close it

chapter
two

The employee name list workbook for the new Kansas City store is ready to be used.

Summary

▶ You can create new, blank workbooks by clicking the Blank Workbook link in the task pane.

▶ You can create a new workbook based on an existing workbook by clicking the New command on the File menu, then clicking the Choose workbook link in the New Workbook task pane.

▶ You enter data by keying the information directly into the active cell or in the Formula Bar. You can enter text and numbers in a variety of formats.

▶ You edit data by keying new data in a cell, double-clicking a cell to edit directly in the cell, or pressing the F2 key and using the Formula Bar to edit the cell's contents.

▶ You can use the Undo list to quickly undo as many as 16 actions at once, including formatting, data entry, editing, and deletion.

▶ The Zoom command zooms a worksheet in and out, making it easier to read or display more data at one time.

▶ You can rename and recolor worksheet tabs to make it easier to find data.

Commands Review

Action	Menu Bar	Shortcut Menu	Toolbar	Task Pane	Keyboard
Create a new workbook	File, New	Right-click Null application window, click New	▢	Blank workbook link in New Workbook task pane	CTRL + N ALT + F, N
Create a new workbook based on another workbook				Choose workbook link in New Workbook task pane	
Edit a cell					F2
Accept a cell entry			✓		ENTER
Cancel a cell entry			✕		ESC
Undo the previous action	Edit, Undo		↶		CTRL + Z ALT + E, U
Redo an undo action	Edit, Redo		↷		CTRL +Y ALT + E, R
Zoom	View, Zoom		100% ▾		ALT + V, Z
Rename a worksheet tab	Format, Sheet, Rename	Right-click sheet tab, click Rename			ALT + O, H, R
Change a worksheet color tab	Format, Sheet, Tab Color	Right-click sheet, tab, click Tab Color			ALT + O, H, T

Concepts Review

Circle the correct answer.

1. To cancel an entry in a cell, press the:
[a] TAB key.
[b] ENTER key.
[c] ESC key.
[d] DELETE key.

2. To accept an entry in a cell:
[a] press the CTRL + ALT + ESC keys.
[b] stop keying and wait for the previous value to return.
[c] press the ESC key.
[d] press the ENTER key.

3. You can undo or redo:
[a] as many as 1 operation.
[b] as many as 10 operations.
[c] as many as 16 operations.
[d] an unlimited number of operations.

4. When you activate a cell containing data and begin keying new data, the new data:
[a] is added to the end of the old data.
[b] is added in front of the old data.
[c] is rejected since there is already data in the cell.
[d] replaces the old data.

5. Pressing the DELETE key when the insertion point is blinking in a cell or in the Formula Bar:
[a] deletes the entire value.
[b] deletes one character to the right.
[c] deletes one character to the left.
[d] does nothing.

6. Pressing the BACKSPACE key when the insertion point is blinking in a cell or in the Formula Bar:
[a] deletes the entire value.
[b] deletes one character to the right.
[c] deletes one character to the left.
[d] does nothing.

7. Which of the following values would be treated as a text value?
[a] 111-22-3333
[b] 11,122,333
[c] 111.22333
[d] $111,223.33

8. When you make a mistake while entering data, you should immediately:
[a] save the workbook.
[b] close the workbook without saving your changes.
[c] reopen the workbook.
[d] use the Undo command.

9. Which of the following is not an option when using the Zoom command?
[a] 200%
[b] 50%
[c] Selection
[d] 1%

10. The default action that occurs when you press the ENTER key when entering cell data is to:
[a] accept the entry and move the active cell down one.
[b] accept the entry and move the active cell to the left.
[c] discard the changes and revert the cell's contents back to the way they were.
[d] accept the entry and move the active cell to the right.

chapter two

Circle **T** if the statement is true or **F** if the statement is false.

T F   1. The Undo command can undo any command in Excel.

T F   2. If you rename a sheet tab, you cannot change its color.

T F   3. To edit a cell entry, you must double-click it first.

T F   4. You cannot use the Undo command until you have first used the Redo command.

T F   5. You can zoom in to 1600% using the Zoom button on the Standard toolbar.

T F   6. When you create a new workbook from an existing workbook, a number is added to the end of the filename.

T F   7. Pressing the ESC key is a valid means of accepting an entry in a cell.

T F   8. The Cancel and Enter buttons do not appear on the Formula Bar until you are entering data in a cell.

T F   9. The insertion point appears while you are editing a cell to indicate where the next character you key will go.

T F   10. Using any of the navigation keys is a valid way of accepting data entry in a cell.

Skills Review

Exercise 1

1. Create a new workbook and enter the data below on Sheet1. Enter the text "TIME SHEET" in cell A1. (*Hint:* Enter the dates with forward slashes and the times with colons. Use 24-hour clock times, as shown in the table.)

TIME SHEET		
Date	Start Time	End Time
5/10/2003	8:00	17:00
5/11/2003	8:05	16:30
5/12/2003	8:00	16:55

2. Save the workbook as *Time Sheet*, and print it.

3. Close the workbook.

Exercise 2

1. Create a new workbook based on the *Employee Time Sheet* workbook located on the Data Disk.

2. Save the workbook as *Employee Time Sheet Revised*.

3. Change the value in cell A2 to your name.

4. Change the start time for 5/10/2003 to 8:15.

5. Change the end time for 5/12/2003 to 17:35.

6. Enter the following data in row 7:

   5/13/2003   8:45   17:00

7. Save your changes, and print the worksheet.

8. Close the workbook.

Exercise 3

1. Create a new workbook based on the *Employee Time Sheet Revised* workbook that you created in Exercise 2.

2. Save the workbook as *Multiple Employees Time Sheets.*

3. Rename Sheet2 as "Lori Jones."

4. Rename Sheet3 as "Kaili Muafala."

5. Rename Sheet1 as your name.

6. Change the sheet tab color of each worksheet to a different color.

7. Save your changes, and print the worksheet.

8. Close the workbook.

Exercise 4

1. Create a new workbook and enter the data below on Sheet1. Enter the label "CHECKBOOK TRANSACTIONS" in cell A1.

CHECKBOOK TRANSACTIONS			
Date	Description	Credit	Debit
10/12/2003	Paycheck	1542.90	
10/14/2003	Groceries		142.57
10/20/2003	Bonus	300.00	
10/21/2003	House payment		842.50

2. Save the workbook as *Checkbook Transactions*, and print it.

3. Close the workbook.

Exercise 5

1. Create a new workbook based on the *Checkbook Transactions* workbook that you created in Exercise 4.

2. Change cell A1 to read "PERSONAL CHECKBOOK TRANSACTIONS."

3. Save the file as *Personal Checkbook Transactions.*

4. Delete the four transactions found in cells A3 through D6.

5. Save and print the workbook, then close it.

chapter two

Exercise 6

1. Create a new workbook and enter the data below on Sheet1. Enter the label "STATE CAPITALS" in cell A1.

STATE CAPITALS	
State	Capital City
Utah	Salt Lake City
Delaware	Dover
California	Los Angeles
Arizona	Tempe
New York	Albany
Florida	Miami
Texas	Dallas
Colorado	Denver

2. Rename Sheet1 as "Capitals."

3. Recolor the Capitals sheet tab to red.

4. Save the workbook as *State Capitals*, and print it.

5. Close the workbook.

Exercise 7

1. Create a new workbook based on the *State Capitals* workbook that you created in Exercise 6.

2. Save the workbook as *Corrected State Capitals*.

3. Display the Web toolbar, if necessary, by clicking the <u>V</u>iew menu, pointing to <u>T</u>oolbars, then clicking Web.

4. Search the Web for a list of state capitals.

5. Correct any errors you find in the workbook.

6. Rename the Capitals sheet tab as "Corrected Capitals," and change the sheet tab color to green.

7. Save and print the workbook, then close it.

Exercise 8

1. Use the Internet to search for movie times in your area.

2. Create a new workbook with column headings for "Movie Title," "Time," and "Theater."

3. Record the start times for at least five different movies you would like to see.

4. Save the workbook as *Movie Times*, and print it.

5. Close the workbook.

Case Projects

Project 1

You are the office manager of a small business. One of your duties is to keep track of the office supplies inventory. Create a workbook using fictitious data for at least 20 items. Include a column for each of the following: name of item, current amount in stock, and estimated price. Save the workbook as *Office Supplies Inventory*, and print and close it.

Project 2

As the payroll clerk at a college bookstore, you must calculate the hours worked by each student employee during the week. Create a new workbook based on the workbook *Employee Work Hours* located on the Data Disk. In row 1 of columns B, C, D, E, and F, list the days Monday through Friday. List the number of hours that each student works each day. Save the workbook as *Employee Work Hours Revised*, and then print and close it.

Project 3

You are a teacher who uses Excel to record student scores. Create a workbook containing 15 fictitious student names with five assignment columns and a total column. Record data indicating each student's scores for the five assignments. Switch to Sheet2 to enter data from another class. Enter 15 more student names and five assignment columns. Record new data as you did before. Rename Sheet1 as "Class 1" and Sheet2 as "Class 2." Change the color of the two sheet tabs to red. Save the workbook as *Student Scores*, and then print and close it.

Project 4

You are thinking of investing money in the stock market. Connect to the Internet and search the Web to find the most current stock price of five companies in which you are interested. Create a new workbook to record the company name, company stock ticker symbol, current share price, yesterday's share price, and the date. Rename the worksheet as "Stocks." Save the workbook as *Stock Prices*, and then print and close it.

Project 5

You make purchasing recommendations for computer systems to your boss. Connect to the Internet and search the Web to obtain prices for systems offered by at least three different vendors. Create a new workbook to record the vendor name, Web address, system price, processor speed, amount of RAM, hard drive size, and monitor size. When you enter a Web address, Excel automatically formats it with blue text and underline. Rename the sheet tab with today's month and day; for example, Jan 4. Save the workbook as *Computer Prices*, and then print and close it.

Project 6

You are planning a road trip. Connect to the Internet and search the Web to find the driving distance from your city to at least five other cities you would like to visit. (*Hint:* Search for the keywords "driving directions.") Create a new workbook to record the starting city, destination city, and driving distance. Save the workbook as *Road Trip*, and then print and close it.

Project 7

You are working on a statistics project. Over the next five days, count the number of students attending each of your classes. Create a new workbook. In row 1, enter the dates you used for your survey. In column A, enter the class names. Enter the data you collected each day for each class. Save the workbook as *Attendance Statistics*, and then print and close it.

Project 8

You are a runner training for a marathon. You keep track of your progress by recording the date, mileage, and time of your runs. Create a new workbook to record fictitious data. Rename Sheet1 as "Week 1," Sheet2 as "Week 2," and Sheet3 as "Week 3." Give each sheet tab a different color. On the Week 1 worksheet, record fictitious data for one week. Save the workbook as *Running Log*, and then print and close it.

chapter two

Building Worksheets

Chapter Overview

Most worksheets do much more than store data. Data needs to be analyzed, calculated, and presented. To perform most of this work, functions and formulas work tirelessly behind the scenes, calculating and recalculating every time data is changed in your worksheets. Reorganizing worksheets by moving and copying data is a regular task. In this chapter, you learn how to accomplish this efficiently.

LEARNING OBJECTIVES

▶ Create and revise formulas
▶ Use cut, copy, and paste
▶ Copy formulas with relative, absolute, and mixed cell references
▶ Use basic functions
▶ Use the Insert Function dialog box
▶ Use 3-D references in formulas

Case profile

One of your duties at Super Power Computers is to calculate sales commissions and bonuses and send this information back to the store managers. Excel makes this simple by allowing you to use formulas to do the calculations. You can also use specialized Excel functions, which help you use your time more effectively. You can then copy and paste the formulas to quickly build your worksheets.

chapter three

3.a Creating and Revising Formulas

Formulas provide much of the true power of a spreadsheet. A **formula** is a mathematical expression that calculates a value. Some formulas are simple, such as those that add, subtract, multiply, and divide two or more values; for example, 2+2. Other formulas can be very complex and include a sequence of **functions**, or predefined formulas. All formulas require **operands**, which can be either values or references to cells containing values. Most formulas require **operators** to indicate the type of calculation that will take place. Common mathematical operators include + for addition, – for subtraction, * for multiplication, / for division, and ^ for exponentiation.

Following Formula Syntax and Rules of Precedence

Formulas follow a syntax. The **syntax** is the proper structure, or order, of the elements (operands and operators) in a formula. Excel follows the **rules of precedence**: it evaluates formulas from left to right, first evaluating any operations between parentheses, then any exponentiation, then multiplication and division, followed by addition and subtraction. Consider the following examples: 5+2*3 and (5+2)*3. In the first formula, 2*3 is calculated first and then added to 5, giving a result of 11. In the second example, 5+2 is calculated first and then multiplied by 3, giving a result of 21.

Entering Formulas

The real power of formulas lies in their ability to use cell references. Using cell references allows you to quickly change values, leaving the formula intact. Sales representatives at Super Power Computers are paid a commission based on the total sales. You need to calculate the sales commission for each employee. To enter a formula:

| Step 1 | *Open* | the *Super Power Computers - Bonus* workbook located on the Data Disk |
| Step 2 | *Save* | the workbook as *Super Power Computers - Bonus Revised* |

This workbook contains sales data from each of the Super Power Computer stores.

| Step 3 | *Activate* | cell D4 on the Store #1 worksheet |

chapter
three

All formulas begin with an equal sign = to indicate to Excel that the following expression needs to be evaluated.

| Step 4 | *Key* | =c4*0.05 |

You do not have to capitalize column references. Excel performs this task for you automatically when you enter a formula.

| Step 5 | *Click* | the Enter button ✓ on the Formula Bar |

This simple mathematical formula multiplies the value in cell C4 by 0.05 and displays the result, $1,726.55. The Formula Bar displays the formula, not the calculated result. Your screen should look similar to Figure 3-1.

FIGURE 3-1
Formula Displayed in the
Formula Bar

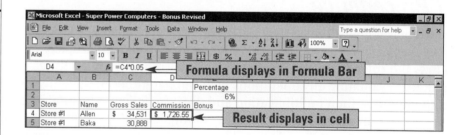

Editing Formulas Using the Formula Bar

Because Super Power Computers has had a good year, the sales commission has been increased to 6%. You can edit the formula to reflect this change. To edit a formula:

Step 1	*Verify*	that cell D4 is the active cell
Step 2	*Drag*	to select 5 in the Formula Bar
Step 3	*Key*	6
Step 4	*Press*	the ENTER key

Cell D4 displays the new result of the calculation, $2,071.86.

| Step 5 | *Save* | the workbook |

QUICK TIP

The blue box that appears around cell C4 is called a **range finder**. It highlights cells that are referenced in a formula.

3.b Using Cut, Copy, and Paste

Moving and copying data helps you organize and prepare worksheets quickly. When data is moved, or **cut**, from a worksheet, it is removed from its original location and placed on the **Clipboard**, which holds data temporarily. To finish moving the data that you cut to another location, you **paste** it from the Clipboard. When data is **copied**, the original data remains in place and a copy of the data is placed on the Clipboard. Data that you cut or copy stays on the Clipboard until you cut or copy more data, or until you exit Excel.

Copying Data Using Copy and Paste

The formula you added to cell D4 needs to be copied for each employee. To copy data using copy and paste:

Step 1	*Activate*	cell D4
Step 2	*Click*	the Copy button 📋 on the Standard toolbar
Step 3	*Click*	cell D5
Step 4	*Click*	the Paste button list arrow 📋▾ on the Standard toolbar
Step 5	*Click*	Formulas

This is the default command if you simply click the Paste button. Clicking Values in the list would paste the value from cell D4 instead of the formula.

Step 6	*Press*	the ESC key to end the Copy command

The formula in the Formula Bar has changed to reflect that this cell is in row 5 instead of in row 4. In other words, the formula references cell C5 instead of cell C4.

Copying Data Using the Fill Handle

Using the fill handle, you can quickly copy the contents of a cell to adjacent cells. The fill handle is the small black square that appears in the lower-right corner of a selected cell. To copy a formula using the fill handle:

Step 1	*Activate*	cell D5, if necessary

chapter
three

| Step 2 | *Drag* | the fill handle to cell D17 |

Make sure you drag only to cell D17 and not to cell D18.

| Step 3 | *Release* | the left mouse button |

The formula is copied to cells D6:D17. Your screen should look similar to Figure 3-2.

FIGURE 3-2
Formulas Copied Using the Fill Handle

C   *Moving Data Using Cut and Paste*

When you cut data from cells, a flashing border surrounds the selected area. The status bar provides instructions about how to select a destination cell. The destination can be on another worksheet or even another open workbook. To move data by using cut and paste:

Step 1	*Select*	the range E1:E2
Step 2	*Click*	the Cut button ✂ on the Standard toolbar
Step 3	*Activate*	cell F1
Step 4	*Click*	the Paste button 📋 on the Standard toolbar

The Cut command in Excel differs from that in other programs, such as Microsoft Word. Excel does not remove the selected text until you take one of two actions: (1) complete the move by selecting a destination and performing the Paste command or (2) press the DELETE key. If you press the DELETE key instead of completing the Paste operation, you do not place the data on the Clipboard; it is removed permanently. If you change your mind before pasting or deleting, press the ESC key to cancel the cut operation.

Using Drag-and-Drop to Cut, Copy, and Paste

Another way to move and copy data is to use **drag-and-drop**. To drag selected cells, click the selection border using the left mouse button. Hold the left mouse button down as you *drag* the cells to a new location. The mouse pointer changes to a four-headed arrow pointer, indicating the cells are being moved. Then *drop* them by releasing the left mouse button. To move data by using drag-and-drop:

Step 1	*Select*	cells A3:E19
Step 2	*Move*	the pointer over the border of your selection
Step 3	*Drag*	the range to cells A1:E17

A ScreenTip and a range outline guide you in moving the cells. Your screen should look similiar to Figure 3-3.

> ### CAUTION TIP
> When moving data with drag-and-drop, Excel prompts you if the move will overwrite data. However, Excel does *not* warn you of this when copying using drag-and-drop, and it overwrites any data in the target cells.

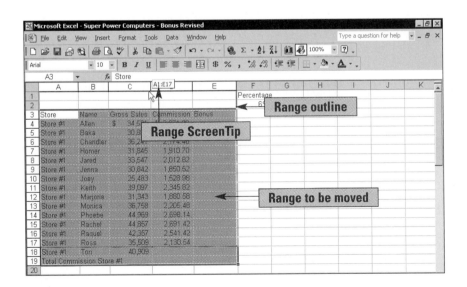

FIGURE 3-3
Dragging and Dropping to Copy Cells

| Step 4 | *Release* | the mouse button |

You can use a similar process to copy data. To copy data using drag-and-drop:

Step 1	*Select*	cell D15
Step 2	*Press & hold*	the CTRL key
Step 3	*Move*	the pointer over the border of your selection
Step 4	*Observe*	the plus sign in the mouse pointer, indicating that you are creating a copy of the selected data
Step 5	*Drag*	the selection to cell D16
Step 6	*Release*	the mouse button and the CTRL key

Using the Office Clipboard to Paste Data

Every time you cut or copy a piece of data, it replaces the data that was previously on the Clipboard. Office has its own Clipboard, called the Office Clipboard, which holds up to 24 items from any open application. You can then select the item you want and paste it into another Office document. You need to activate the Office Clipboard before you can collect cut or copied items on it. To activate the Office Clipboard:

Step 1	*Click*	<u>E</u>dit
Step 2	*Click*	Office Clip<u>b</u>oard
Step 3	*Observe*	that the Clipboard task pane opens
Step 4	*Copy*	the range F1:F2

A portion of the selected data appears on the Clipboard, as shown in Figure 3-4.

FIGURE 3-4
Clipboard Items

| Step 5 | *Activate* | cell F1 on the Store #2 sheet tab |

The top item on the Office Clipboard is the last item cut or copied.

| Step 6 | *Point to* | Percentage 6% in the Clipboard task pane |

A list arrow appears. If you click the list arrow, a submenu opens with <u>P</u>aste and <u>D</u>elete on it. Clicking the item on the Clipboard is the same as clicking the list arrow and then clicking <u>P</u>aste.

| Step 7 | *Click* | the Percentage 6% Clipboard item |

A copy of your data is placed in cells F1:F2 on the Store #2 worksheet.

| Step 8 | *Click* | the Close button on the Clipboard task pane title bar |
| Step 9 | *Save* | the workbook |

3.c Copying Formulas with Relative, Absolute, and Mixed Cell References

Excel uses three types of cell references: absolute, relative, and mixed. When you copy a formula containing a **relative reference**, the references change relative to the cell from which the formula is being copied. If cell C1 contains the formula =A1+B1 and is copied to cell D2, the formula changes to =B2+C2. Cell D2 is one row down and one row over from cell C1; the references B2 and C2 are correspondingly one row down and one row over from cells A1 and B1. When you copied the formulas in column D earlier in this chapter, you copied relative references, so the formulas were automatically updated to reflect the new row they were copied to.

When you need a formula to refer to a specific cell, no matter where the formula is copied, you use an **absolute reference**. Absolute cell references prefix the column and row with a dollar sign ($). A better way to set up the formula in column D is to use an absolute reference to cell F2, so that if the sales commission must be adjusted, it only has to be changed in one place. The formula for cell D2 would be =**C2*F2**.

chapter
three

When this formula is copied, the first, relative, reference changes, while the second, absolute, reference does not. To edit the formula and add an absolute reference:

Step 1	*Click*	the Store #1 sheet tab
Step 2	*Enter*	=C2*F2 in cell D2
Step 3	*Use*	the fill handle to copy cell D2 to cells D3:D16

The formula as well as its format is pasted into cell D3:D16. You don't want to copy the formatting.

Step 4	*Click*	the Auto Fill Options button on the worksheet
Step 5	*Click*	Fill Without Formatting
Step 6	*Observe*	that the dollar signs disappear from cell D3:D16
Step 7	*Click*	cell D3

Note in the Formula Bar that the relative reference in the formula was correctly updated to the proper row number, while the absolute reference remained fixed on cell F2.

| Step 8 | *Save* | the workbook |

In addition to absolute and relative references, Excel uses mixed references. A **mixed cell reference** maintains a reference to a specific row or column. For example, to maintain a reference to column A while allowing the row number to increment, use the mixed reference $A1. To maintain a reference to a specific row number while allowing the column letter to increment, use the mixed reference A$1.

3.d Using Basic Functions

Functions are predefined formulas that reduce complicated formulas to a function name and several required arguments or operands. An **argument** is some sort of data, usually numeric or text, that is supplied to a function. For example, to find the average of a series of numerical values, you must divide the sum by the number of values in the series. The AVERAGE function does this automatically when you supply the series of values as arguments. Arguments can be supplied to functions by keying the value in directly, or by using cell references. You can use formulas, or even other functions, as some or all of the arguments of a function.

To enter a function in a cell, you key the = sign, the name of the function, and then any required and/or optional arguments used by the function enclosed in parentheses. If the function is part of a longer formula, you key the = sign only at the beginning of the formula. The first function you learn about, the **SUM** function, uses the following syntax:

=**SUM**(**number1**, number2, ...)

Required arguments are listed in bold. Certain functions, such as the SUM function, allow you to supply as many optional arguments as you like, indicated by the ellipses (...).

notes
Throughout this book function names are capitalized to distinguish them from other text. Function names are not actually case-sensitive, so =count, =Count, and =COUNT are all valid ways to enter the function name.

Using the SUM Function

The SUM function, which adds two or more values, is one of the most commonly used functions. You need to add the total amount to be paid in sales commissions. To start keying the SUM function:

Step 1	*Activate*	cell D17

Step 2	*Key*	=SUM(

The Argument ScreenTip appears with the syntax of the formula you've started entering. You can enter individual values separated by commas, enter a range, or simply select cells. You select a range of cells.

Step 3	*Drag*	to select cells D2:D16

Your screen should look similar to Figure 3-5. The range D2:D16 is the number1 argument of the SUM function.

chapter
three

FIGURE 3-5
Using the SUM Function

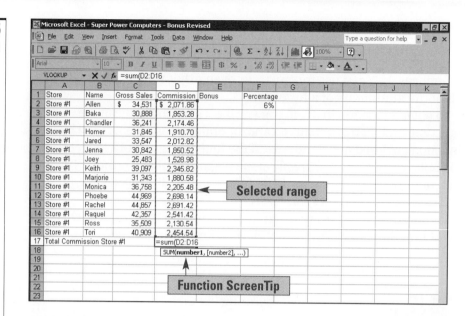

| Step 4 | *Click* | the Enter button ☑ on the Formula Bar |

The total commission for Store #1, $32,350.56, appears in cell D17. Note in the Formula Bar that the end parenthesis was automatically added when you accepted the entry. If you want to sum the values in a second range, separate each range with a comma. For example, to sum the ranges A3:D3 and A14:D14, the SUM function would be written as =SUM(A3:D3, A14:D14).

Entering Functions Using the AutoSum Command

To quickly insert commonly used functions, you can use the AutoSum button on the Standard toolbar. When you use the AutoSum button, Excel inserts the selected function and scans cells above and to the left for arguments. If it detects a continuous series of cells containing values, the reference is selected and added as an argument. To enter the SUM function using the AutoSum button:

Step 1	*Click*	the Store #2 sheet tab
Step 2	*Click*	cell D17
Step 3	*Click*	the AutoSum button list arrow Σ ▾ on the Standard toolbar

Five common functions are listed on the AutoSum button list.

Step 4	*Click*	S̲um

The range D2:D16 is automatically selected, and the function =SUM(D2:D16) is inserted in cell D17.

Step 5	*Press*	the ENTER key
Step 6	*Observe*	that the result, $35,396.04, appears in cell D17
Step 7	*Save*	the workbook

3.e Using the Insert Function Dialog Box

Excel provides many more functions in addition to the five listed on the AutoSum button. The Insert Function dialog box helps you enter values or cell references for each of the required arguments in the correct order. For convenience, Excel divides functions into categories, such as statistical, date and time, and financial. In this section you preview a few of the many functions available.

Using the Date Function DATE

Date and time values are calculated in Excel by using special values called **serial numbers**. A value of 1 represents the first day that Excel can use in calculations, January 1, 1900. Hours, minutes, and seconds are portions of a day, so 12:00 PM is calculated using a value of .5. Most of the time, you enter the actual date, such as 1/1/1900, and Excel hides the serial value by formatting the cell with a date or time format. At times you may need to convert a given date to its serial number. For example, you need to update your workbook every 60 days, so you want to add the update date to the workbook. You can do this by using the DATE function to change the date to its serial value, and then adding 60 to the result. The **DATE** function returns the serial number value of a date. Its syntax is as follows:

=DATE(year, month, day)

The required arguments, year, month, and day, must be supplied as individual values. To calculate this date using the DATE function:

Step 1	*Activate*	cell C22 on the Store #1 worksheet

chapter
three

Mouse **T**ip

You can open the Insert
Function dialog box by
clicking More Functions
on the AutoSum
button list.

FIGURE 3-6
Insert Function Dialog Box

Step 2	*Key*	Updated
Step 3	*Press*	the TAB key
Step 4	*Click*	the Insert Function button [fx] on the Formula Bar

The Insert Function dialog box displays a list of Function categories
and function names. Your dialog box should look similar to Figure 3-6.

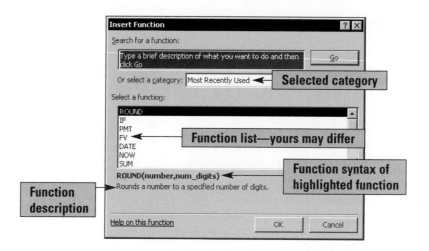

Step 5	*Click*	the Or select a category: list arrow
Step 6	*Click*	Date & Time

The Select a function: list changes to an alphabetical list of all the
functions in the Date & Time category.

Step 7	*Click*	Date in the Select a function: list
Step 8	*Click*	OK

The Function Arguments dialog box opens, and guides you through
the entry of each argument of the selected function. A description of
the function is located in the middle of the dialog box. Each text box is
an argument of the function. If the name of the argument is in bold,
then it is a required argument. The Year text box is selected, as
indicated by the blinking insertion point. A description of the selected
argument appears below the function description. See Figure 3-7.

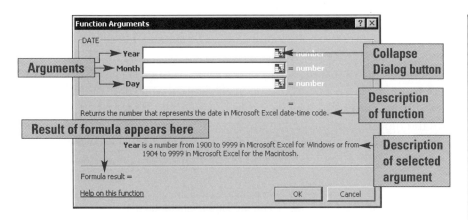

FIGURE 3-7
Function Arguments

Step 9	*Key*	2003 in the Year text box
Step 10	*Press*	the TAB key to move to the Month text box
Step 11	*Key*	5 in the Month text box
Step 12	*Press*	the TAB key to move to the Day text box
Step 13	*Key*	1 in the Day box
Step 14	*Observe*	the formula result at the bottom of the dialog box
Step 15	*Click*	OK

Next, you need to add 60 to the result of the function. To add a formula to a function:

Step 1	*Press*	the F2 key
Step 2	*Key*	+60
Step 3	*Press*	the ENTER key

The result of the formula, 6/30/2003, appears in cell D22.

Using the Financial Function PMT

Financial functions are used to calculate values for all types of investments and loans, as well as to calculate depreciation of assets. The **PMT** function is used to calculate the payment of a loan based on constant payments and a constant interest rate.

Luis Alvarez, the owner of the Super Power Computers chain of stores, is considering borrowing some money to expand its headquarters, and he wants to get his managers' opinions on the loan, so you want to include

chapter
three

this information in the workbook. You need to calculate how much monthly payments on the loan will be. The syntax of the PMT function is:

=PMT(rate,nper,pv,fv,type)

Rate is the interest rate, *nper* is the total number of payments for the loan, and *pv* is the present value of the loan; that is, how much is owed. *Fv* (future value) and *type* (whether the payment is due at the beginning of the month or at the end of the month) are both optional arguments because they have default values of 0 for *fv* and 0 for *type*, indicating payment will be made at the end of the month. To use the PMT function:

Step 1	*Activate*	cell E3 on the Financial worksheet
Step 2	*Click*	the Insert Function button f_x on the Formula Bar
Step 3	*Click*	the Or select a <u>c</u>ategory: list arrow
Step 4	*Click*	Financial
Step 5	*Double-click*	PMT in the Select a functio<u>n</u>: list

Instead of keying arguments into the Function Arguments dialog box, you can click cells on the worksheet.

Step 6	*Drag*	the Function Arguments dialog box title bar to move the dialog box so you can see row 3
Step 7	*Click*	cell A3

Because the interest rate is expressed in terms of a year, you must divide the rate by 12, and supply this result as the rate argument.

Step 8	*Key*	/12
Step 9	*Press*	the TAB key to move to the Nper text box
Step 10	*Click*	cell B3
Step 11	*Press*	the TAB key to move to the Pv text box
Step 12	*Click*	cell C3
Step 13	*Click*	OK

The monthly payment for this loan is calculated at $3,945.94. It appears in parentheses and in red because it is a negative value (an expense to the company). This is common accounting notation.

CAUTION TIP

When using many financial functions, it is important that the *rate* and *nper* arguments "agree." A loan at 8.5% usually means that you are paying 8.5% interest on the loan over the course of the entire year—not monthly. Because you usually make monthly payments on a loan, the *nper* argument is most likely expressed in months. For a three-year loan, the number of periods, or payments, is 36. To calculate the interest correctly, you must show the interest rate in months, not years. Using a formula, you can divide the interest rate by 12 to bring it into agreement with the number of periods, or payments, on the loan.

Using the Logical Function IF

Logical functions test data using a true/false evaluation. Think of a true/false evaluation is as a yes/no choice. For example, bonuses are paid to a Super Power Computer's sales representative if his or her sales are greater than $37,500. The question "Are the total sales for this employee greater than or equal to $37,500?" has only two answers, "Yes" or "No."

The **IF** function is used to evaluate whether a given statement is true. If the logical test is true, the function returns one value; otherwise, it returns a different value. The IF function has the following syntax:

=IF(logical_test,value_if_true,value_if_false)

The first argument identifies the logical test. The second argument indicates the formula's value if the logical test is true. The last argument identifies the formula's value if the logical test is false. Sometimes it is easier to create logical functions by writing them in statement form first:

> **If** sales are greater than or equal to 37,500, **then** the bonus is 500, **else** (otherwise) the result is 0.

Now, you can put your sentence into something resembling function syntax:

> =IF(sales>=37500, then bonus is 500, else bonus is 0)

Finally, create your formula using named ranges, cell references, or values. To use the IF function:

M E N U   T I P

To open the Insert Function dialog box, click the _Function_ command on the Insert menu.

Step 1	*Activate*	cell E2 on the Store #1 worksheet
Step 2	*Click*	the Insert Function button f_x on the Formula Bar
Step 3	*Double-click*	the IF function in the Logical category
Step 4	*Key*	C2>=37500 in the Logical_test text box
Step 5	*Press*	the TAB key
Step 6	*Key*	500
Step 7	*Press*	the TAB key
Step 8	*Key*	0
Step 9	*Click*	OK

Q U I C K   T I P

If you see #NUM! in a cell, then you used an unacceptable argument in a function requiring a numeric argument. This error also arises if a formula produces a number too large (greater than $1*10^{307}$) or too small (less than $-1*10^{307}$) to be represented in Excel.

Because the value in cell C2 ($34,531) is less than 37500, the value of cell E2 evaluates to 0.

| Step 10 | *Copy* | the formula in cell E2 to cells E3:E16 |

**chapter
three**

C 3.f Using 3-D References in Formulas

Cell references are used in formulas to ensure that when a data value changes, the formula recalculates and displays the new result automatically. The simple formula =A1+B1, for example, links to cells A1 and B1 to calculate the sum of the values contained in those cells. **Linking** formulas link to the cells on another worksheet. The linked formulas maintain a connection to the worksheet that holds the original formula.

In complex workbooks with many worksheets, you may need to perform calculations that use cell references from several worksheets. This type of cell reference is called a **3-D reference**. 3-D references span not only columns and rows, but worksheets as well.

You need to find the minimum and maximum commissions for all four stores. The syntax of the MAX and MIN functions is similar to that of the SUM function:

=**MAX(number1,** *number2, …*)
=**MIN(number1,** *number2, …*)

To add the MAX function to a worksheet using 3-D references:

Step 1	*Click*	cell B19 on the Store #1 worksheet
Step 2	*Key*	Maximum commission
Step 3	*Press*	the TAB key twice
Step 4	*Click*	the AutoSum button list arrow on the Standard toolbar
Step 5	*Click*	Max
Step 6	*Press & hold*	the SHIFT key
Step 7	*Click*	the Store #4 sheet tab

This selects all the worksheets from Store #1 to Store #4.

| Step 8 | *Select* | the range D2:D16 |

In the formula, you see the 3-D reference =MAX('Store #1:Store #4'!D2:E16). The worksheet names are enclosed by apostrophes (') and separated from the cell references by an exclamation point (!).

Step 9	*Click*	the Enter button  on the Formula Bar

The result, 2936.46, is correctly identified as the highest value among the selected cells on the four store worksheets.

To add the MIN function to a worksheet using 3-D reference:

Step 1	*Click*	cell B20 on the Store #1 worksheet
Step 2	*Key*	Minimum commission
Step 3	*Press*	the TAB key twice
Step 4	*Click*	the AutoSum button list arrow ∑ ▾ on the Standard toolbar
Step 5	*Click*	Min
Step 6	*Press & hold*	the SHIFT key
Step 7	*Click*	the Store #4 sheet tab
Step 8	*Select*	the range D2:D16
Step 9	*Click*	the Enter button on the Formula Bar

The result, 1506.66, is correctly identified as the lowest value among the selected cells on the four store worksheets.

Step 10	*Save*	the workbook and close it

Your workbook is ready for distribution to the four stores.

chapter
three

Summary

▶ You can create formulas to calculate values. Formulas can use cell references to update information whenever the referenced cell's data changes.

▶ All formulas have a syntax; when Excel calculates results, it follows the rules of precedence.

▶ Functions are built-in formulas used to perform a variety of calculations. Most functions require arguments, which you can supply as values, cell references, or even formulas.

▶ You use the cut, copy, and paste operations to move or copy information.

▶ Use the Office Clipboard to store up to 24 items. These items can be pasted into other workbooks, or even into documents created in other applications.

▶ You can drag selection borders to move data. Press the CTRL key and drag selection borders to copy data. Press the ALT key to move or copy data to another worksheet.

▶ Relative cell references change relative to the source cell when copied.

▶ Absolute cell references always refer to the same cell when a formula is copied. Absolute cell references use the dollar sign ($) in front of the column and row identifiers: A1.

▶ Mixed cell references always refer to a specific row or column when the formula is copied. Mixed references use the dollar sign ($) in front of either the row or column identifier: $A1 or A$1.

▶ Insert Function and the Function Palette work together as a function wizard, providing helpful information to guide you through the construction of complex formulas.

▶ Basic functions, such as SUM, MAX, and MIN, can be inserted by using the AutoSum button.

▶ Date and time functions, including DATE, allow you to perform calculations using dates.

▶ Financial functions, such as PMT, allow you to calculate values for investments and loans.

▶ Logical functions, such as IF, test data using a true/false evaluation. The calculated result depends on the result of the evaluation.

▶ Formulas can use 3-D cell references—cell references from other worksheets or other workbooks.

Commands Review

Action	Menu Bar	Shortcut Menu	Toolbar	Task Pane	Keyboard
Cut	E̲dit, Cut	Cut	✂		CTRL + X ALT + E, T
Copy	E̲dit, C̲opy	C̲opy	📋		CTRL + C ALT + E, C
Paste	E̲dit, P̲aste	P̲aste	📋	Click item in palette in Office Clipboard task pane	CTRL + V ALT + E, P
Insert common functions using AutoSum			Σ ▾		
Insert Function	Insert, F̲unction		*fx*		SHIFT + F3 ALT + I, F
Cycle reference type between absolute, mixed, and relative					F4

Concepts Review

Circle the correct answer.

1. **To copy a selection while dragging, press and hold the:**
   [a] SHIFT key.
   [b] END key.
   [c] CTRL key.
   [d] ALT key.

2. **To copy a selection to another worksheet, press and hold the:**
   [a] SHIFT + CTRL keys.
   [b] CTRL + ALT keys.
   [c] SHIFT + ALT keys.
   [d] CTRL + SPACEBAR keys.

3. **Which of the following cell references is an absolute reference?**
   [a] A1
   [b] $A1
   [c] A1
   [d] A$1

4. **Copying the formula =A1+B1 from cell C1 to cell E3 would make what change to the formula?**
   [a] =A1+B1
   [b] =A1+C3
   [c] =B3+C1
   [d] =C3+D3

5. **Copying the formula =$A1+B$2 from cell C1 to cell E3 would make what change to the formula?**
   [a] =$A3+D$2
   [b] =$A1+B$2
   [c] =$A2+E$2
   [d] =$A3+C$2

6. **Identify the type of reference for the row and column of the following cell reference: X$24.**
   [a] absolute, absolute
   [b] absolute, relative
   [c] relative, absolute
   [d] relative, relative

7. **The DATE function returns the:**
   [a] serial value of a date.
   [b] current date.
   [c] current time.
   [d] current system status.

8. **The proper syntax for an IF formula is:**
   [a] =IF(condition,value_if_false,value_if_true).
   [b] =IF(condition,value_if_true,value_if_false).
   [c] =IF(value_if_true,value_if_false,condition).
   [d] =IF(value_if_false,value_if_true,condition).

chapter three

9. Which of the following formulas returns the value 60?
   [a] =10*2+4
   [b] =(10*2)+4
   [c] =10*(2+4)
   [d] =10+(2*4)

10. All formulas start with:
   [a] @.
   [b] the keyword "Formula".
   [c] =.
   [d] $$.

Circle **T** if the statement is true or **F** if the statement is false.

T   F   1. The Formula Arguments dialog box displays the results of the formula as you add values for each of the arguments.

T   F   2. A good way to create a logical formula is to write it out in statement form first.

T   F   3. Skipping optional arguments in a function is acceptable.

T   F   4. Changing the order of required arguments in a function is acceptable, as long as they are all there.

T   F   5. The formula =(5+5)*2 gives the same result as the formula =5+5*2.

T   F   6. Formulas are only updated when you press the F9 key.

T   F   7. You can use the F4 key to cycle through cell reference options when editing formulas.

T   F   8. As soon as you cut data from a worksheet, it disappears, whether you paste it somewhere else or not.

T   F   9. A cut-and-paste operation is the same as dragging a selection border to another location.

T   F   10. The Office Clipboard provides access to only the last eight items copied or cut.

notes   Several of the following Skills Review exercises introduce functions not covered in the chapter. Use the Insert Function tool to guide you through the use of new functions. For additional information, use online Help.

Skills Review

SCANS

Exercise 1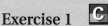

1. Create a new workbook.

2. Enter "Test Scores" in cell A1.

3. Using the values 100, 121, 135, 117, 143, 122, 125, 118, 111, and 135, use statistical functions (*Hint:* check the Statistical function category) to perform the following tasks:

   a. Determine the minimum value.

   b. Determine the maximum value.

   c. Find the average value by opening the Insert Function dialog box, double-clicking Average in the Statistical category, dragging to select the numbers you entered, then clicking OK.

d. Find the 50th percentile by opening the Insert Function dialog box, double-clicking Percentile in the Statistical category, dragging to select the numbers you entered, typing 0.5 in the K box, then clicking OK.

e. Count the number of items by opening the Insert Function dialog box, double-clicking Count in the Statistical category, dragging to select the numbers you entered, then clicking OK.

4. Save the workbook as *Test Scores*. Print and close the workbook.

Exercise 2   C

1. Create a new workbook.

2. Enter "Enter a Date:" in cell A2.

3. Enter "Is it a Friday?" in cell A4.

4. The WEEKDAY function, in the Date & Time category, returns a number indicating a day of the week for a given date, 1 = Sunday, 2 = Monday, and so on. In cell A5, create a formula using an IF statement that determines whether any given date since January 1, 1900 in cell A3 is a Friday. If the date is a Friday, the formula should return "Yes." If not, the formula should return "No."

5. Enter several dates in cell A3 until you find one that is a Friday. Cell A5 should show the value "Yes."

6. Save the workbook as *Day Finder*. Print and close the workbook.

Exercise 3   C

1. Create a new workbook.

2. Enter "The Quick Brown Fox" in cell A2.

3. In cell A3, enter "Jumped Over the Lazy Dog."

4. Use text functions to perform the following tasks:

a. Join the content of cells A2 and A3 in cell A6. To do this, insert the CONCATENATE function from the Text category. Click cell A2 as the first argument, key " " (quotation mark, a space, and another quotation mark) as the second argument, then click cell A3 as the third argument.

b. In cell A8, convert the value of cell A6 to uppercase. To do this, insert the UPPER function from the Text category, and click cell A6 as the argument.

c. In cell A10, locate the character position of the letter "Q" in cell A6. To do this, insert the FIND function from the Text category, enter "Q" as the first argument, and click cell A6 as the second argument.

5. Save the workbook as *Text Practice*. Print and close the workbook.

Exercise 4   C

1. Open the *Depreciation Calculator* workbook located on the Data Disk.

2. In cell B12, a financial function called SLN has been entered using relative cell references. This formula was copied to cells C12:K12, resulting in errors. Change the cell references in cell B12 to absolute references.

3. Copy the revised formula in cell B12 to cells C12:K12.

4. In cell L12, total cells B12:K12.

5. Save the workbook as *Depreciation Calculator Revised*. Print and close the workbook.

chapter three

Exercise 5   C

1. Create a new workbook.

2. Enter "Year" in cell A1 and "Roman" in cell B1.

3. Enter the following numbers in column A: 1900, 1941, 1999, 2000, 2010.

4. In column B, use the ROMAN function from the Math & Trig category to convert the numbers to ROMAN numerals by using the cells in column A as the argument.

5. Save the workbook as *Roman Conversion*. Print and close the workbook.

Exercise 6   C

1. Create a new workbook.

2. Using the RAND function in the Math & Trig category, generate five random numbers in column A. The RAND function takes no arguments, so simply enter the function in each cell.

3. In column B, create a formula to generate whole numbers between 1 and 100 using the RAND and ROUND functions. To do this, open the Insert Functions dialog box, double-click the ROUND function in the Math & Trig category, type RAND()*100 in the Number argument box, and enter 0 as the Num_digits argument.

4. Save the workbook as *Random Numbers*. Print and close the workbook.

Exercise 7   C

1. Enter the following data in a new workbook on the Sheet1 worksheet:

Employee Name	Current Wage	Proposed Wage	Increase per Month
Mark Havlaczek	$7.50	$8.00	
Roberta Hernandez	$8.25	$9.00	
Loren Mons	$12.00	$13.00	
Total Increase (all stores)			

2. Rename the Sheet1 worksheet to "Downtown Store."

3. Enter the following data on the Sheet2 worksheet:

Employee Name	Current Wage	Proposed Wage	Increase per Month
Eric Wimmer	$8.25	$8.85	
Micah Anderson	$7.75	$8.50	
Allyson Smith	$9.50	$10.35	

4. Rename the Sheet2 worksheet "Uptown Store."

5. On the Downtown Store worksheet, create a formula in cell D2 that calculates how much *more* each employee will make per month as a result of the proposed wage increase. Assume that each employee works 168 hours per month. (*Hint:* Subtract the Current Wage from the Proposed Wage, then multiply the result by 168.)

6. Copy the formula to cells D3:D4.

7. Copy the formulas in cells D2:D4 on the Downtown Store worksheet to the same cells on the Uptown Store worksheet.

8. In cell D5 on the Downtown Store worksheet, "enter = sum(".

9. Press and hold the SHIFT key, then click the Uptown Store worksheet.

10. Select cells D2:D4 and press the ENTER key.

11. Save the workbook as *Proposed Wage Increase*. Print and close the workbook.

Exercise 8

1. Open the *Proposed Wage Increase* workbook you created in Exercise 7.

2. Using drag-and-drop, move cells D1:D5 on the Downtown Store worksheet to G1:G5.

3. Using cut and paste, move cells C1:C4 on the Downtown Store worksheet to E1:E4.

4. Using your choice of move commands, move cells B1:B4 on the Downtown Store worksheet to cells C1:C4.

5. Repeat Steps 2 through 4 on the Uptown Store worksheet.

6. On the Downtown Store worksheet, activate cell G5.

7. Change the cell reference D2:D4 in the Formula Bar to G2:G4.

8. Save the workbook as *Proposed Wage Increase Revised*. Print and close the workbook.

Case Projects

Project 1

You work for an insurance company processing accident claims. One of your tasks is to determine how many days have elapsed between the date of an accident and the date that a claim was filed. You know that Excel stores dates as numbers, so you must be able to create a formula that calculates this information. Use the Ask A Question Box to look up more information about how Excel keeps track of dates. Can you figure out the trick? Create a workbook with column labels for Accident Date, Claim Filed Date, and Elapsed Days. Enter two fictitious accident dates and two corresponding claim filed dates. Save the workbook as *Claim Lapse Calculator*, and then print and close it.

Project 2

You are a college entrance administrator. To gain admittance to your school, a prospective student must score in the 80th percentile on the school's entrance exam. In a new workbook, use the RAND function in the Math & Trig category to generate a list of 100 random test scores between 30 and 100.

Once you've generated the random scores, copy and paste the values over the formulas in the scores column to keep them from changing. (*Hint:* Use Copy, Paste Special.) Use statistical functions to find the average test score, the median test score, and the 80th percentile of the scores. Use an IF function with the PERCENTILE function to display "Yes" if the score is higher than the 80th percentile, or "No" if the score is lower than the 80th percentile. Save the workbook as *College Entrance Exam Scores*, and then print and close it.

Project 3

Connect to the Internet and search the Web to locate a timeline showing major events of the twentieth century. Create a workbook to record the date and a description of the event. Include at least one event from each decade of the twentieth century. Do not include more than three events from any decade. Save the workbook as *20th Century Timeline*, and then print and close it.

chapter three

Project 4

Connect to the Internet and search the Web to locate information about current events. Create a workbook to list the date(s) of the event, the place, and a brief description of the event. Save the workbook as *Current Events*, and then print and close it.

Project 5

The CONVERT function is used to convert units of measurement from one system to another. You work as a lab technician in a bioengineering firm, and you need to convert temperatures from Fahrenheit to Celsius and to Kelvin. Create a workbook with 10 Fahrenheit temperatures in column A. In column B, use the CONVERT function to convert the temperatures to Celsius. In column C, convert from Celsius to Kelvin. Save the workbook as *Temperature Conversion*, and print and close it. (*Hint:* If the CONVERT function is not available, enable it by clicking the Tools menu, then clicking Add-Ins. Click the Analysis ToolPak check box, then click OK.)

Project 6

You are considering a loan for $8,000 to buy a car. The loan will be paid back in 36 months at an interest rate of 6.5%. Calculate the monthly payment using the PMT function. Then, calculate the amount of interest and principal for each payment of the loan using the IPMT and PPMT functions. Save the workbook as *Car Loan Payments*, and then print and close it.

Project 7

Use the Ask A Question Box to locate and print a list of conversion units.

Project 8

You are the personnel manager of a large bookstore. Each employee is given one week (five days) of vacation after he or she has been employed for at least six months (180 days). After that time, one day of vacation is added for every 45 days the employee works. Create a new workbook that will calculate the number of vacation days an employee has earned by subtracting the employee's hire date from today's date. (*Hint:* Use the TODAY function to automatically insert today's date.) Save the workbook as *Holiday Calculator*, and then print and close it.

Enhancing Worksheets

Chapter Overview

Worksheets hold and process a lot of data. The goal of well-designed worksheets is to provide information in a clear, easy-to-read fashion. Thoughtful application of formatting styles can enhance the appearance of your worksheets on-screen and in printed documents. In this chapter, you explore how to format worksheets and cell data, and how to filter a list of data so that only relevant data appears. You also learn to extend the power of pasting far beyond simply copying data from one location to another.

LEARNING OBJECTIVES

- ▶ Create worksheet and column titles
- ▶ Format cells, rows, and columns
- ▶ Use Paste Special
- ▶ Define and apply styles
- ▶ Manipulate rows, columns, and cells
- ▶ Filter lists using AutoFilter

Case profile

One of your jobs at Super Power Computers is to prepare last year's quarterly sales reports for distribution. The workbook must be easy to use and logically present the information so that company managers can quickly summarize the data and report to the president.

chapter four

4.a Creating Worksheet and Column Titles

Titles provide a clear indication of what type of information can be found on the worksheet. You can add titles to a worksheet or column to indicate the type of information in each column.

Merging and Splitting Cells

To add visual impact, titles are often centered at the top of a worksheet. To do this quickly, you can use the Merge and Center command. To merge cells and create a worksheet title:

Step 1	*Open*	the *Super Power Computers - Quarterly Sales Report 2002* workbook on the Data Disk
Step 2	*Save*	The workbook as *Super Power Computers - Quarterly Sales Report 2002 Revised*

This workbook contains a summary of 2002 sales on the Sales Summary worksheet. The Source Data worksheet contains the raw data from the stores. The error message ####### indicates that a numerical value is too long to display using the current column width. You increase the width of the column later in this chapter.

Step 3	*Select*	the range A1:F1
Step 4	*Click*	the Merge and Center button on the Formatting toolbar

The selected cells are merged into a single cell whose cell reference is the cell in the upper-left corner of the selection—in this case, cell A1— and the contents of cell A1 are centered in the new cell.

Step 5	*Repeat*	Steps 3 and 4 twice to merge and center cells A2 and A3 across the ranges A2:F2 and A3:F3

You didn't mean to center the data in cell A3.

Step 6	*Click*	cell A3
Step 7	*Click*	the Merge and Center button on the Formatting toolbar

The data in cell A3 is no longer centered across cells A3:F3. Your worksheet should look similar to Figure 4-1.

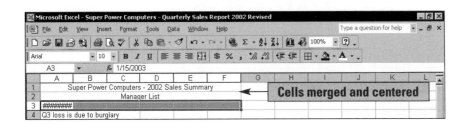

FIGURE 4-1
Merge and Center Titles

Using AutoFill to Create Column Titles

The **AutoFill** command creates a series of values. AutoFill can automatically increment numerical values, cells containing a mixture of text and numbers, days of the week, months of the year, and even custom series you define. To use AutoFill to add column labels:

Step 1	*Activate*	cell B5
Step 2	*Move*	the pointer over the fill handle
Step 3	*Drag*	the fill handle to cell E5

As you drag the fill handle, a ScreenTip displays the new values being added. Your screen should look similar to Figure 4-2. Excel correctly identifies the quarter numbers and increments them as you drag.

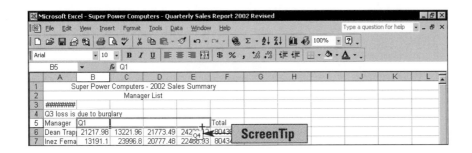

FIGURE 4-2
AutoFill Numbers

| Step 4 | *Release* | the mouse button |

When you release the mouse button, the column headings Q1 through Q4 appear in cells B5:E5.

| Step 5 | *Save* | the workbook |

> **MENU TIP**
>
> Not all fill options are available when you drag to use the AutoFill feature. To see additional AutoFill options, use the Edit menu, Fill, Series command to open the Series dialog box.

> **MOUSE TIP**
>
> Click the AutoFill Options button on the screen to change how the cells are filled when you drag the fill handle.

chapter
four

4.b **Formatting Cells, Rows, and Columns**

Careful application of formatting to rows, columns, and cells transforms a mundane, hard-to-decipher worksheet into a vehicle for sharing information. In this section, you learn about many of the formatting tools available.

Applying AutoFormats to Worksheets

AutoFormats are predefined combinations of shading, cell borders, font styles, and number formatting that quickly give worksheets a stylized look. To apply AutoFormats:

Step 1	*Select*	the range A5:F10
Step 2	*Click*	F<u>o</u>rmat
Step 3	*Click*	<u>A</u>utoFormat

The AutoFormat dialog box displays a list of available AutoFormat styles and should look similar to Figure 4-3.

FIGURE 4-3
AutoFormat Dialog Box

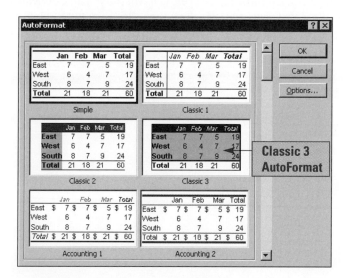

Step 4	*Click*	the Classic 3 AutoFormat
Step 5	*Click*	OK
Step 6	*Click*	any cell in the worksheet to deselect the range

The AutoFormat is applied to the selected area. You don't like the way the AutoFormatted worksheet looks, so you format it yourself.

| Step 7 | *Click* | the Undo button 🔙 on the Standard toolbar |

Applying Fonts and Font Styles

A **font** is a set of printed characters that share a common typeface. A **typeface** is the design and appearance of the font in printed form. The **style** refers to whether the font is displayed with *italic*, **bold**, an underline, or normal print. The **point size** refers to the print height. You can also add **effects**, such as strikethrough, superscripts, and subscripts. Some common typefaces include the following:

Arial   Times New Roman   Courier New   Book Antiqua

To maintain consistency in its documents, Super Power Computers has selected the Impact font style, set to point size 14, for worksheet titles. To change the font and font size:

Step 1	*Select*	cell A1
Step 2	*Click*	the Font button list arrow [Arial ▾] on the Formatting toolbar to display the available fonts
Step 3	*Click*	Impact (or another font if Impact is not available on your system)
Step 4	*Click*	the Font Size button list arrow [10 ▾] on the Formatting toolbar
Step 5	*Click*	14

Usually, when you increase the font size in a cell, the row height automatically increases to accommodate the larger font; however, when you increase the font size in a merged cell, it does not. You adjust this later in this chapter. You decide to make the Total label stand out more.

| Step 6 | *Change* | the font in cell A10 to Arial Black |

Another way to add emphasis is to change the font color. To change the font color:

| Step 1 | *Activate* | cell A1 |

CAUTION TIP

To make your worksheets look as professional as possible, avoid using more than three or four fonts. Too many fonts may look comical and detract from an otherwise well-designed layout.

MENU TIP

Click the Cells command on the Format menu, then click the Font tab to choose a font, font size, font style, and font color.

---

chapter
four

| Step 2 | *Click* | the Font Color button list arrow ⬜▾ on the Formatting toolbar |

| Step 3 | *Point to* | the Blue square (second row, sixth column) |

A ScreenTip displays the color name under the pointer.

| Step 4 | *Click* | the Blue square |

You can also use bold, italics, or underlining to draw attention to or emphasize certain cells. To change the font style:

Step 1	*Select*	the range B5:F5
Step 2	*Click*	the Bold button **B** on the Formatting toolbar
Step 3	*Select*	the range A6:A10
Step 4	*Click*	the Italic button *I* on the Formatting toolbar

Modifying the Alignment of Cell Content

You can change the alignment of values within a cell. The default horizontal alignment in a cell is for text values to be left-aligned, and numbers, dates, and times to be right-aligned. The default vertical alignment is for data to be aligned at the bottom of a cell. Typically, column labels are centered in the column, while row labels are left-aligned. To change the alignment of cells:

| Step 1 | *Select* | the range B5:F5 |
| Step 2 | *Click* | the Center button ▦ on the Formatting toolbar |

Applying Number Formats

Understanding how and when to apply number formats is very important. Using the extensive set of number formats in Excel, you can display numerical values such as times, dates, currency, percentages, fractions, and more. When you apply a numerical format to a value, the manner in which the value is displayed may vary dramatically, but the actual value held by the cell remains the same. Table 4-1 illustrates how a common numerical value of 1054.253 would be displayed with different number formats applied.

MOUSE TIP

The Formatting toolbar is extremely helpful when you only need to apply one or two settings to a range. When you need to make several formatting adjustments, use the Format Cells dialog box.

TABLE 4-1
Comparing Number
Formats

Category	Description	Default Display (Value = 1054.253)
General	No specific number format	1054.253
Number	Default of two decimal places; can also display commas for thousand separators	1054.25
Currency	Default of two decimal places, comma separators, and $ (the U.S. dollar sign)	$1,054.25
Accounting	Aligns currency symbol, displays two decimal places and comma separators	$ 1,054.25
Date	Displays serial equivalent of date	11/19/1902
Time	Displays serial equivalent of time	11/19/1902 6:00 AM
Percentage	Multiplies value by 100 and displays the result with % sign	105425%
Fraction	Displays decimal portion of value as a fraction	1054 1/4
Scientific	Displays the number in scientific notation	1.05E+03

The comma format automatically sets the numerical display to two decimal places, inserts a comma when needed for thousands, millions, and so on, and adjusts the alignment of the cell(s) to line up on the decimal. To change the formatting to the comma format:

Step 1	*Select*	the range B6:E10
Step 2	*Click*	the Comma Style button ⬚ on the Formatting toolbar

The cells are updated to display the new formatting, including a slight, automatic column width adjustment to accommodate the extra formatting. (You format the Total column later in this chapter.)

Currency style is commonly used when dealing with money. There are several ways to adjust currency style, including changing the font color to red for negative numbers. You can also insert other symbols, such as those for the euro (E) and the yen (¥). To use currency style:

Step 1	*Verify*	that the range B6:E10 is still selected
Step 2	*Click*	the Currency Style button 🬀 on the Formatting toolbar

chapter
four

This looks fine, but you want the negative values to stand out even more. To adjust the currency format, you use thc Format Cells dialog box. To change formatting using the Format Cells dialog box:

| Step 1 | *Click* | F̲ormat |
| Step 2 | *Click* | C̲ells |

The Format Cells dialog box opens. Each tab contains a different category of formatting options that you can apply to selected cells.

| Step 3 | *Click* | the Number tab, if necessary |
| Step 4 | *Click* | Currency in the C̲ategory: list |

The Number tab in the Format Cells dialog box permits you to change a variety of options for each of the available number formats. When the Currency category is selected, you can choose how negative numbers are displayed. The dialog box on your screen should look similar to Figure 4-4.

FIGURE 4-4
Format Cells Dialog Box

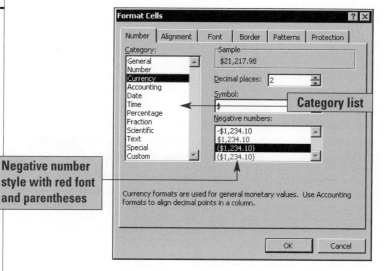

Negative number style with red font and parentheses

Category list

| Step 5 | *Click* | the fourth item in the N̲egative numbers: list, red text and parentheses |
| Step 6 | *Click* | OK |

The loss in cell D8 is now easy to see.

Adjusting the Decimal Place

You can adjust the number of decimal places displayed in all number formats except General, Date, Time, and Text. To change the number of decimal places displayed in a cell:

Step 1	*Verify*	that the range B6:E10 is still selected
Step 2	*Click*	the Decrease Decimal button ⌗ on the Formatting toolbar twice

The data in the selected cells is rounded to the nearest whole dollar. Although the cells display rounded numbers, the original value is stored in each cell and appears in the Formula Bar when the cell is active.

Indenting, Rotating, and Wrapping Text in a Cell

To give more visual appeal to your worksheets, you can indent, rotate, or wrap values in a cell. The employee names would be easier to distinguish if they were indented in the cells. To indent cell content:

Step 1	*Select*	the range A6:A9
Step 2	*Click*	the Increase Indent button ⌗ on the Formatting toolbar

Sometimes rotating text is a good way to make it stand out. To rotate text in a cell:

Step 1	*Select*	the range B5:E5
Step 2	*Right-click*	the selected range
Step 3	*Click*	Format Cells
Step 4	*Click*	the Alignment tab

Your dialog box should look similar to Figure 4-5. The Alignment tab is used to control various alignment settings, including rotation.

M OUSE TIP

To increase the indent more, click the Increase Indent button on the Formatting toolbar again. To decrease the indent, click the Decrease Indent button on the Formatting toolbar.

chapter
four

FIGURE 4-5
Alignment Tab in the
Formal Cells Dialog Box

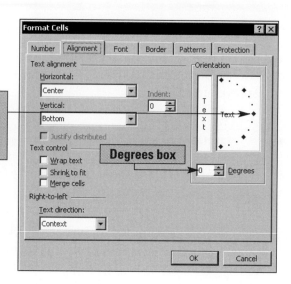

Diamond can be dragged to change the orientation of the data

Degrees box

| Step 5 | *Drag* | the red diamond in the Orientation box up until the Degrees box displays 45 |
| Step 6 | *Click* | OK |

The column labels rotate 45 degrees, and the row height increases to display the rotated value.

When data is too long for the column width, it is displayed as long as neighboring cells are empty. You can adjust the column width, but this isn't always desirable for long entries. Instead, you can use wrapping to maintain column width, while displaying all the data entered in a particular cell. **Wrapping** allows longer cell entries to continue to the next "line" within a single cell. To turn on text wrapping:

Step 1	*Activate*	cell A4
Step 2	*Open*	the Alignment tab in the Format Cells dialog box
Step 3	*Click*	the Wrap text check box
Step 4	*Click*	OK

The text is wrapped to fit within the column width. The row height might adjust automatically. If not, you adjust it later.

Applying Cell Borders and Shading

Cell borders and shading are two of the more dramatic visual effects available to enhance your worksheets. Borders can be used to separate row and column labels from data. Shading can be used to emphasize important cells. Although you see grid lines on your screen, the default for printed worksheets is for no grid lines to appear. If you want grid lines to appear on your printed pages, you need to apply a border. Borders can be applied to a range of selected cells or to individual cells. To add a border:

Step 1	**Select**	the range B6:E9
Step 2	**Click**	the Borders button list arrow ▦ ▾ on the Formatting toolbar
Step 3	**Click**	the All Borders button ⊞

The All Borders command applies a border to all edges surrounding and within the selection. Your screen should look similar to Figure 4-6.

QUICK TIP

You are not limited to the 12 choices appearing on the Borders list button. Use the Borders tab in the Format Cells dialog box to select different line styles, change line colors, and choose additional border options, such as inserting diagonal lines and applying borders to only the inside of a selection.

FIGURE 4-6
All Borders Added to the Selection

One way you can make row 5, which contains the column labels, stand out is to use a "reverse text" effect. To create this effect, you apply a dark fill color to the cells, then change the font color to white. To add shading to a cell:

Step 1	**Select**	cells A5:F5
Step 2	**Click**	the Fill Color button list arrow 🎨 ▾ on the Formatting toolbar
Step 3	**Select**	the Blue square (second row, sixth column)
Step 4	**Click**	the Font Color button list arrow 𝐀 ▾ on the Formatting toolbar
Step 5	**Select**	the White square (last row, last column)
Step 6	**Activate**	cell A1 to deselect the cells

chapter
four

Drawing Cell Borders

You can also draw cell borders exactly where you want them. To draw cell borders:

Step 1	*Click*	the Borders button list arrow [ ] on the Formatting toolbar
Step 2	*Click*	D̲raw Borders to display the Borders toolbar
Step 3	*Click*	the Line Style button list arrow [ ] on the Borders toolbar to drop down a list of line styles
Step 4	*Click*	the double-line style
Step 5	*Drag*	across the bottom of cells B9:E9

A double-line is added to the bottom of the cells. To deactivate the Draw Border button, click the button again or turn off the toolbar.

Step 6	*Click*	the Close button [X] on the Borders toolbar

Using the Format Painter

The Format Painter copies formats from one cell to another. To use the Format Painter:

Step 1	*Select*	the range E6:E10
Step 2	*Click*	the Format Painter button [ ] on the Standard toolbar
Step 3	*Select*	the range F6:F10

The currency formatting and borders from cells E6:E10 are copied to cells F6:F10.

Clearing Formats

Occasionally, you need to remove formatting from a cell or cells, while maintaining the data in the cell. To clear formatting from cells:

Step 1	*Activate*	cell A10

Step 2	*Click*	E̲dit
Step 3	*Point to*	Cle̲ar
Step 4	*Click*	F̲ormats

All formatting is removed from the cell, and the font is changed to the default style of 10-point Arial.

| Step 5 | *Save* | the workbook |

4.c Using Paste Special

The Paste S̲pecial command provides you with extra options when you copy or move data in Excel. The best quarter for each manager is listed in row 12. To create the column labels for this data, you copy and transpose the names listed in column A to row 12. To use the Paste Special command:

Step 1	*Copy*	cells A6:A9
Step 2	*Right-click*	cell B12
Step 3	*Click*	Paste S̲pecial

The Paste Special dialog box should look similar to Figure 4-7.

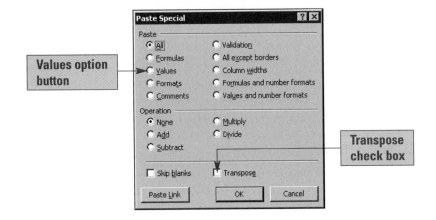

Values option button

Transpose check box

FIGURE 4-7
Paste Special Dialog Box

chapter
four

The Paste Special dialog box contains options for pasting data, formulas, and formats in cells. Some of these options are explained in Table 4-2.

TABLE 4-2
Paste Special Options

Paste Option	Description
All	Pastes content and formulas from source cell
Formulas	Pastes only formulas from source cell
Values	Pastes only values from source cell, converting formulas into latest result
Formats	Pastes only formats from source cell, leaving content of destination cell in place
Operation (add, subtract, multiply, divide)	Performs operation on value from source cell with value of destination cell to create new value without a formula

Step 4	*Click*	the Values option button
Step 5	*Click*	the Transpose check box to insert a check mark
Step 6	*Click*	OK
Step 7	*Press*	the ESC key to end the Copy command

The names are transposed to row 12 without the formatting from the source cells.

4.d Defining and Applying Styles

To create a consistent corporate identity, many companies use certain styles whenever a workbook is created. **Styles** can cover a variety of settings, such as number format, alignment settings, font type, cell borders, and cell patterns. You already used some of the built-in styles in Excel when you applied the comma and currency number styles. In addition to numerical styles, you can also define your own styles, which can then be applied to other cells and copied into other workbooks. To create a new style:

Step 1	*Activate*	cell A2
Step 2	*Click*	Format
Step 3	*Click*	Style

QUICK TIP

To create a style from a previously formatted cell, select the cell, then open the Style dialog box. The format settings for the style of the cell you selected will be listed in the dialog box.

The Style dialog box opens, displaying the settings for the Normal style, as shown in Figure 4-8. To create a new style, type a new style name in the Style name: box, then modify the settings as necessary.

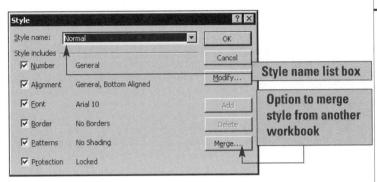

Style name list box

Option to merge style from another workbook

| Step 4 | *Key* | Worksheet Subtitle in the Style name: text box |
| Step 5 | *Click* | Modify |

The familiar Format Cells dialog box opens.

Step 6	*Click*	the Font tab
Step 7	*Click*	Impact in the Font: list
Step 8	*Click*	12 in the Size: list
Step 9	*Click*	the Color: list arrow
Step 10	*Click*	the Red square (third row, first column)

You can apply alignment options, borders, and numerical formats to your style as well.

Step 11	*Click*	the Alignment tab
Step 12	*Click*	the Horizontal: list arrow
Step 13	*Verify*	that Center is selected

This command centers the value in the cell. It was already selected because you applied the Merge and Center command to cell A2 earlier. When the style is applied to cell A2, it centers, the value in the merged cell. If the style is applied to a cell that isn't merged, it centers the data only in the cell you apply the style to.

MOUSE TIP

You can copy styles from workbook to workbook by using the Format Painter. Open both workbooks. In the source workbook, select a cell with the formatting style you want to copy, and click Format Painter. Switch to the target workbook, then click the cell to which you want to apply the formatting. The style is automatically transferred to the Style list of the target workbook.

QUICK TIP

You can copy styles from workbook to workbook by using the Copy and Paste commands. Open both workbooks, copy the cell in the source workbook containing the desired style, then use the Paste Special command and select the Formats option to paste it into the target workbook.

chapter
four

Step 14	*Click*	OK to close the Format Cells dialog box

Step 15	*Click*	OK to close the Style dialog box and apply the style to the active cell

To apply this style to other cells in this workbook, activate the cell(s), reopen the Style dialog box, select the style you wish to apply, then click OK. A real advantage of using named styles is that when you modify a named style, all cells with that style applied are updated automatically.

4.e Manipulating Rows, Columns, and Cells

As you organize worksheets, you will find many occasions when you need to insert a few cells into a list—or entire rows or columns—to add new information to a worksheet. You may also need to delete cells, rows, or columns.

Inserting and Deleting Rows and Columns

You decide to insert a blank row above row 5. To insert a new row:

Step 1	*Right-click*	the row 5 heading

Step 2	*Click*	Insert

The data in row 5 and below is shifted down to accommodate the new row. When a column is inserted, all data is shifted to the right.

Upon reviewing your worksheet, you realize that you don't need the extra row after all. To delete rows or columns:

Step 1	*Right-click*	the row 5 heading

Step 2	*Click*	Delete to delete the newly added row

Changing Column Width and Row Height

If the data in a cell is too long for the column width, Excel allows the value to spill over into the next cell, as long as the neighboring cell is empty. If the neighboring cell contains data, Excel shows only the first part of the data. By changing the column width, you can show more or less data.

As you adjusted the font height, or turned on the wrap text feature, you may have noticed that the row height increased to show the data in the cell. Although this change is generally automatic, sometimes you need more precise control of the row height.

You need to resize rows 1 and 2 to accommodate the larger font size. To AutoFit a row to the largest point size:

Step 1	**Double-click**	the boundary between row headings 1 and 2
Step 2	**Double-click**	the boundary between row headings 2 and 3

Rows 1 and 2 increase in height to fit the entries in cells A1 and A2. You also might need to adjust the height of row 4 if it did not automatically resize to accomodate the wrapped text in cell A1.

Step 3	**Double-click**	the boundary between row headings 4 and 5, if necessary

Next you need to adjust column widths to display the widest entries. To manually change the column width:

Step 1	**Right-click**	the column A heading
Step 2	**Click**	Column Width
Step 3	**Key**	15 in the Column width: text box
Step 4	**Click**	OK

You can also use the AutoFit feature to automatically adjust the width to fit the longest entry in the column. To AutoFit a column to the longest entry:

Step 1	**Move**	the mouse pointer over the boundary between the column B and column C headings
Step 2	**Double-click**	the boundary

The column automatically resizes so it is wide enough to display the value in cell B12, the widest entry in column B.

Step 3	**Repeat**	Step 2 to AutoFit columns C, D, and E

QUICK TIP

To change the width of several columns at once, select them before opening the Column Width dialog box.

MOUSE TIP

To change the formatting in a newly inserted row or column, click the Insert Options button that appears after you insert the row or column.

MENU TIP

To adjust the width of a column, click Format, point to Columns, then click Width. To AutoFit the row height, select AutoFit instead of Height.

To adjust the height of a row by using menus, click Format, point to Row, then click Height. To AutoFit the row height, select AutoFit instead of Height.

chapter
four

Now you need to decrease the height of row 4. To manually adjust the height of a row:

Step 1	Right-click	the row 4 header
Step 2	Click	Row Height
Step 3	Key	25.5 in the Row height: text box
Step 4	Click	OK

The row height decreases to fit the entry in cell A4.

Inserting and Deleting Cells

In some instances, you may need to insert extra cells without inserting an entire row or column. The Store Data worksheet has an error in column D. The data in rows 27–37 should actually be in rows 28–38. To insert extra cells:

Step 1	Click	the Store Data sheet tab
Step 2	Scroll	the Store Data worksheet so you can view rows 27–38
Step 3	Right-click	cell D27
Step 4	Click	Insert

The Insert dialog box opens.

Step 5	Verify	that the Shift cells down option button is selected
Step 6	Click	OK

The data in column D below row 26 shifts down one cell.

Step 7	Enter	1104 in cell D27

Hiding and Unhiding Rows and Columns

You can hide columns and rows when extraneous data does not need to be displayed. To hide a row or column:

Step 1	Right-click	the column D heading on the Store Data sheet tab

MENU TIP

To delete cells, select the cells you want to delete, right-click them, and click Delete. The Delete dialog box contains the same options as the Insert dialog box.

QUICK TIP

Click the Insert Options button that appears on screen after inserting new cells to adjust the formatting of the newly inserted cell.

Step 2	Click	Hide

Column E slides left, hiding column D. To unhide a column or row:

Step 1	Select	both column headings surrounding column D
Step 2	Right-click	either column heading
Step 3	Click	Unhide

Column D reappears.

Freezing and Unfreezing Rows and Columns

When working with large worksheets, it can be helpful to keep row and column labels on the screen as you scroll through your worksheet. The Freeze Panes command freezes the rows above and the columns to the left of the active cell and prevents them from scrolling off the screen. The Store Data worksheet contains more data than will fit on the screen at once. To freeze the columns and row headings:

Step 1	Activate	cell A5
Step 2	Click	Window
Step 3	Click	Freeze Panes

A thin, black line appears on your workbook, indicating that the rows above row 5 are frozen and will not scroll with the rest of your worksheet. This black line will not print when you print the worksheet.

Step 4	Press & hold	the DOWN ARROW key until your worksheet begins scrolling down

The worksheet scrolls, but the column labels stay fixed at the top of the worksheet. When you no longer need the frozen panes, you can unfreeze them. To unfreeze panes:

Step 1	Click	Window
Step 2	Click	Unfreeze Panes

MOUSE TIP

You can drag a hidden column into view. Move the mouse pointer to the hidden column boundary by positioning the mouse pointer slightly to the right of the boundary between the two columns on either side of the hidden column. The pointer changes to two black horizontal arrows with a gap between them, indicating that it is on the right boundary of the hidden column. Drag to the right to drag the hidden column into view.

QUICK TIP

To freeze columns, position the active cell to the right of the columns you want to freeze, then use the Freeze Panes command.

chapter
four

Step 3	**Save**	the workbook

The panes are removed, permitting normal worksheet scrolling.

4.f Filtering Lists Using AutoFilter

Excel is often used to store lists of data, similar to a database table. The Store Data sheet tab in your workbook contains a list of sales data. Sometimes, you want to look at data that meets some criteria. **Filtering** a list allows you to screen out any data that does not meet your **criteria**, or conditions that you specify. You can apply more than one filter so as to reduce the list even more. When you apply a filter, only the data meeting the specified criteria are displayed. While the filter remains on, you can format, edit, chart, and print the filtered list. When you have finished, turn the filter off and the rest of the records in the list will appear.

The AutoFilter command offers a fast, easy way to apply multiple filters to a list. To apply AutoFilter:

Step 1	**Activate**	any cell in the list
Step 2	**Click**	Data
Step 3	**Point to**	Filter
Step 4	**Click**	AutoFilter

The filter list arrow appears next to each column label. Clicking any of these arrows displays a list of AutoFilter options.

Step 5	**Click**	the Filter list arrow next to Store in cell A4
Step 6	**Click**	Store #2

The list is filtered for any entries in column A that contain "Store #2"; your screen should look similar to Figure 4-9. The filter list arrows of the filtered columns and the row headings appear in blue. All other entries are hidden.

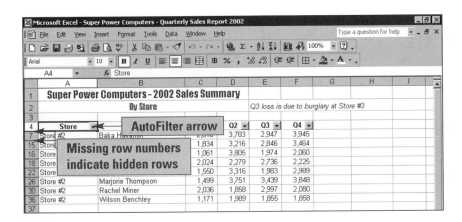

FIGURE 4-9
Applying AutoFilter to a List

When you want to display all of the records again, use the Show all command. To clear the filters:

Step 1	Click	the Filter list arrow next to Store in cell A4
Step 2	Click	(All) to restore the entries

When you have finished filtering a list, you can turn off AutoFilter. To turn off AutoFilter:

Step 1	Click	Data
Step 2	Point to	Filter
Step 3	Click	AutoFilter
Step 4	Save	the workbook and close it

Your formatted worksheets are much easier to read than the unformatted worksheets were.

MENU TIP

You can also clear the filters by pointing to Filter on the Data menu, and then clicking Show All.

chapter
four

Summary

► You can use the Merge and Center command to create worksheet titles.

► AutoFill fills in series of numbers, alphanumeric combinations, and day and month names.

► Judicious use of fonts and font styles can enhance a worksheet's appearance and make it easier to read.

► Align cell contents to enhance visual clarity. The default for text is left-alignment. For numeric entries, such as currency, dates, and times, the default is right-alignment.

► Number formats change how cells' numerical contents are displayed. Excel detects date, time, and currency entries and formats the cell accordingly.

► Rotate text to add visual interest or to decrease the width of a column. Indent text to provide visual breaks or to indicate that a list has a certain hierarchical structure. Use the alignment tab of the Format Cells dialog box to apply these settings.

► Borders and shading can add major visual impact to worksheets.

► Format Painter enables you to copy formats to other cells.

► You can clear cell contents, formats, or both using the Clear command on the Edit menu.

► AutoFormat applies stylized formatting to a selection of cells.

► Paste Special includes many options for pasting. Use Paste Special to paste only formats, to paste only values, to perform calculations automatically, or to transpose data from rows to columns.

► You can create and modify styles to reuse throughout a worksheet and in other workbooks.

► You can insert and delete rows and columns as needed to organize worksheets.

► You can change column width and row height to display more or less data.

► You can insert and delete cells by shifting the remaining cells up, down, left, or right when necessary to maintain surrounding information.

► You should hide columns and rows when extraneous data does not need to be displayed. Unhide them when you want to display the data again.

▶ You can freeze columns and rows to prevent them from scrolling along with the worksheet.

▶ You can use AutoFilter to display only data belonging to a certain category.

Commands Review

Action	Menu Bar	Shortcut Menu	Toolbar	Task Pane	Keyboard
Merge and Center					
AutoFill Series	Edit, Fill, Series				ALT + E, I, S
AutoFormat	Format, AutoFormat				ALT + O, A
Format cells	Format, Cells	Right-click selected range, Format Cells			CTRL + 1 ALT + O, E
Font Color	Format, Cells, Font tab				ALT + O, E
Bold	Format, Cells, Font tab				ALT + O, E CTRL + B
Italics	Format, Cells, Font tab				ALT + O, E CTRL + I
Underline	Format, Cells, Font tab				ALT + O, E CTRL + U
Align cell contents	Format, Cells, Alignment tab				ALT + O, E
Apply number formats	Format, Cells, Number tab				ALT + O, E
Rotate text	Format, Cells, Alignment tab				ALT + O, E
Increase/decrease indent	Format, Cells, Alignment tab				ALT + O, E
Add borders	Format, Cells, Borders tab				ALT + O, E
Add shading to cells	Format, Cells, Patterns tab				ALT + O, E
Use Format Painter					
Clear formats	Edit, Clear, Formats				ALT + E, C, F
Apply AutoFormat	Format, AutoFormat				ALT + O, A
Paste Special	Edit, Paste Special	Right-click cell, Paste Special			ALT + E, S
Define or Merge Format Style	Format, Style				ALT + O, S ALT + '
Insert rows	Insert, Rows	Right-click row, Insert			ALT + I, R
Insert columns	Insert, Columns	Right-click column, Insert			ALT + I, C
Delete rows and columns	Edit, Delete	Right-click row or column, Delete			ALT + E, D
Change column width	Format, Columns, Width Format, Columns, AutoFit Selection				ALT + O, C, W ALT + O, C, A

chapter four

Action	Menu Bar	Shortcut Menu	Toolbar	Task Pane	Keyboard
Change row height	Format, Rows, Height Format, Rows, AutoFit Selection				ALT + O, R, H ALT + O, R, A
Insert cells	Insert, Cells	Right-click cell, Insert			ALT + I, E CTRL + SHIFT + + (plus key)
Delete cells	Edit, Delete	Right-click cell, Delete			ALT + E, D
Hide rows or columns	Format, Row, Hide Format, Column, Hide				ALT + O, R, H ALT + O, C, H
Unhide rows or columns	Format, Row, Unhide Format, Column, Unhide				ALT + O, R, U ALT + O, C, U
Freeze/unfreeze rows and columns	Window, Freeze Panes Window, Unfreeze Panes				ALT + W, F
Use AutoFilter	Data, Filter, AutoFilter				ALT + D, I, F

Concepts Review

Circle the correct answer.

1. **Which of the following commands can you use to copy formatting only from one selection to another?**
   [a] Copy, Paste Special (Formats option)
   [b] Copy, Paste
   [c] Cut, Paste
   [d] Paste Special, Copy

2. **To apply multiple changes to a font, use the _____ tab of the Format Cells dialog box.**
   [a] Font
   [b] Border
   [c] Patterns
   [d] Number

3. **To apply custom border styles, use the _____ tab of the Format Cells dialog box.**
   [a] Font
   [b] Border
   [c] Patterns
   [d] Number

4. **To insert a cell in the middle of existing data:**
   [a] click Format, then click Add Cells.
   [b] right-click the row header, then click Insert.
   [c] right-click the column header, then click Insert.
   [d] right-click the cell where you want a new blank cell to appear, then click Insert.

5. **To prevent a row from scrolling, you should:**
   [a] hide the row.
   [b] freeze the row.
   [c] insert a new row.
   [d] filter the list.

6. **AutoFill can be used to fill series of:**
   [a] day names.
   [b] month names.
   [c] alphanumeric combinations.
   [d] All of the above.

7. **To maintain a set column width while still displaying all of a cell's content, you must:**
   [a] indent the text.
   [b] rotate the text.
   [c] edit the content until it fits.
   [d] wrap the text.

8. **Using the Font tab of the Format Cells dialog box, you can:**
   [a] change numerical style settings.
   [b] add borders to cells.
   [c] change the alignment of text in a cell.
   [d] change font settings, such as font, size, style, and color.

9. **Cell A1 contains a value of .25. If the currency style is applied to cell A1, the cell displays:**
   [a] 25%.
   [b] 0.25%.
   [c] $0.25.
   [d] 2.50E-01.

10. **Cell A2 contains a value of 45.26 and has been formatted to display 0 decimal places. What is displayed in cell A2?**
    [a] $45.26
    [b] $45.00
    [c] 45
    [d] 45%

Circle **T** if the statement is true or **F** if the statement is false.

T   F   1. To delete a range of cells, you must first delete the rows or columns that contain the cells.

T   F   2. You can apply a border diagonally across a cell (or cells).

T   F   3. AutoFilter has certain preset categories, but does not automatically add categories based on the data in your worksheet.

T   F   4. Increasing the font size automatically increases the row height.

T   F   5. Rotating text automatically adjusts the row height.

T   F   6. AutoFill cannot fill a series of values containing a mixture of text and numbers, such as "Apollo 11."

T   F   7. The Merge and Center command merges only the value in the upper-left cell of your selection.

T   F   8. Changing a cell's number format alters the actual value of the cell.

T   F   9. You can create your own cell styles.

T   F   10. You can copy styles created in one workbook to another workbook.

Skills Review

Exercise 1

1. Open the *Project Expense Log* workbook located on the Data Disk.

2. Change the numeric format of column A to the MM/DD/YY date format.

3. Change the number format of column C to Currency Style.

4. Merge and center cell A1 across cells A1:C1.

5. Center the column labels in row 3.

6. Turn on AutoFilter and filter the Place column for Phoenix, AZ.

7. Save the workbook as *Project Expense Log Revised*. Print and close the workbook.

chapter four

Exercise 2 C

1. Open the *Wage Increase* workbook located on the Data Disk.

2. Use the Format Cells dialog box to format the column labels as follows:

   a. Change the font to Times New Roman.

   b. Increase the font size to 12.

   c. Change the font color to blue.

   d. Change the font style to bold.

   e. Turn on Wrap Text.

3. Center the column labels.

4. Make cells A7:D7 bold and add a Gray-25% shade.

5. Add a thick bottom border to cells A1:D1.

6. Indent cell A7.

7. Adjust the column widths using AutoFit.

8. Hide the row containing Micah Anderson.

9. Delete the range A4: D4.

10. Insert cells above the range A3: D3.

11. Enter the following in row 3: Jared Wright, 8.50, 8.75.

12. Copy the formula from cell D2 to cell D3.

13. Change the format of the range B3: D3 to Accounting with two decimal places and no dollar sign.

14. Save the workbook as *Wage Increase Revised*. Print and close the workbook.

Exercise 3 C

1. Open the *Number Formatting* workbook on the Data Disk.

2. Apply the List 1 AutoFormat to the data.

3. Use the number format indicated by each column label to format the columns. Use the default settings unless otherwise directed.

   a. In the Number column, select the Use 1000 Separator (,) check box in the Number format settings.

   b. In the Date column, set the Date type to 3/14/2001. (Excel converts numbers into dates, starting with 1 equal to 1/1/1900.)

   c. In the Time column, set the Time type to 3/14/2001 1:30 PM. (*Hint:* If you don't have this format, set it as 3/14/01 1:30 PM.)

   d. In the Fraction column, set the Fraction type to Up to two digits (21/25). (*Hint:* Because many of the numbers are whole numbers, no fraction will appear in this column in the worksheet, but the numbers will move to the left side of the cell to allow proper alignment of fractions when needed.)

4. Save the workbook as *Number Formatting Revised*. Print and close the workbook.

Exercise 4 [C]

1. Create a new workbook.

2. Enter the data as shown in the table below:

Important Dates of World War II	
Date	**Event**
9/1/1939	Germany invades Poland
6/14/40	German troops occupy Paris
7/10/40	Battle of Britain begins
6/22/1941	German troops invade Russia
12/7/1941	Japan attacks U.S. forces at Pearl Harbor, Hawaii
12/8/1941	U.S. declares war on Japan
12/11/1941	U.S. declares war on Germany and Italy
6/4/1942	Battle of Midway starts (turning point of Pacific war)
1/23/1943	Casablanca Conference decides on Cross Channel Invasion of Continental Europe
7/10/43	Allies invade Sicily
6/6/1944	D-Day Allied invasion of Western Europe commences in France
5/7/1945	Germany surrenders to Allies at Reims, France
7/16/1945	U.S. tests 1st atomic bomb in New Mexico
8/6/1945	U.S. drops atomic bomb on Hiroshima, Japan
8/9/1945	U.S. drops atomic bomb on Nagasaki, Japan
8/14/1945	Japan agrees to surrender
9/2/1945	Japan formally surrenders in Tokyo Bay

3. Merge and center the title in the range A1: B1.

4. Bold and center the titles in the range A2: B2.

5. Change the format of the Date column to the Month DD, YYYY format.

6. Format cell A1 with a black fill and white text.

7. Format the text in cell A1 as bold and increase the font size to 16 points.

8. Format row 2 with a dark gray fill and white text.

9. Use AutoFit to adjust the column widths.

10. Save the workbook as *WWII*. Print and close the workbook.

Exercise 5 [C]

1. Open the *WWII* workbook you created in Exercise 4.

2. Change the width of column B to 45.

3. Turn on wrap text with column B selected.

4. Left align cells A3:A19.

chapter four

5. Italicize cells A3, A7, A13, A14, and A19.

6. Activate cell A1, then save the workbook as *WWII Revised*. Print and close the workbook.

Exercise 6

1. Open the *New Computer Prices* workbook located on the Data Disk.

2. Change the title in row A1 to 16 point, bold text.

3. Merge and center cell A1 across A1:G1.

4. Bold and center the titles in row 3.

5. Resize columns A–G to fit.

6. Format column C with Currency Style and no decimal places.

7. Change the data in columns E and F to right-aligned. (Do not right-align the column labels.)

8. Save the workbook as *New Computer Prices Formatted*. Print and close the workbook.

Exercise 7

1. Open the *Employee Time 1* workbook located on the Data Disk.

2. Insert a new column to the left of column A, on the Revised Data worksheet.

3. Move all of the data (including the column heading) under Project to the new column A.

4. Delete the empty column C.

5. Change column C to Number format with two decimal places.

6. Increase the width of column A to show the project names in full.

7. Bold and center the column labels.

8. Move the title in cell B1 to cell A1, make the title bold, then merge and center it across columns A through C.

9. Delete the blank rows 2, 3, and 4 under the worksheet title.

10. Freeze the column labels. (*Hint:* Freeze rows 1 and 2.)

11. Save the workbook as *Employee Time 2*. Print and close the workbook.

Exercise 8

1. Create a new workbook, and then enter "Title" in cell A1.

2. Change the Font style to Times New Roman, font size 16, and color blue.

3. Fill the cell with the light turquoise color.

4. Create a new style "Title" based on cell A1.

5. Enter "Column Heading" in cell A2.

6. Rotate the text 45 degrees.

7. Change the alignment to center, horizontally and vertically.

8. Add a left and right dashed style border.

9. Create a new style "Column Heading" based on cell A2.

10. Key 1 in cell A5, and key 2 in cell B5.

11. Select A5:B5, then drag the fill handle to cell E5.

12. Save the workbook as *Cell Styles*. Print and close the workbook.

Case Projects

Project 1

You work in a large bank. You are frequently asked about the current exchange rate for U.S. dollars relative to a variety of foreign currencies. Connect to the Internet and search the Web for a site that reports currency exchange rates. Create a new workbook to keep track of recent updates. Include the URL of the site(s) you find in the workbook, which will allow you to access these sites easily later. Record the date and currency exchange rate for converting U.S. dollars into the euro currency and the currencies of at least six countries, including those of Japan, Germany, France, and the United Kingdom. Apply currency formats displaying the appropriate currency symbol for each country (if available). Set up your workbook so that you can monitor the changes in exchange rates over time. Center and bold column labels, and italicize row labels. Make sure your worksheet has a formatted title. Save the workbook as *Foreign Currency Exchange*, and then print and close it.

Project 2 C

Your mom, a quilter, has come to you with an interesting project. She needs to organize her quilt pattern, but because of the number of pieces, it's very difficult to keep track of everything. You know that Excel can shade cells in different colors. That gives you an idea. Can you use shading and borders to create a fun geometrical pattern? Don't be afraid to modify column widths and row heights to achieve a more artistic pattern. Save your workbook as *Quilt*, and then print and close it.

Project 3

You are an instructor at a community college who teaches working adults about Excel. Several of your students have asked you for additional resources. Connect to the Internet and use the Web toolbar to search for Excel books. Create a new worksheet that lists the title, author name, and ISBN number for each book. Add a fourth column that lists the URL where you found the information about each book. (*Hint:* To copy the URL of the current Web page, click in the Address or Location box in your browser window, click Copy on the Edit menu, then paste this into your worksheet.) Add a title to your worksheet and format it nicely. Save the workbook as *Excel Books*, and then print and close it.

Project 4 C

You are the manager of a pizzeria. Create a worksheet with fictitious data that shows how many pizzas were sold last month. Calculate the total sales, figuring that each pizza sold for $8.00. Show the following column headings: Overhead, Labor, Ingredients, Advertising, and Profit. Calculate the amount spent in each category, figuring 15% for overhead, 30% for labor, 25% for ingredients, 10% for advertising, and the remainder for profit. Format the column labels to stand out from the rest of the data, and add a worksheet title. Save the workbook as *Pizzeria*, and then print and close it.

chapter four

Project 5

You plan on selling your car soon and want to find out how much it is worth. Connect to the Internet and use the Web toolbar to search for used car prices. Try finding a listing for your car and two other cars built the same year. (*Hint:* Search for "Blue Book values.") Create an Excel worksheet listing your car and the two cars you found. List the trade-in value of the cars you selected. Format the workbook nicely. Save the workbook as *Blue Book Values*, and then print and close it.

Project 6

You are a major sports fan. Create a workbook with column headings for Team Name, City, and Sport, then list as many pro sports teams as you can think of. Use the Internet to help you. When you finish the list, add AutoFilter to the list so you can filter the list by city or sport. Hide the row of the team you dislike the most. Format the worksheet nicely and add a worksheet title. Save the workbook as *Sports Teams*, and then print and close it.

Problem 7

You are a busy salesperson who is constantly visiting clients in your car, and who therefore, depends on a cellular phone. You want to see if your usage in the last year warrants changing your cellular calling plan. Create a worksheet with columns for local and long-distance minutes. Randomly generate numbers for each month between 0 and 400 for local air time, and numbers between 0 and 150 for long-distance air time. Copy the formula cells, then use the Paste Special command to paste only the values (not the formulas) in the same cells. Add a worksheet title and format the column headings with bold. Change the font color of any monthly total over 400 minutes to red. Save the workbook as *Cell Phone*, and then print and close it.

Project 8

Create a new workbook, enter some data, and then copy the workbook's contents using the Paste Special command. Paste Special provides many ways to copy data from one cell to another. Use the Ask A Question Box to learn about each option. Write a four-paragraph document explaining each of the options. Save the document as *Paste Special Options.doc*, and then print and close it.

Previewing and Printing Worksheets and Workbooks

Chapter Overview

When data needs to be changed or located in a workbook, the Find and Replace commands are at your service. AutoCorrect can simplify data entry and reduce spelling errors by correcting mistakes as you key. Prior to printing, it's a good idea to check for spelling errors. Excel provides many options to help you print exactly what you want. For example, you can print selections, worksheets, or entire workbooks. You also can set up headers and footers using pre-defined styles, or create custom headers and footers. In addition, you can modify page breaks and margin settings to print sheets to fit every need.

LEARNING OBJECTIVES

- ▶ Use Find and Replace
- ▶ Check spelling
- ▶ Set print options and print worksheets
- ▶ Print an entire workbook

Case profile

Every six months, Super Power Computers holds a long-range planning session. In this meeting, the company president, Luis Alvarez, reviews the accomplishments of the last six months and notes the company's progress toward previously set goals. Goals for the next six months are revised and set. You have prepared a calendar in Excel for 2003 that each participant in the meeting can use for notes.

chapter five

C

5.a Using Find and Replace

The Find command locates data and formats in a cell value, formula, or comment. Your calendars are ready to print, but you reread the worksheet, and you realize that the year displayed on each of your calendars is "02" instead of "03." To find and replace items:

Step 1	***Open***	the *12 Month Calendars* workbook located on the Data Disk
Step 2	***Save***	the workbook as *12 Month Calendars Revised*
Step 3	***Click***	Edit
Step 4	***Click***	Find
Step 5	***Click***	Options >> to expand the dialog box to show search options

CAUTION TIP

If the Options button shows two arrows pointing to the left (Options <<), then the dialog box is already expanded.

The Find tab in the Find and Replace dialog box on your screen should look similar to Figure 5-1. This tab provides many options for finding data. You want to search only this worksheet, by rows, and for data entered directly into a cell; it doesn't matter whether you look in Formulas or in Values. The search options are fine in this case. You enter the search text.

FIGURE 5-1
Find and Replace Dialog Box

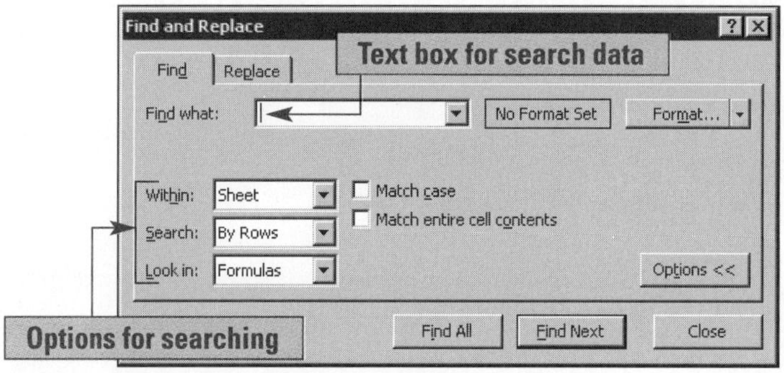

Step 6	***Key***	02 in the Find what: text box
Step 7	***Click***	the Format button list arrow
Step 8	***Click***	Choose Format From Cell
Step 9	***Click***	cell A1

A preview of the format appears to the left of the Format button.

Step 10	***Click***	Find All

At the bottom of the Find and Replace box, a list of cells appears. Each item in this list is a hyperlink to that cell, and you can click any link to jump directly to a cell containing the found item. You want to replace each of these with "03" formatted with bold. The Replace command finds and replaces individual instances or all instances of a given value.

Step 11	*Click*	the Replace tab
Step 12	*Key*	03 in the Replace with: text box
Step 13	*Click*	the Format list arrow in the Replace with: section
Step 14	*Click*	Format
Step 15	*Click*	Bold in the Font style: list on the Font tab
Step 16	*Click*	OK
Step 17	*Click*	Replace All
Step 18	*Click*	OK in the dialog box that opens to tell you that 12 replacements have been made
Step 19	*Click*	Close

The dates are now correct and formatted with bold.

Step 20	*Save*	the workbook

5.b Checking Spelling

Before you print a worksheet, you should proofread it and check the spelling. Excel provides two ways to check the spelling in a worksheet: AutoCorrect and the spell checker.

Using AutoCorrect

AutoCorrect checks your spelling as you go and automatically corrects common typos, such as "teh" for "the." You can turn AutoCorrect into a powerful helper by adding your own commonly used abbreviations in place of longer words or phrases. You decide to set up an abbreviation in AutoCorrect. To set AutoCorrect options:

Step 1	*Click*	Tools
Step 2	*Click*	AutoCorrect Options
Step 3	*Click*	the AutoCorrect tab, if necessary

QUICK TIP

The Find and Replace commands do not search comments, chart objects or sheet tabs.

CAUTION TIP

The Replace All button provides a quick way to replace data, but it may make replacements you didn't intend or expect. If you want to verify each item before you replace it, click the Find Next button to locate the data in the worksheet, then click the Replace button to replace each item one at a time.

chapter five

Your AutoCorrect dialog box should look similar to Figure 5-2.

FIGURE 5-2
AutoCorrect Dialog Box

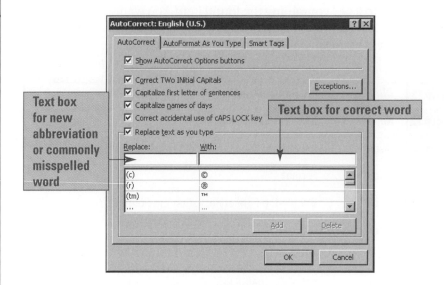

Step 4	*Key*	spc in the Replace: text box
Step 5	*Key*	Super Power Computers in the With: text box
Step 6	*Click*	Add

Now, whenever you key "spc" it will automatically be replaced with "Super Power Computers."

Step 7	*Click*	OK
Step 8	*Insert*	two rows at the top of the worksheet
Step 9	*Key*	spc in cell A1
Step 10	*Press*	the ENTER key
Step 11	*Merge*	and center cell A1 across columns A:O

Another Super Power Computers employee created a style for worksheet titles and copied the style to this workbook, so you can apply it to the title.

Step 12	*Apply*	the Worksheet Title style to cell A1
Step 13	*Save*	the workbook

Checking Spelling

Excel features a powerful spell checker that flags words that are not in the built-in dictionary and suggests alternate spellings. The spell checker does not find words that are spelled correctly but used incorrectly—for example, it will not flag "there" as misspelled when you should have used "their"—so always proofread your worksheets for errors, in addition to running a spell check. To spell check a worksheet:

| Step 1 | Click | the Spelling button ABC✓ on the Standard toolbar |

The spell checker starts at the active cell and checks the active worksheet row by row until it reaches the end of the worksheet. If the active cell is not at the top of the worksheet, Excel asks if you want to start at the top. The Spelling dialog box opens when the spell checker locates a word it doesn't recognize. Suggested corrections appear in the Suggestions: list box, as shown in Figure 5-3. Excel locates the misspelled word, "Wedensday" in the March calendar. The first suggestion in the Suggestions: list box is selected and is correct.

Spelling: English (U.S.)   ? ✕

Not in Dictionary:
Wedensday   [Ignore Once]
                                            [Ignore All]
Flagged word
                                            [Add to Dictionary]
Suggestions:
Wednesday   [Change] ◄
Wednesdays   [Change All]
Suggested corrections   [AutoCorrect]

Dictionary language: English (U.S.) ▼

[Options...] [Undo Last] [Cancel]

Command to replace flagged word with selected suggestion

FIGURE 5-3
Spelling Dialog Box

| Step 2 | Click | Change to replace the misspelled word with the selected suggestion |

There are no more spelling errors in the worksheet, so a dialog box opens, telling you that the spell check is complete.

| Step 3 | Click | OK |
| Step 4 | Save | the workbook |

MENU TIP

You can run the spell checker by clicking the Spelling command on the Tools menu.

QUICK TIP

To spell check multiple worksheets, select the sheet tabs of each sheet you want to check, then click the Spelling button.

CAUTION TIP

Many specialized professions use industry-specific vocabularies that may not be included in the Excel dictionary. Proper names are also not included in the Excel dictionary. Click Ignore Once or Ignore All to skip these items.

chapter
five

C **5.c** Setting Print Options and Printing Worksheets

Excel provides many options for formatting and printing your worksheets. You can change the margins and the orientation, add headers, footers, and print titles, or print multiple ranges or worksheets. You can also set a specific print area.

Setting the Print Area

By default, Excel prints all data on the current worksheet. If you need to print only a portion of a worksheet, however, you can define a print area by using the Set Print Area command. To set the print area:

Step 1	*Select*	the range A1:O11
Step 2	*Click*	File
Step 3	*Point to*	Print Area
Step 4	*Click*	Set Print Area

This action defines a print area covering the worksheet title and the months January-03 and February-03.

Step 5	*Click*	cell A1 to deselect the range

Changing Margins

When the data is not situated properly on the page, you can adjust the margins, or align the data centered on the page. You can change margins in the Print Preview window or in the Page Setup dialog box. To change margins in Print Preview:

Step 1	*Click*	the Print Preview button on the Standard toolbar
Step 2	*Click*	the Margins button on the Print Preview toolbar

Your screen should look similar to Figure 5-4. The dotted lines indicate the margins and the header/footer locations. You can change these margins by dragging the lines.

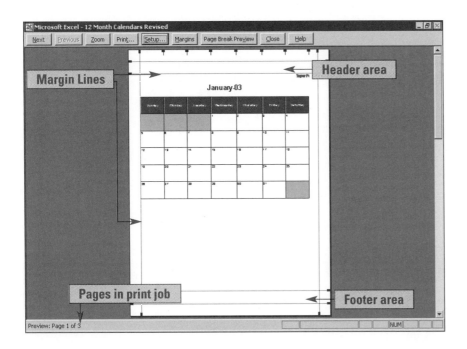

FIGURE 5-4
Adjusting Margins in
Print Preview

MENU TIP

You can click the Print Preview command on the File menu to preview a document.

Step 3	*Move*	the mouse pointer over the left margin line so that it changes to a double-headed arrow
Step 4	*Drag*	the margin line to the right, observing that the status bar indicates the width (in inches) of the margin
Step 5	*Release*	the mouse button when the status bar displays approximately "Left Margin: 1.00"
Step 6	*Click*	the Margins button on the Print Preview toolbar to turn off the margin lines

MOUSE TIP

Drag the scroll box in the vertical scroll bar in the Print Preview window to move to another page.

You also can precisely set margins in the Page Setup dialog box. To adjust the margins using the Page Setup dialog box:

Step 1	*Click*	the Setup button on the Print Preview toolbar
Step 2	*Click*	the Margins tab

QUICK TIP

Zoom in to the worksheet to get more precise control.

chapter
five

Your dialog box should look similar to Figure 5-5.

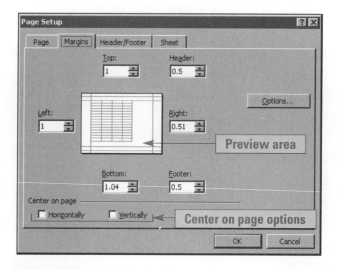

Step 3	*Double-click*	the Right: text box to select the current margin setting
Step 4	*Key*	1
Step 5	*Click*	OK

The right margin is now 1 inch. Luis wants the calendar to print two months to a page and sideways.

Changing Scaling and Page Orientation

The Page Setup dialog box provides many settings through which you can arrange the page, including scaling and orientation. Scaling a document allows you to fit a report to a certain number of pages. To scale the print area:

Step 1	*Click*	the Setup button on the Print Preview toolbar
Step 2	*Click*	the Page tab
Step 3	*Click*	the Fit to: option button

The Page tab in the Page Setup dialog box on your screen should look similar to Figure 5-6. The Fit to option automatically fits your print area to the number of pages you specify.

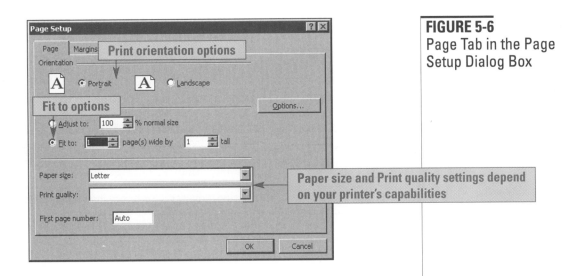

FIGURE 5-6
Page Tab in the Page
Setup Dialog Box

| Step 4 | *Click* | OK |

The print job scales to fit on a single page.

Most business documents, including letters, memos, and financial reports, are printed in **portrait orientation**, or across the width of the page. However, in Excel, you may find **landscape orientation** more suitable, because it prints across the length of the page, as if you were holding the paper sideways. To change the orientation:

Step 1	*Click*	the Setup button on the Print Preview toolbar
Step 2	*Click*	the Landscape option button on the Page tab in the Page Setup dialog box
Step 3	*Click*	OK

The print area appears in landscape orientation and all on one page. Your screen should look similar to Figure 5-7.

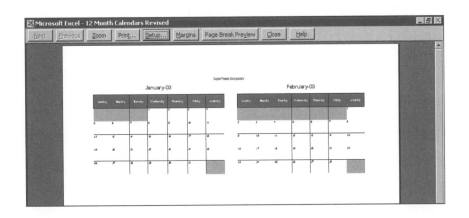

FIGURE 5-7
Calendar in Landscape
Orientation

chapter
five

Centering the Page Horizontally and Vertically

You can use the Page Setup dialog box to center the print area vertically and horizontally on the page. To center a print area on the page:

Step 1	*Click*	the <u>S</u>etup button on the Print Preview toolbar
Step 2	*Click*	the Margins tab
Step 3	*Click*	the Hori<u>z</u>ontally check box to insert a check mark
Step 4	*Click*	the <u>V</u>ertically check box to insert a check mark
Step 5	*Click*	OK to center the print area on the page

Setting Headers and Footers

A **header** appears above the top margin of every page you print. A **footer** appears below the bottom margin of every page you print. Excel has several predefined headers and footers, using common options such as the page number, filename, and date. To add a header:

Step 1	*Click*	the <u>S</u>etup button on the Print Preview toolbar
Step 2	*Click*	the Header/Footer tab
Step 3	*Click*	the He<u>a</u>der: list arrow

The He<u>a</u>der: list contains preset headers to print the current page number, total number of pages to be printed, worksheet name, company name, date, filename, and user name, as well as several variations and combinations of these elements.

Step 4	*Click*	12 Month Calendars Revised

This choice prints the filename as the header. The mini-preview above the He<u>a</u>der: list shows how your header will look. You also can create a custom header and footer. To add a custom footer to your document:

Step 1	*Click*	C<u>u</u>stom Footer

The Footer dialog box opens with the blinking insertion point in the <u>L</u>eft section: text box. The Header and Footer dialog boxes, which look identical, contain buttons to insert special print codes. See Table 5-1.

To	Use	Code Inserted
Change the text font	A	
Insert a page number	#	&[Page]
Insert the total number of pages		&[Pages]
Insert the current date		&[Date]
Insert the current time		&[Time]
Insert the workbook path and filename		&[Path]&[File]
Insert the workbook filename		&[File]
Insert the worksheet name		&[Tab]
Insert a picture		&[Picture]
Format a picture		

TABLE 5-1
Header and
Footer Buttons

Step 2	*Key*	your name in the <u>L</u>eft section: text box
Step 3	*Click*	in the <u>R</u>ight section: text box
Step 4	*Click*	the Date button
Step 5	*Click*	in the <u>C</u>enter section: text box
Step 6	*Click*	the Page Number button
Step 7	*Press*	the SPACEBAR
Step 8	*Key*	of
Step 9	*Press*	the SPACEBAR
Step 10	*Click*	the Total Pages button

QUICK TIP

Text you key in the <u>L</u>eft section: text box will be left aligned, text in the <u>C</u>enter section: text box will be center aligned, and text in the <u>R</u>ight section: text box will be right aligned.

The Footer dialog box on your screen should look similar to Figure 5-8.

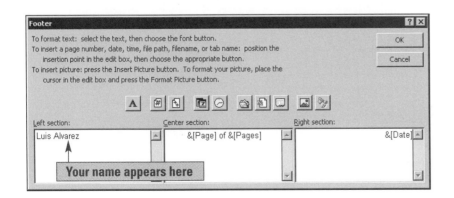

FIGURE 5-8
Footer Dialog Box

chapter
five

| Step 11 | *Click* | OK |

Your footer appears in the Footer: list box, and the mini-preview below the Footer: list box shows what the footer will look like.

| Step 12 | *Click* | OK to apply the header and footer |

The preview shows that one page of the calendar with two months on it will print. However, you need all 12 months to print.

| Step 13 | *Click* | the Close button on the Print Preview toolbar |

Setting Multiple Print Ranges

To print more than one area of a worksheet, you can specify multiple ranges in the Page Setup dialog box. You key a comma between each range to separate them. To set multiple print ranges:

Step 1	*Click*	File
Step 2	*Click*	Page Setup
Step 3	*Click*	the Sheet tab, if necessary

The dialog box on your screen should look similar to Figure 5-9.

FIGURE 5-9
Sheet Tab in the Page
Setup Dialog Box

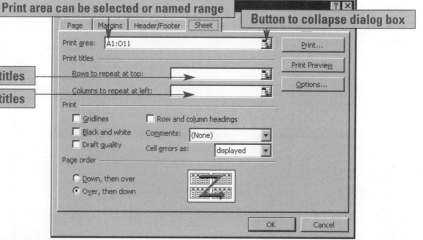

| Step 4 | *Click* | after the "11" in the Print area: text box |

A flashing border in your worksheet indicates the current print area.

Step 5	*Key*	, (a comma)
Step 6	*Click*	the Collapse dialog box button
Step 7	*Select*	A13:O21
Step 8	*Click*	the Expand dialog box button
Step 9	*Click*	Print Preview in the Page Setup dialog box
Step 10	*Click*	the Next button on the Print Preview toolbar
Step 11	*Click*	the Close button on the Print Preview toolbar

Two pages are now set to print. There is another way to print more than one page at a time.

Inserting and Removing Page Breaks

To quickly print all the data on a worksheet, you can use Page Break Preview. When a worksheet contains data that will print on more than one page, you may need to adjust the position of page breaks so that information appears on the correct page. Because you have already defined a print area and set the print setting to Fit to, first you need to clear those settings. To clear the print area and change the Fit to option:

Step 1	*Click*	File
Step 2	*Point to*	Print Area
Step 3	*Click*	Clear Print Area
Step 4	*Open*	the Page tab in the Page Setup dialog box
Step 5	*Key*	6 in the box next to tall
Step 6	*Click*	OK

Your print job fits on six pages, two months per page. To change to Page Break Preview:

Step 1	*Click*	View
Step 2	*Click*	Page Break Preview
Step 3	*Click*	OK to close the Welcome to Page Break Preview dialog box, if necessary

chapter
five

Your screen should look similar to Figure 5-10. Dashed blue lines represent the automatic page breaks in Excel. A light gray page number indicates the order in which pages will print. You can drag the page break to a new location to change how pages are printed.

notes Because of differences in printer margins, the exact row number you use may differ in the steps that follow.

| Step 4 | *Scroll* | the worksheet until you see the dashed line, near row 22 |
| Step 5 | *Drag* | the dashed blue page break line from near row 22 to row 11 |

The dashed blue line changes to a solid blue line, representing a manually adjusted page break.

Step 6	*Follow*	Steps 4 and 5 to manually position a page break at rows 21, 31, and 41
Step 7	*Activate*	cell A52
Step 8	*Click*	Insert
Step 9	*Click*	Page Break

In Normal view, the page breaks appear as dotted black lines. To switch back to Normal view:

Step 1	*Click*	View
Step 2	*Click*	Normal

Check to make sure that your calendar will now print two months per page.

Step 3	*Click*	the Print Preview button [icon] on the Standard toolbar
Step 4	*Click*	the down scroll arrow five times to scroll through the preview
Step 5	*Drag*	the scroll box back to the top of the scroll bar
Step 6	*Close*	Print Preview

The worksheet title, "Super Power Computers," appears on page 1, but not on the rest of the pages. You can set a print title to appear on each page.

Setting Print Titles

Print titles are useful when you need column or row labels to appear on every printed page. You set print titles from the Page Setup dialog box, but this command is not available when you open the dialog box with the Print Preview window open. To create print titles:

Step 1	*Open*	the Sheet tab in the Page Setup dialog box
Step 2	*Click*	in the Rows to repeat at top: text box
Step 3	*Select*	row 1 in your worksheet
Step 4	*Click*	Print Preview in the Page Setup dialog box
Step 5	*Scroll*	through the pages to verify that the title repeats on every page
Step 6	*Close*	Print Preview

CAUTION TIP

In Normal view, the dotted black page break lines can be turned on and off using the Options dialog box. Click the Options command on the Tools menu, click the View tab, and then click the Page breaks check box in the Window options group to turn this option on or off.

chapter
five

Printing a Worksheet

Now that you have adjusted the page setup options and set the page breaks, you are ready to print. To print a worksheet:

Step 1	*Click*	<u>F</u>ile
Step 2	*Click*	<u>P</u>rint

The Print dialog box on your screen should look similar to Figure 5-11.

FIGURE 5-11
Print Dialog Box

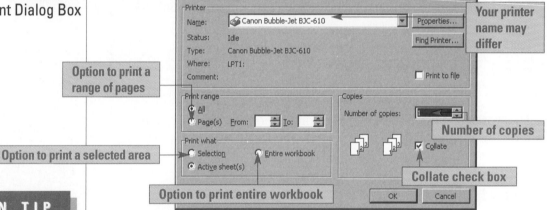

By default, the Active Sheet(s) option prints the entire worksheet. However, if you set a print area, or define page breaks, the Acti<u>v</u>e Sheet refers to these manually defined print areas. If you select a region, then click the Print button, that area is printed by default instead of the print areas you may have defined.

Step 3	*Verify*	that the Acti<u>v</u>e Sheet(s) option button is selected in the Print what section

Step 4	*Click*	OK

The 2003 worksheet prints, two months per page.

Until now, you have been working with areas on only one worksheet. In the next section, you learn how to print multiple worksheets.

CAUTION TIP

The Print button on the Standard toolbar uses the current page setup options to print your worksheet. Before printing, verify the current print area settings and which printer will print the worksheet.

5.d Printing an Entire Workbook

Luis wants everyone to have a 2004 calendar at the meeting as well. It is just for reference, so it can be printed six months to a page. When you print multiple worksheets, each worksheet has its own page break settings. To print the entire workbook:

Step 1	*Click*	the 2004 sheet tab
Step 2	*Switch to*	Page Break Preview
Step 3	*Drag*	the vertical page break line to the right of column O
Step 4	*Drag*	the horizontal page break near row 22 to below row 29
Step 5	*Right-click*	cell A40
Step 6	*Click*	Remove Page Break
Step 7	*Remove*	the other page break at row 50
Step 8	*Switch to*	Normal view
Step 9	*Click*	File
Step 10	*Click*	Print
Step 11	*Click*	the Entire workbook option button in the Print what section
Step 12	*Change*	the Number of copies text box to 2
Step 13	*Click*	Preview
Step 14	*Verify*	that the pages will print as desired
Step 15	*Verify*	that your instructor wants you to print two copies of all eight pages
Step 16	*Click*	the Print button on the Print Preview toolbar
Step 17	*Click*	OK
Step 18	*Save*	the workbook and close it

You're all set for the meeting!

CAUTION TIP

When you print multiple worksheets, remember to check the page breaks on every page.

QUICK TIP

The Collate check box in the Print dialog box organizes the order of your print job. Select it when you are printing more than one copy of a multiple-page worksheet to print a complete copy of the document before starting the next copy.

chapter
five

Summary

▶ The Find and Replace commands enable you to locate and change data.

▶ AutoCorrect corrects common spelling errors as you type. Add AutoCorrect entries to replace abbreviations with long words, titles, or phrases.

▶ You should always spell check workbooks before printing them. Remember that the spell checker does not detect incorrect usage, such as "your" for "you're." Always proofread your document after spell checking it.

▶ You can define print areas by clicking the File menu, pointing to Print area, and then clicking Set Print Area.

▶ You can set margins by dragging them in Print Preview or by using the Margins tab in the Page Setup dialog box.

▶ You can use the Page tab in the Page Setup dialog box to set scaling options and to change the orientation of the page.

▶ You can use the Margins tab in the Page Setup dialog box to select page centering options.

▶ You can use the Header/Footer tab to add a header or footer to a printed worksheet.

▶ You can set multiple print ranges on the Sheet tab in the Page Setup dialog box.

▶ You can manually adjust page breaks in Page Break view.

▶ You can select rows and columns to repeat on every printed page on the Sheet tab in the Page Setup dialog box.

▶ You can print a workbook by clearing print areas, then selecting the Entire Workbook option in the Print dialog box.

Commands Review

Action	Menu Bar	Shortcut Menu	Toolbar	Task Pane	Keyboard
Find	Edit, Find				ALT + E, F CTRL + F
Replace	Edit, Replace				ALT + E, E CTRL + H
Add AutoCorrect entries	Tools, AutoCorrect options				ALT + T, A
Check spelling	Tools, Spelling				ALT + T, S F7
Set print area	File, Print Area, Set Print Area				ALT + F, T, S
Clear print area	File, Print Area, Clear Print Area				ALT + F, T, C
Preview the workbook to be printed	File, Print Preview		🔍		ALT + F, V
Set print options	File, Page Setup				ALT + F, U
View page breaks	View, Page Break Preview				ALT + V, P
Switch to Normal view	View, Normal				ALT + V, N
Print	File, Print		🖨		CTRL + P ALT + F, P

Concepts Review

Circle the correct answer.

1. To create multiple ranges for printing, press and hold the:
[a] SHIFT key while selecting ranges.
[b] END key while selecting ranges.
[c] CTRL key while selecting ranges.
[d] ALT key while selecting ranges.

2. To set centering options for a printed report, open the Page Setup dialog box and use the:
[a] Page tab.
[b] Margins tab.
[c] Header/Footer tab.
[d] Sheet tab.

3. To set a page to print in landscape orientation, open the Page Setup dialog box and use the:
[a] Page tab.
[b] Margins tab.
[c] Header/Footer tab.
[d] Sheet tab.

4. When you include the print formula "&[Page]" in a header or footer, it prints:
[a] "&[Page]" on every page.
[b] the total page count on every page.

[c] the current page number on each page.
[d] a box where you can write in the page number by hand.

5. In Normal view, page breaks are indicated by a:
[a] heavy blue line.
[b] heavy black line.
[c] dotted black line.
[d] thin blue line.

6. In Page Break Preview view, default page breaks are indicated by a:
[a] dotted blue line.
[b] heavy black line.
[c] solid blue line.
[d] thin blue line.

7. Replace can replace values in which of the following?
[a] chart objects
[b] comments
[c] formulas
[d] chart objects, comments, and formulas

chapter five

8. **You set up page breaks on Sheet1 of a workbook and select Entire workbook from the Print dialog box. Sheet2 doesn't print correctly. What should you do?**
   [a] Click the Print button again to see whether the problem goes away.
   [b] Check to see whether the printer is working properly.
   [c] Clear the print area.
   [d] Use Page Break Preview mode to check the page breaks on both worksheets.

9. **To set collating options for a print job, you use the:**
   [a] Page Setup dialog box.
   [b] Page Break Preview.
   [c] Print dialog box.
   [d] Options button in the Page Setup dialog box.

10. **When you manually adjust page break lines, Page Break Preview displays a:**
   [a] dotted blue line.
   [b] heavy black line.
   [c] solid blue line.
   [d] thin blue line.

Circle **T** if the statement is true or **F** if the statement is false.

T   F   1. You should always preview before you print.

T   F   2. Clicking the Print button on the Standard toolbar opens the Print dialog box.

T   F   3. The dotted black page preview lines cannot be turned off.

T   F   4. You must select named ranges by opening the Page Setup dialog box from the File menu.

T   F   5. Once you change page break locations, you can't undo them.

T   F   6. You can see page breaks only in Page Break Preview mode.

T   F   7. You should always proofread your worksheet in addition to checking spelling.

T   F   8. Headers and footers must use the same font.

T   F   9. AutoCorrect can be used to replace a shortcut with a longer word or phrase.

T   F   10. You need to set footer options for each page in your printed report.

Skills Review

SCANS

Exercise 1   C

1. Open the *24 Month Calendar* workbook located on the Data Disk.

2. Select the Jan-03, Feb-03, Jun-03, and Jul-03 calendars.

3. Set the print area with these ranges selected.

4. Preview the worksheet.

5. Print the worksheet if instructed to do so.

6. Change the view to Normal view.

7. Activate cell A1.

8. Save the workbook as *24 Month Calendar Revised* and close it.

Exercise 2 [C]

1. Open the *Sales Rep Data* workbook located on the Data Disk.

2. Add a custom header "Sales Rep Data" using 16-point, bold text, and center it in the header area.

3. Use Page Break Preview to set page breaks after every 30 rows. Pull down the top page break to prevent the two blank rows from printing.

4. Center the print area horizontally, and set row 3 to repeat at the top of each page.

5. Preview your print job, and print the worksheet if instructed to do so.

6. Save the workbook as *Sales Rep Data Revised* and close it.

Exercise 3

1. Open the *Cookie Sales* workbook located on the Data Disk.

2. Replace all instances of the word "chip" with the work "chunk."

3. Use the Replace command to change all cells containing "Totals" to "Total" formatted with 12-point red font.

4. Run the spell checker.

5. Set the print area to cover all the data in the worksheet.

6. Change the print orientation to landscape.

7. Use the Fit to: option to print all of the data on one page.

8. Set the print options to center the data vertically and horizontally.

9. Print the worksheet if instructed to do so.

10. Save the workbook as *Cookie Sales Revised* and close it.

Exercise 4 [C]

1. Open the *Home Loan* workbook located on the Data Disk (click OK if a dialog box opens warning you about macros).

2. Switch to the Loan Amortization Table worksheet.

3. Use Page Break Preview to print 50 payments per page. Insert new page breaks as necessary.

4. Print the worksheet if instructed to do so.

5. Save the workbook as *Home Loan Revised* and close it.

Exercise 5 [C]

1. You will be distributing the *24 Month Calendar Revised* to all employees in your company. Write a step-by-step description explaining how to print only the January-03 calendar. Save the document as *Printing a Calendar*. Include the following instructions:

　　a. Explain how to add **2003** as the header for the printed report.

　　b. Explain how to print the calendar in Landscape orientation.

2. Print your document or e-mail it to a classmate. Have your classmate follow your directions *exactly* and print the report. See how well he or she was able to follow your instructions.

3. Save and close the *Printing a Calendar.doc* document.

chapter five

Exercise 6

1. Open the *Sweet Tooth Q2 2003 Sales* workbook located on the Data Disk.

2. Set print options to print the worksheet centered horizontally and vertically using Portrait orientation.

3. Print the worksheet.

4. Set print options to print the worksheet centered horizontally, but not vertically, using Landscape orientation.

5. Print the worksheet.

6. Save the workbook as *Sweet Tooth Q2 2003 Sales Revised* and close it.

Exercise 7

1. Open the *Sweet Tooth Q3 2003 Sales* workbook located on the Data Disk.

2. Change the top and bottom margins to 3 inches.

3. Create a custom footer displaying the filename on the left, the date in the center, and the time on the right.

4. Print the worksheet.

5. Save the workbook as *Sweet Tooth Q3 2003 Sales Revised* and close it.

Exercise 8

1. Open the *Sweet Tooth 2003 Sales* workbook located on the Data Disk.

2. Add the abbreviation "sw" to the AutoCorrect list. Replace the abbreviation with "Sweet Tooth."

3. Use the AutoCorrect abbreviation "sw" to add "Sweet Tooth" to cell A1 on each of the worksheets.

4. Set the print scale to 150% on all four worksheets.

5. Set the print options on all four worksheets to print in Landscape orientation, with a 2-inch top margin, and centered horizontally.

6. Print the worksheet if instructed to do so.

7. Save the workbook as *Sweet Tooth 2003 Sales Revised* and close it.

Case Projects

Project 1

Your job is to train employees in the use of Excel. Search the Internet for Excel tips to include in your weekly "Excel Training Letter." Select one tip and create a Word document of at least two paragraphs describing it. Provide the URL of any sites that you used as references for your tip. Save the document as *Excel Training Letter.doc* and then print and close it.

Project 2

As part of your job, you track inventory at a used car dealership. You must record the number of cars sold by type per month. Create a worksheet providing fictitious sales data on at least four different types of cars for a period of four months. Set page breaks to print each month's data on a separate page. Center the data horizontally on each page. Print the worksheet title and column labels on each page. Save the workbook as *Car Sales* and close it.

Project 3

You're an office manager for a busy construction company. You have a lot of names, phone numbers, and addresses to manage. You keep the data for each state on separate worksheets. Create a new workbook. At the top of each worksheet create the following column headings: Last Name, First Name, Address, City, State, Zip, Phone number. On each worksheet, enter fictitious data for at least five people from the same state. Include a footer on each page with your company's name. Print the entire workbook in landscape orientation. Save the workbook as *Phone List* and close it.

Problem 4

You are a travel agent. To stay competitive, you use the Internet to find out about your competitors' offers. Connect to the Internet, and use the Web toolbar to locate at least three Web sites offering five- to seven-night packages to Cancun, Mexico. Print pages showing information about each of these packages. Create a workbook listing the name of each package, and enter the Web address where you located the vacation package. Save the workbook as *Vacation to Cancun*. Print it in an attractive format, and then close it.

Problem 5

You are interested in increasing your productivity while using Excel. Using the Ask A Question Box, search for the topic "keyboard shortcuts." Print one of the pages containing keyboard shortcuts for any of the shortcut key categories. Instructions for printing are included on each page in the Help file.

Problem 6

You need to purchase a workgroup class laser printer (16+ pages a minute, 600 dpi or better) for your publishing company. Connect to the Internet and search the Web for a review of this type of printer. Create a workbook and list your findings on three of the printers. Be sure to include the manufacturer, model, pages per minute, dpi if higher than 600, cost, and the Web address where you found the review. Save the workbook as *Workgroup Printer*, print it in an attractive format, and close it.

Project 7

In order to be better organized, you decide to create a daily planner. Create a worksheet that breaks the day into one-hour segments, starting from when you get up in the morning and ending when you go to bed at night. Fill in the planner with your usual schedule for seven days. Print the worksheet(s) in an attractive format. Save the workbook as *Daily Planner* and close it.

Project 8

You are the accounts manager of a graphic design company. Create a list of 10 clients who owe your company money. Use fictitious client names and amounts due (between $500 and $2,000). Add a column indicating how many days the account is overdue. Print the worksheet it in an attractive format. Save the workbook as *Overdue Accounts* and close it.

chapter five

Creating Charts and Sharing Information

Chapter Overview

Charts offer a great way to summarize and present data, providing a colorful, graphic link to numerical data collected in worksheets. Graphics can add visual interest to your worksheet. Creating such an explicit relationship helps other people analyze trends, spot inconsistencies in business performance, and evaluate market share. Sharing information electronically is an essential task. In this chapter, you learn how to create and modify charts, add graphics, add comments to worksheets, use the Web Discussion feature, and save Excel documents as Web pages.

LEARNING OBJECTIVES

- ▶ Use the Chart Wizard to create a chart
- ▶ Format and modify a chart
- ▶ Insert, resize, and move a graphic
- ▶ Work with embedded charts
- ▶ Preview and print charts
- ▶ Use workgroup collaboration
- ▶ Use Go To

Case profile

Each quarter, Super Power Computers' regional managers meet with the company president, Luis Alvarez, to review sales figures and set goals for the next quarter. You have collected data from each of the regional offices and are now ready to compile a report for the meeting. You decide to use charts to show the company's final sales figures.

chapter six

6.a Using the Chart Wizard to Create a Chart

A chart provides a graphical interface to numerical data contained in a worksheet. Almost anyone can appreciate and understand the colorful simplicity of a chart. The data found in the *Super Power Computers - Sales Data Q1 2003* workbook represents Super Power Computers' sales for the first quarter. Your job is to create and format a chart for use in tomorrow's sales meeting. To open the workbook and save it with a new name:

Step 1	*Open*	the *Super Power Computers - Sales Data Q1 2003* workbook located on the Data Disk
Step 2	*Save*	the workbook as *Super Power Computers - Sales Data Q1 2003 Revised*

The Chart Wizard walks you step by step through a series of four dialog box boxes to quickly create a chart. You can create charts as separate workbook sheets called **chart sheets,** or you can place them directly on the worksheet page as **embedded charts.** One type of chart, called a column chart, helps you compare values across categories. To create a chart using the Chart Wizard:

Step 1	*Activate*	cell A5 on the Summary worksheet
Step 2	*Click*	the Chart Wizard button 📊 on the Standard toolbar

The Chart Wizard dialog box on your screen should look similar to Figure 6-1. In Step 1, you select the type of chart you want to create from the list of chart types on the left side of the dialog box. You click a chart type on the left to display chart subtypes on the right side of the dialog box. A description of the chart subtype appears below the preview box. You want to create a three-dimensional chart, which is an interesting visual alternative to two-dimensional charts.

QUICK TIP

The fastest way to create a chart is to press the F11 key. This shortcut key creates a default two-dimensional column chart on a separate chart sheet.

MOUSE TIP

The Chart Wizard automatically detects the range you want to include in your chart when you activate any cell within the range.

chapter
six

FIGURE 6-1
Step 1 of the Chart Wizard

QUICK TIP

By default, data is plotted with the longest edge along the *x*-axis—in this case, the column labels. If the chart doesn't show the data the way you expected, click the other option button in the Series in: section in Step 2 of the Chart Wizard to reverse the way data is plotted in the chart—in this case, by row labels.

MOUSE TIP

You can change a chart to a different type at any time. Right-click the chart you want to change, click Chart type on the shortcut menu, select a new chart type and subtype, then click the OK button.

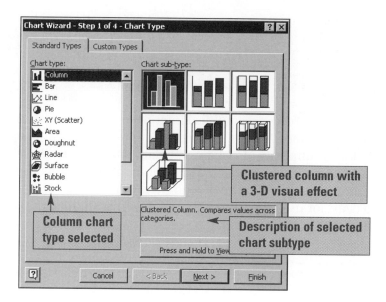

Step 3	*Verify*	that Column is selected in the Chart type: list
Step 4	*Click*	the Clustered column with a 3-D visual effect from the Chart sub-type: box (first column, second row)
Step 5	*Click*	Next >

In Step 2 of the Chart Wizard, you select or modify the chart's source data. A preview of the selected data appears at the top of the Data Range tab. Notice the flashing border surrounding the chart data in the worksheet behind the Chart Wizard.

Step 6	*Click*	Next >

The Titles tab in Step 3 of the Chart Wizard on your screen should look similar to Figure 6-2.

FIGURE 6-2
Step 3 of the Chart Wizard

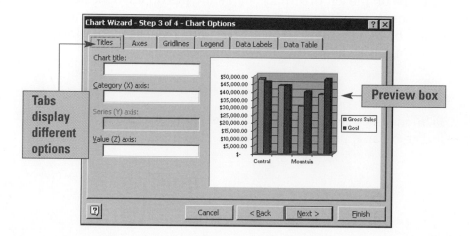

You enter chart options such as titles, legends, and data labels. The tabs vary depending on the chart type you selected.

Step 7	*Click*	in the Chart title: text box
Step 8	*Key*	Gross Sales by Region

The title you just keyed appears in the Preview box after a few seconds.

Step 9	*Press*	the TAB key to move to the Category (X) axis: text box
Step 10	*Key*	Region Name
Step 11	*Click*	the Legend tab
Step 12	*Click*	the Bottom option button
Step 13	*Click*	Next >

The dialog box on your screen should look similar to Figure 6-3. In Step 4 of the Chart Wizard, you specify the location of the new chart. You can create the chart as a new sheet or as an object in another worksheet.

Step 14	*Click*	the As new sheet: option button
Step 15	*Key*	Gross Sales by Region Chart in the As new sheet: text box
Step 16	*Click*	Finish

The chart appears on a new worksheet in your workbook, and the Chart toolbar appears. Your screen should look similar to Figure 6-4.

MOUSE TIP

Change your mind while using the Chart Wizard? Step backward at any time by clicking the < Back button. Make any changes, then click the Next > button to continue. The wizard leaves all other settings intact.

FIGURE 6-3
Step 4 of the Chart Wizard

MOUSE TIP

You can change the location of a chart by right-clicking the chart and clicking Location.

chapter
six

FIGURE 6-4
Chart Created with
Chart Wizard

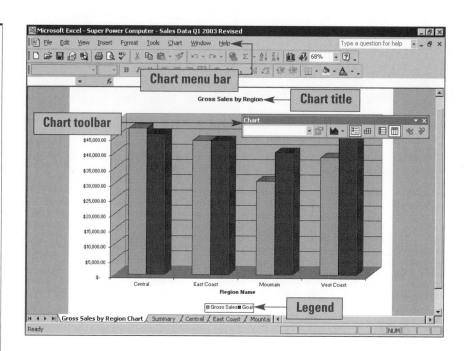

MENU TIP

Do you use a certain type of chart most of the time? You can change the default chart type. First, create a chart. Click Chart Type on the Chart menu, select the type of chart and the subtype that you use most often, then click the Set as default chart button.

When you create a chart, the Chart toolbar appears, and the Chart menu replaces the Data menu in the menu bar. The Chart menu bar and toolbar contain chart-specific tools to help you create and modify charts.

C 6.b Formatting and Modifying a Chart

MOUSE TIP

To select a data point in a chart, click it, then click it again. Do not double-click the data point.

Every element of a chart, such as the title, legend, and plot area, is considered an object. An **object** is a graphical element added to a worksheet that you can manipulate by moving, resizing, or reformatting it. Each chart object can be formatted by double-clicking or right-clicking the object, then clicking Format *object* (where *object* is the name of the selected object). The Format dialog box displays options unique to each object.

Some of the more important chart objects are defined here. The **legend** is the key used to identify the colors assigned to categories in a chart. **Tick marks** are small marks on the edges of the chart that delineate the scale or separate the data categories. **Data points** represent the numerical data in your worksheet. In the current chart type, the data points are represented by horizontal columns. Data points, however, can also be represented by bars, columns, pie slices, and a variety of other shapes and marks. A **data series** represents all related data points in a set. On your chart, the Gross Sales columns are a data series, as are the Goal columns. A **data label** displays the actual value of each data point on the chart. The **plot area** of a chart is the area that includes only the chart itself.

Changing Chart Fonts

You can change font settings for all text on the chart simultaneously, or you can select individual text objects and then customize their font settings. You want the title to stand out from the other elements of the chart. To change fonts for individual objects:

Step 1	*Move*	the mouse pointer over the Chart Title object at the top of the chart to display the ScreenTip
Step 2	*Right-click*	the Chart Title object
Step 3	*Click*	Format Chart Title
Step 4	*Click*	the Font tab in the Format Chart Title dialog box, if necessary
Step 5	*Click*	Impact in the Font: list
Step 6	*Click*	20 in the Size: list
Step 7	*Click*	the Color: list arrow
Step 8	*Click*	the Blue square (second row, sixth column)
Step 9	*Click*	the Patterns tab
Step 10	*Click*	the Automatic option button in the Border section
Step 11	*Click*	OK
Step 12	*Press*	the ESC key to deselect the Chart Title object

The chart title is now formatted with your selections. Next, you format one of the axes.

Formatting the Axes

You can modify both axes of the chart. The **category axis**, sometimes called the *x*-axis, is the axis along which you normally plot categories of data. This axis runs horizontally along the bottom of many chart types. The **value axis**, or *y*-axis, usually runs vertically along the left side of a chart, and is the axis along which you plot values associated with various categories of data.

Excel gives you full control over the scale of the axes, the number format, and the appearance of the axis labels. You decide to modify the number format of the value axis by dropping the decimal amount. To modify the value axis scale:

| Step 1 | *Right-click* | the value axis along the left side of the chart |
| Step 2 | *Click* | Format Axis |

chapter
six

Step 3	*Click*	the Number tab in the Format Axis dialog box
Step 4	*Click*	the down spin arrow in the Decimal places: text box twice to set it to 0
Step 5	*Click*	OK

Your screen should look similar to Figure 6-5.

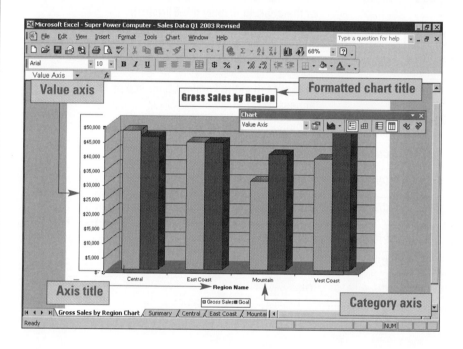

FIGURE 6-5
Changing Value
Scale Options

Adding a Data Table to a Chart

A **data table** displays the actual data used to create the chart. For small data sets, you may find it helpful to show this information on the chart worksheet. To add a data table to the chart:

| Step 1 | *Click* | the Data Table button ⊞ on the Chart toolbar |

The data table is added beneath the value axis. Your screen should look similar to Figure 6-6.

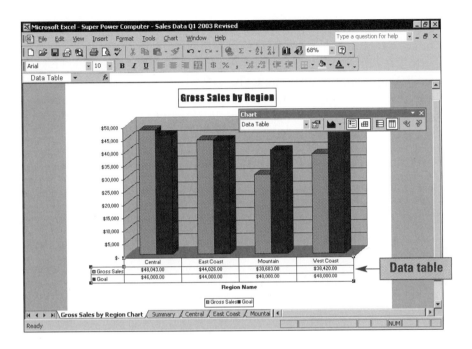

FIGURE 6-6
Adding a Data Table to a Chart

> **MOUSE TIP**
>
> You can add data labels by right-clicking the data series, clicking the Data Labels tab, selecting an option button, then clicking the OK button.

> **QUICK TIP**
>
> When a chart object is selected, you can cycle to other chart objects by pressing the ARROW keys.

| Step 2 | *Save* | the workbook |

The Gross Sales by Region chart is complete. Next, you insert the company logo on the chart.

6.c Inserting, Resizing, and Moving a Graphic

You can insert other types of objects into a chart. For example, you can place text, lines, or pictures to further enhance your chart. To insert an object into a chart:

| Step 1 | *Click* | the Drawing button on the Standard toolbar to display the Drawing toolbar, if necessary |
| Step 2 | *Click* | the Insert Picture From File button  on the Drawing toolbar |

The Insert Picture dialog box opens.

chapter
six

| Step 3 | *Click* | SPC Logo on the Data Disk |
| Step 4 | *Click* | Insert |

The image object is inserted in your chart. The Picture toolbar might appear. The small circles around the image are **sizing handles**. The image is too large. Pressing the CTRL key while dragging a sizing handle resizes the object uniformly from the center of the object. As you drag the object handle, the Name Box displays a scale percentage.

Step 5	*Press & hold*	the CTRL key
Step 6	*Drag*	the lower-right sizing handle up and to the left
Step 7	*Release*	the mouse button when the object is approximately 45% of its original size

To move the object:

| Step 1 | *Move* | the mouse pointer over the image object |
| Step 2 | *Drag* | the object to position it to the left of the chart title |

The chart on your screen should look similar to Figure 6-7.

FIGURE 6-7
Inserting and Positioning a
Chart Object

| Step 3 | *Press* | the ESC key to deselect the logo |
| Step 4 | *Save* | the workbook |

QUICK TIP

To insert clip art, click the Insert Clip Art button on the Drawing toolbar. To insert other types of objects, click the Object command on the Insert menu.

MOUSE TIP

To resize an object proportionally from the edge, press and hold the SHIFT key while you drag a selection handle.

QUICK TIP

To delete a chart object, select it and then press the DELETE key.

6.d Working with Embedded Charts

Embedded charts are charts placed directly into a worksheet, rather than on a separate sheet tab. You decide to create an embedded chart in your workbook. To create an embedded chart:

Step 1	*Select*	the range A5:B8 on the Central worksheet
Step 2	*Click*	the Chart Wizard button on the Standard toolbar
Step 3	*Click*	Pie in the Chart type: list
Step 4	*Click*	Finish

The default chart type is an embedded chart, so there is no need to click all the way through the Chart Wizard. The chart is embedded in your worksheet, but it needs a little work. To resize and move an embedded chart:

| Step 1 | *Verify* | that the chart is still selected |

Sizing handles appear around the edges of the chart when it is selected.

Step 2	*Drag*	the sizing handle in the middle of the left edge of the chart object
Step 3	*Release*	the mouse button near the divider line between columns D and E
Step 4	*Position*	the mouse pointer anywhere in the white chart area (ScreenTip displays Chart Area)
Step 5	*Drag*	the chart object so that the chart is vertically centered next to the worksheet data

Your screen should look similar to Figure 6-8.

QUICK TIP

To delete an embedded chart, select the chart, and then press the DELETE key.

chapter
six

FIGURE 6-8
Resizing and Moving an
Embedded Chart

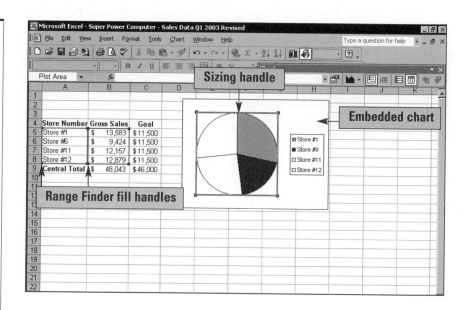

The data you charted is surrounded by colored boxes, called **Range Finder**. You can use Range Finder to adjust the data used by the chart. You don't want to include the total row in the chart. To modify the chart using Range Finder:

Step 1	*Position*	the mouse pointer over one of the Range Finder fill handles at the bottom of row 8

The pointer changes to a double-headed arrow.

Step 2	*Drag*	the fill handle up to just below row 7

The chart displays only three sets of data.

Step 3	*Press*	the ESC key to deselect the chart
Step 4	*Save*	the workbook

QUICK TIP

If you have an object selected within the chart, you may need to press the ESC key a few times until a cell in the worksheet becomes active.

C 6.e Previewing and Printing Charts

Before you print your chart for the meeting, you should preview it in Print Preview to make sure that everything looks the way you expected. You can preview a chart, change print setup options, and print the chart from the Print Preview window.

Printing Chart Sheets

Printing charts on separate worksheets is very similar to printing any worksheet data. To preview the chart sheet, change chart printing options, and print a chart:

Step 1	*Click*	the Gross Sales by Region Chart sheet tab
Step 2	*Click*	the Print Preview button 🔍 on the Standard toolbar
Step 3	*Click*	the Setup button on the Print Preview toolbar
Step 4	*Click*	the Chart tab in the Page Setup dialog box

The Scale to fit page option scales the chart until either the height or the width of the chart hits a page margin. The Use full page option scales the chart until both the height and the width touch the page margins on all sides of the page.

Step 5	*Click*	the Scale to fit page option button
Step 6	*Click*	OK
Step 7	*Click*	the Print button on the Print Preview toolbar
Step 8	*Click*	OK

Printing an Embedded Chart

You have a few choices to make when printing embedded charts. One option is to print the chart by itself. Another option is to print the chart as part of the worksheet, and the final option is to exclude the chart from printing at all. By default, an embedded chart prints as part of the worksheet, as long as it is not specifically excluded from a print area. If Print Preview does not show a chart you expected to print, try clearing the print area, or adjusting the page breaks in Page Break Preview. When you select a chart, Excel assumes that you want to print only the chart.

Because of all these print options, it is especially important that you preview the document before printing it when you work with embedded charts. To preview the worksheet with the embedded chart:

| Step 1 | *Click* | the Central sheet tab |

QUICK TIP

You can print an embedded chart by itself or with the data on the worksheet. To print an embedded chart by itself, select the chart by clicking it once, then click the Print Preview button on the Standard toolbar.

chapter
six

Step 2	*Click*	the Print Preview button on the Standard toolbar
Step 3	*Click*	the Print button on the Print Preview toolbar
Step 4	*Click*	OK
Step 5	*Save*	the workbook

C

6.f Using Workgroup Collaboration

Sharing information electronically is no longer an option; it's an essential part of doing business. To effectively communicate with colleagues and coworkers, you can use comments, engage in Web discussions, and publish pages to a Web server for periodic review.

You need to send the workbook with the finished charts to the regional managers for their comments and suggestions.

Adding and Editing Comments

You can add comments to any cell to provide a simple, effective way to share explanatory information with others. Comments can highlight important cells or explain complex formulas. To add a comment:

Step 1	*Right-click*	cell C9 on the Central sheet tab
Step 2	*Click*	Insert Comment
Step 3	*Key*	Consider revising goal in Q2 to $52,500
Step 4	*Click*	cell C9 to close the comment

A small red triangle appears in the upper-right corner of cells containing comments. To read comments:

| Step 1 | *Move* | the mouse pointer over cell C9 |

The yellow comment note that appears on your screen should look similar to Figure 6-9.

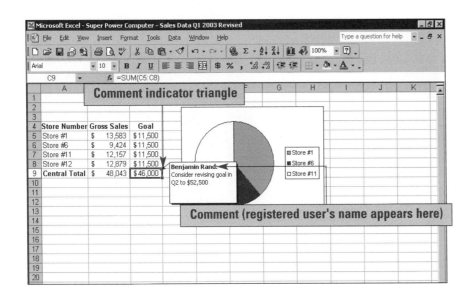

FIGURE 6-9
Reading a Comment

You can add or modify the text in a comment. To edit a comment:

Step 1	*Right-click*	cell C9
Step 2	*Click*	Edit Comment
Step 3	*Select*	$52,500
Step 4	*Key*	$54,000
Step 5	*Click*	cell C9

Inserting Hyperlinks

Another helpful collaboration tool is the ability to insert hyperlinks in a document. A **hyperlink** is a link to another place in the current workbook, to another file on your computer or on your network, or to a Web page, or it can be a mailto link. When clicked, a **mailto link** automatically starts a new message using the user's default e-mail program. To insert a hyperlink in a document:

Step 1	*Right-click*	cell A1 on the Summary worksheet
Step 2	*Click*	Hyperlink
Step 3	*Click*	E-mail Address in the Link to: list

The Insert Hyperlink dialog box on your screen should look similar to Figure 6-10. When you click an option in the Link to: list, the dialog box options change. When you clicked the E-mail Address option, the dialog box provides text boxes to enter an e-mail address and a message subject.

chapter
six

FIGURE 6-10
Insert Hyperlink
Dialog Box

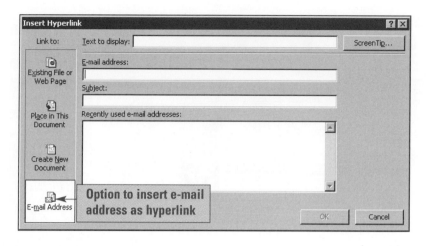

Step 4	*Key*	your e-mail address (or a fictitious e-mail address) in the E-mail address: text box
Step 5	*Key*	Review Chart in the Subject: text box
Step 6	*Select*	the text in the Text to display: text box
Step 7	*Key*	Contact me in the Text to display: text box
Step 8	*Click*	OK

MOUSE TIP

To delete a hyperlink, right-click the link, then click Remove Hyperlink on the shortcut menu.

The hyperlink appears in cell A1 as blue, underlined text. When you click this link, your e-mail program opens with the e-mail address you added in the Insert Hyperlink dialog box in the To text box (in this case, it's your e-mail address). To test the link:

Step 1	*Click*	the Contact me hyperlink in cell A1
Step 2	*Observe*	the message window with your e-mail address in the To text box
Step 3	*Close*	your e-mail program without sending a message or saving changes to the message

Creating and Responding to Discussion Comments

Discussions allow users to post and respond to comments made by other users. For example, one user might post a question about how to perform a certain task in Excel. Other users can then respond to the question.

notes To use the Discussion feature, you must have access to a discussion server and user rights to view and contribute to discussions.

You display the Web Discussions toolbar to create and respond to topics. For a new topic you enter a subject and message, and then post the topic to the discussion server, where other users can log in, read, and respond to the topic. To create and post a discussion comment:

Step 1	*Click*	<u>T</u>ools
Step 2	*Point to*	O<u>n</u>line Collaboration
Step 3	*Click*	<u>W</u>eb Discussions to display the Web Discussions toolbar
Step 4	*Click*	the Insert Discussion about the Workbook button on the Web Discussions toolbar
Step 5	*Key*	Review Sales Figures in the Discussion <u>S</u>ubject: text box
Step 6	*Press*	the TAB key to move to the message text box
Step 7	*Key*	Please review sales figures for your region and respond with any corrections.
Step 8	*Click*	OK
Step 9	*Click*	the <u>C</u>lose button Close to close the Web Discussions toolbar

Previewing and Saving a Workbook or a Worksheet as a Web Page

You post the Gross Sales chart on the company's intranet to allow other employees to see the company's progress. You can save a workbook in HTML format for publication on the Web. To preview a workbook as a Web page:

Step 1	*Click*	the Gross Sales by Region Chart sheet tab
Step 2	*Click*	<u>F</u>ile
Step 3	*Click*	We<u>b</u> Page Preview

A copy of your workbook appears in HTML format in your Web browser. Your screen should look similar to Figure 6-11.

> ### CAUTION TIP
>
> You may not be able to create a discussion comment if you do not have proper access to a discussion server. If you cannot log on, you cannot complete the steps in this section.

chapter
six

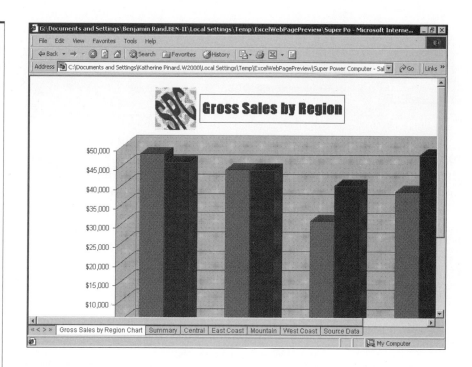

It's a good idea to avoid
using spaces and
uppercase letters in
filenames for pages
intended for the Web
because many Web
servers cannot properly
handle them.

Step 4	*Close*	your Web browser

You want to publish only the chart page. To save the chart worksheet
as a Web page:

Step 1	*Click*	File
Step 2	*Click*	Save As Web Page
Step 3	*Click*	the Selection: Chart option button
Step 4	*Key*	sales_data_chart in the File name: text box
Step 5	*Click*	Save

The chart is saved and ready to be uploaded to a Web server. You can
save your page directly to a Web server by clicking the Publish button
instead of the Save button in the Save As dialog box.

6.g Using Go To

A quick way to select cells is to use the Go To command. Using Go
To, you can select ranges, named ranges, and cells based on certain
characteristics, such as selecting all cells that contain formulas.

To use Go To:

Step 1	*Click*	the Central sheet tab
Step 2	*Click*	<u>E</u>dit
Step 3	*Click*	<u>G</u>o To

The Go To dialog box opens. You can enter a range, select a named range, or click the <u>S</u>pecial button to locate cells that share common characteristics.

| Step 4 | *Click* | <u>S</u>pecial |

The Go To Special dialog box on your screen should look similar to Figure 6-12. It provides additional search options.

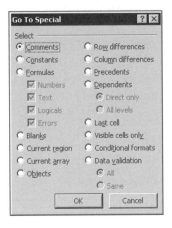

FIGURE 6-12
The Go To Special
Dialog Box

| Step 5 | *Click* | the <u>F</u>ormulas option button |
| Step 6 | *Click* | OK |

All of the cells containing formulas on the Central worksheet are highlighted.

| Step 7 | *Save* | and close the workbook |

You can use Go To to find and select cells or ranges based on content.

chapter
six

Summary

► The Chart Wizard enables you to create a chart. You can create a new default chart by pressing the F11 key.

► Charts can be placed on a separate chart tab, or they can be embedded in a worksheet. A chart location can be changed at any time.

► Charts contain many types of objects, including titles, legends, data tables, and plot areas. Each of these objects can be formatted independently.

► You can change formatting elements for all chart objects at any time by using the Format dialog box.

► You can add a data table to a chart to show the actual data used to create the chart.

► Drawing objects, such as pictures or text boxes, can be inserted into a chart. Drag selection handles to resize them. Drag entire objects to new locations.

► You can move and resize embedded worksheets as you like.

► It is a good idea to preview charts before printing them so you can set print options. Embedded charts can be printed separately or as part of the active worksheet.

► Comments enable you to highlight important cells or explain formulas. You can edit existing comments.

► Hyperlinks can be added to cell content to provide easy links to Web pages, files, or e-mail addresses.

► Discussion comments can be added to any file if you have a connection to a discussion server.

► Workbooks or worksheets can be previewed and saved as Web pages.

► Go To enables you to find and select cell ranges or cells based on the type of content.

Commands Review

Action	Menu Bar	Shortcut Menu	Toolbar	Task Pane	Keyboard
Use the Chart Wizard	Insert, Chart				ALT + I, H
Create a default chart					F11 ALT + F1
Format a selected chart object	Format, Selected (chart object name)	Right-click chart object, Format (chart object name)	Select object from the Chart Objects list box, ; double-click object		ALT + O, E CTRL + 1
Change chart type	Chart, Chart Type	Right-click chart, Chart Type			ALT + C, T
Change chart options	Chart, Chart Options	Right-click chart, Chart Options			ALT + C, O
Show the Chart toolbar	View, Toolbars, Chart				ALT + V, T
Add a data table to a chart					
Show the Drawing toolbar	View, Toolbars, Drawing				ALT + V, T
Insert a picture	Insert, Picture, From File				ALT + I, P, F
Insert clip art	Insert, Picture, Clip Art				ALT + I, P, C
Insert an object	Insert, Object				ALT + I, O
Preview a chart	File, Print Preview				ALT + F, V
Print a chart	File, Print				CTRL + P ALT + F, P
Add a comment	Insert, Comment	Right-click, Insert Comment			ALT + I, M
Edit a comment	Insert, Edit Comment	Right-click comment, Edit Comment			ALT + I, E
Delete a comment	Insert, Delete Comment	Right-click comment, Delete Comment			ALT + I, M
Insert a hyperlink	Insert, Hyperlink	Right-click text Hyperlink			ALT + I, I CTRL + K
Remove a hyperlink		Right-click hyperlink, Remove Hyperlink			
Insert discussion comments	Tools, Online Collaboration, Web Discussions				ALT + T, N, W
Preview a worksheet as a Web page	File, Web Page Preview				ALT + F, B
Save a worksheet as Web Page	File, Save As Web Page				ALT + F, G
Use Go To	Edit, Go to				ALT + E, G CTRL + G

chapter six

Concepts Review

SCANS

Circle the correct answer.

1. A data label:
[a] displays the name of a chart object when the mouse pointer is over that object.
[b] displays the actual data used to create a chart.
[c] is a key used to identify patterns, colors, or symbols associated with data points on a chart.
[d] displays the value of a data point on a chart.

2. A legend:
[a] displays the name of a chart object when the mouse pointer is over that object.
[b] displays the actual data used to create a chart.
[c] is a key used to identify patterns, colors, or symbols associated with data points on a chart.
[d] can show the value of a data point on a chart.

3. A mailto link opens:
[a] a Web browser.
[b] a Web page.
[c] a new e-mail message and addresses it.
[d] none of the above.

4. A data point:
[a] represents a series of data.
[b] represents a single value.
[c] identifies the colors assigned to categories in a chart.
[d] separates the data categories.

5. Which of the following does *not* bring up the Format (chart object) Properties dialog box?
[a] double-click (chart object)
[b] right-click (chart object), select Format (chart object)

[c] select object, click Edit, click Format (chart object)
[d] click the Chart Objects list arrow on the Chart toolbar to select the chart object, then click the Format (chart object) button on the Chart toolbar

6. The F11 shortcut key allows you to:
[a] create an embedded chart.
[b] choose whether to use the Chart Wizard.
[c] create a default chart sheet chart.
[d] create either an embedded chart or a chart sheet chart.

7. The Chart Wizard allows you to:
[a] create either an embedded chart or a chart sheet chart.
[b] create only an embedded chart.
[c] create only a chart sheet chart.
[d] edit an existing chart.

8. If you change your mind while using the Chart Wizard, you can click the:
[a] Cancel button and start over.
[b] Finish button, delete the chart, and start over.
[c] Next button.
[d] Back button.

9. To change the location of a chart, right-click the chart and click:
[a] Chart Type.
[b] Source Data.
[c] Chart Options.
[d] Location.

10. The value axis of a chart represents:
[a] the actual data values of each category.
[b] the categories of data.
[c] nothing.
[d] the chart height and width.

Circle **T** if the statement is true or **F** if the statement is false.

T   F   1. Charts make data easier to understand.

T   F   2. Embedded charts cannot be moved on the worksheet.

T   F   3. A data point is a graphical means of displaying numerical data.

T   F   4. The <u>G</u>o To command is one way to select all cells that contain formulas.

T   F   5. The Format (chart object) dialog box is the same no matter which object is selected.

T   F   6. Hyperlinks cannot be linked to files on your computer.

T   F   7. The Use Full Page print option scales a chart in both directions to fill the entire page.

T   F   8. You can't print an embedded chart by itself.

T   F   9. Web Page Preview is a good way to see what your workbook will look like as a Web page.

T   F   10. You do not need access to a discussion server to add comments to a discussion.

Skills Review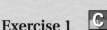

Exercise 1

1. Open the *Sales Data* workbook located on the Data Disk.

2. Using the data on the Summary tab, create a new Clustered Column chart with a three-dimensional effect.

3. Title the chart "Sales by Region."

4. Insert the chart on a new chart sheet called "Sales by Region Chart."

5. Print the Sales by Region Chart.

6. Switch to the Source Data worksheet, then use the <u>G</u>o To command to highlight all cells containing a formula.

7. Save the workbook as *Sales Data Revised* and close it.

Exercise 2

1. Open the *Sales Data Revised* workbook that you created in Exercise 1.

2. Look at the embedded chart on the West Coast tab, then find two other types of charts that present the data in a clear manner.

3. Find two types of charts that make it more difficult to understand the data.

4. Using Microsoft Word, write at least two paragraphs describing why certain types of charts worked well to illustrate the data and why others did not. Try to discern from the chart type description what type of information is needed for each type of chart and why your data did or did not work.

5. Save the document as *Chart Types.doc* and then print and close it. Close the workbook.

Exercise 3

1. Open the *Exports by Country* workbook located on the Data Disk.

2. Activate cell A2.

3. Create a line with markers chart using the Chart Wizard.

4. Title the chart "Exports by Country."

5. Add "2003" to the Category (X) axis.

6. Create the chart as an object on Sheet1.

7. Preview and print your chart as part of the worksheet. (*Hint:* Move the chart or change the paper orientation as necessary.)

8. Use Go To to select the last cell in the worksheet.

9. With your instructor's permission, connect to the Internet, and search the Web for a picture of a flag of one of the countries used in your chart. Be sure to verify that the image is one you can use for free.

10. In your Web browser, right-click the picture, then click Save Picture <u>A</u>s and save the picture.

11. Insert the picture on your chart.

12. Save the workbook as *Exports by Country Chart,* print the chart sheet, and then close the workbook.

Exercise 4   C

1. Open the *Exports by Country Chart* workbook that you created in Exercise 3.

2. Add the following data to row 5: Japan, $6,438,945.00, $2,345,743.00, $5,098,760.00, $3,198,245.00.

3. Select the chart and use the Range Finder to add Japan's data to the chart.

4. Save the workbook as *Exports by Country Chart Revised,* print the chart sheet, and close the workbook.

Exercise 5   C

1. Open the *Expenses* workbook located on the Data Disk. Activate cell A2.

2. Create a Bar of Pie type chart using the Chart Wizard (in the Pie chart type category). This type of chart uses a selected number of values from the bottom of a list of values to create a "breakout" section. In this case, the breakout section is the category Taxes.

3. Title the chart "Expenses."

4. Show the percentage data labels.

5. Create the chart as an embedded chart.

6. Save the workbook as *Expenses Chart,* print the worksheet, and close the workbook.

Exercise 6   C

1. Open the *Computer Comparison* workbook located on the Data Disk.

2. Create a new chart, using the Line – Column on 2 Axes custom type of chart. (*Hint:* Click the Custom Types tab in Step 1 of the Chart Wizard.)

3. Title the chart "Computer Price/Speed Comparison."

4. Title the *x*-axis "System."

5. Title the *y*-axis "Price."

6. Title the secondary *y*-axis "Speed."

7. Create the chart as a new sheet.

8. Preview the Web page, then save the chart sheet as a Web page called *computer_comparison_chart.htm.*

9. Save the workbook as *Computer Comparison Chart,* print the chart sheet, and close the workbook.

Exercise 7

1. Open the *Computer Comparison Chart* workbook that you created in Exercise 6.

2. Show the data table on the chart.

3. Click the Athlon 1.2 GHz data point two times to select it (do not double-click it). Drag the data point handle at the top-middle of the data point down until the value reads $2,650.

4. Modify the value of the PIII 1 GHz data point to $2,400 by dragging the data point handle.

5. Print the chart.

6. Add comments in cells B3 and B5 indicating that the value of each of these cells was changed.

7. Save the workbook as *Computer Comparison Chart Revised*.

8. Print the chart sheet and the worksheet, and then close the workbook.

Exercise 8

1. Open the *Class Attendance* workbook located on your Data Disk.

2. Create a new chart with the Chart Wizard.

3. Use the Custom Types tab to select the Colored Lines chart type.

4. Title the chart "Class Attendance."

5. Put the chart on a new sheet called "Attendance Chart."

6. Change the area fill of the Chart Area to Automatic (white).

7. On the data page, include a hyperlink to your favorite search engine.

8. Print the chart, save your workbook as *Class Attendance Chart,* and close it.

Case Projects

Project 1

As the entertainment editor for a local newspaper, you publish a weekly chart of the top five films based on their box office revenues for the week. Connect to the Internet and use the Web toolbar to search the Web for information on the top five movies from the last week. Create a worksheet listing each of the titles and showing how much each film grossed in the last week. Add another column to show total revenues to date for each film. Insert comments next to two of the films indicating whether you want to see the film, or what you thought of it if you have already seen it. Create a chart that best illustrates the data. Save the workbook as *Box Office*, and then print and close it.

Project 2

Use the Ask A Question Box to find out how to add a text box to a chart. Create a Word document and use your own words to describe step by step how to accomplish this task. Save the document as *Adding a Text Box to a Chart.doc,* and print and close it.

Project 3

As the owner of a mall-based cookie store, you want to track your cookie sales by type and month to determine which cookies are bestsellers and what the best time of the year is for cookie sales. Create a worksheet with 10 types of cookies (examples: chocolate chip, oatmeal, walnut, peanut butter). Include fictitious data for cookie sales for

chapter six

each type of cookie during the past 12 months. Create charts showing overall cookie sales by month and overall cookie sales by type. With your instructor's permission, connect to the Internet and search the Web for a picture of your favorite type of cookie. Verify that the file you want to use is an image you can use for free, then save the picture, and then insert it on your chart. Save the workbook as *Cookie Sales,* and print and close it.

Project 4

Connect to the Internet and use the Web toolbar to search the Web for different types of charts. Look for charts showing sales volume, stock prices, or percentages of sales by category. Create a workbook containing hyperlinks to five different charts. Save your workbook as *Charts on the Web,* and print and close it.

Project 5

Stock price charts are usually displayed using a high-low-close style chart, which requires three columns of data. Connect to the Internet and use the Web toolbar to search the Web for stock prices for three companies whose products you use. Locate price histories for the last five days for each stock, including the high, low, and closing prices for each day. Create a High Low Close chart (stock category) for each company, showing the price plotted against the date. Save the workbook as *High Low Close,* and print and close it.

Project 6

Create a worksheet showing one month's expenses for at least 10 expense categories in your

household (estimate your expenses or supply fictitious data). Create a three-dimensional pie chart, and separate the largest expense from the pie. Use data labels to display the label and value of each expense. Save the workbook as *Family Expenses,* and print and close it.

Project 7

As the weather editor of a local newspaper, your job is to create a chart of the five-day forecasts for your city. Connect to the Internet, and locate a Web site that provides a five-day forecast for your area. Enter the data in a new worksheet and create a chart showing the high and low temperatures for each day. Place the chart on a separate worksheet page. Save the workbook as *Temperature Forecast*, print it, save it as a Web page named *temperature_forecast.htm*, and then close the workbook.

Project 8

You are interested in finding out how the government spends the money in its budget. Connect to the Internet, and search the Web for a site that shows where the government spends tax revenue. Create a new workbook and pie chart showing the information you find. Include at least five categories. If you have access to a discussion server, set up a discussion and include a comment about your budget findings. Have classmates add comments to the discussion. Save your workbook as *Government Spending,* and print and close it.

Working with Windows 2000

T Appendix **Overview**

he Windows 2000 operating system creates a workspace on your computer screen, called the desktop. The desktop is a graphical environment that contains icons you click with the mouse pointer to access your computer system resources or to perform a task such as opening a software application. This appendix introduces you to the Windows 2000 desktop by describing the default desktop icons and showing how to access your computer resources, use menu commands and toolbar buttons to perform a task, and review and select dialog box options.

appendix

A.a Reviewing the Windows 2000 Desktop

Whenever you start your computer, the Windows 2000 operating system automatically starts. You are prompted to log on with your user name and password, which identify your account. Then the Windows 2000 desktop appears on your screen. To view the Windows 2000 desktop:

| Step 1 | *Turn on* | your computer and monitor |

The Log On to Windows dialog box opens, as shown in Figure A-1.

FIGURE A-1
Log On to Windows
Dialog Box

Step 2	*Key*	your user name in the <u>U</u>ser name: text box
Step 3	*Key*	your password in the <u>P</u>assword: text box
Step 4	*Click*	OK
Step 5	*Click*	the Exit button in the Getting Started with Windows 2000 dialog box, if necessary
Step 6	*Observe*	the Windows 2000 desktop work area, as shown in Figure A-2

The Windows 2000 desktop contains three elements: icons, background, and taskbar. The icons represent Windows objects and shortcuts to opening software applications or performing tasks. Table A-1 describes some of the default icons. The taskbar, at the bottom of the window, contains the Start button and the Quick Launch toolbar, and tray. The icon types and arrangement, desktop background, or Quick Launch toolbar on your screen might be different.

QUICK TIP

If you don't see the Log On to Windows dialog box, you can open the Windows Security window at any time by pressing the CTRL + ALT + DELETE keys. From this window, you can log off the current user and log back on as another user. You can also change passwords, shut down Windows 2000 and your computer, and use the Task Manager to shut down a program.

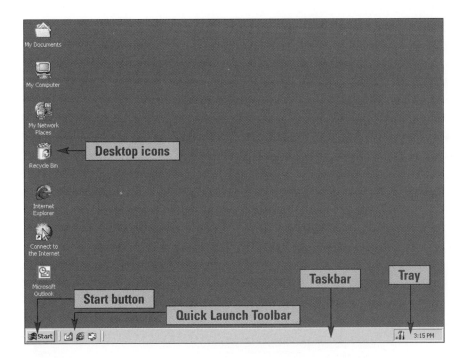

FIGURE A-2
Windows 2000 Desktop

TABLE A-1
Common Desktop Icons

Icon	Name	Description
	My Computer	Provides access to computer system resources
	My Documents	Stores Office documents (by default)
	Internet Explorer	Opens Internet Explorer Web browser
	Microsoft Outlook	Opens Outlook 2002 information manager software
	Recycle Bin	Temporarily stores folders and files deleted from the hard drive
	My Network Places	Provides access to computers and printers net worked in your workgroup

The Start button on the taskbar displays the Start menu, which you can use to perform tasks. By default, the taskbar also contains the **Quick Launch toolbar**, which has shortcuts to open the Internet Explorer Web browser and Outlook Express e-mail software, and to switch between the desktop and open application windows. You can customize the Quick Launch toolbar to include other shortcuts.

appendix
A

QUICK TIP

An **active desktop** can contain live Web content. You can create an active desktop by adding windows to the desktop that contain automatically updated Web pages. To add Web pages to your desktop, right-click the desktop, point to Active Desktop, click Customize my Desktop, and click the Web tab in the Display Properties dialog box. For more information on Active Desktop features, see online Help.

A.b Accessing Your Computer System Resources

The My Computer window provides access to your computer system resources. Double-click the My Computer desktop icon to open the window. To open the My Computer window:

Step 1	*Point to*	the My Computer icon 🖥 on the desktop
Step 2	*Observe*	a brief description of the icon in the box, called a ScreenTip
Step 3	*Double-click*	the My Computer icon 🖥 to open the My Computer window shown in Figure A-3

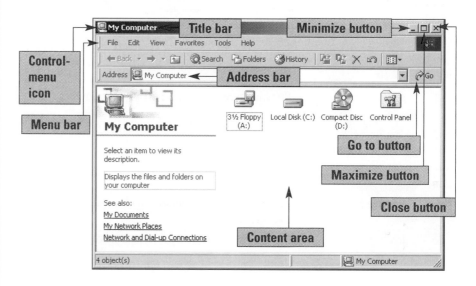

FIGURE A-3
My Computer window

A window is a rectangular area on your screen in which you view operating system options or a software application, such as Internet Explorer. Windows 2000 has some common window elements. The **title bar**, at the top of the window, includes the window's Control-menu icon, the window name, and the Minimize, Restore (or Maximize), and Close buttons. The **Control-menu icon**, in the upper-left corner of the window, accesses the Control menu that contains commands for restoring, moving sizing, minimizing, maximizing, and closing the window. The **Minimize** button, near the upper-right corner of the window, reduces the window to a taskbar button. The **Maximize** button, to the right of the Minimize button, enlarges the window to fill the entire screen viewing area above the taskbar. If the window is already maximized, the Restore button appears in its place. The **Restore** button reduces the window size. The **Close** button, in the upper-right corner, closes the window. To maximize the My Computer window:

| Step 1 | *Click* | the Maximize button ▢ on the My Computer window title bar |
| Step 2 | *Observe* | that the My Computer window completely covers the desktop |

When you want to leave a window open, but do not want to see it on the desktop, you can minimize it. To minimize the My Computer window:

| Step 1 | *Click* | the Minimize button ▬ on the My Computer window title bar |
| Step 2 | *Observe* | that the My Computer button remains on the taskbar |

The minimized window is still open but not occupying space on the desktop. To view the My Computer window and then restore it to a smaller size:

Step 1	*Click*	the My Computer button on the taskbar to view the window
Step 2	*Click*	the Restore button ▣ on the My Computer title bar
Step 3	*Observe*	that the My Computer window is reduced to a smaller window on the desktop

You can move and size a window with the mouse pointer. To move the My Computer window:

Step 1	*Position*	the mouse pointer on the My Computer title bar
Step 2	*Drag*	the window down and to the right approximately ½ inch
Step 3	*Drag*	the window back to the center of the screen

Several Windows 2000 windows—My Computer, My Documents, and Windows Explorer—have the same menu bar and toolbar features. When you size a window too small to view all its icons, a vertical or horizontal scroll bar may appear. A scroll bar includes scroll arrows and a scroll box for viewing different parts of the window contents.

appendix
A

To size the My Computer window:

Step 1	*Position*	the mouse pointer on the lower-right corner of the window
Step 2	*Observe*	that the mouse pointer becomes a black, double-headed sizing pointer
Step 3	*Drag*	the lower-right corner boundary diagonally up until the horizontal scroll bar appears and release the mouse button
Step 4	*Click*	the right scroll arrow on the horizontal scroll bar to view hidden icons
Step 5	*Size*	the window to a larger size to remove the horizontal scroll bar

You can open the window associated with any My Computer icon
by double-clicking it. The windows open in the same window, not
separate windows. To open the Control Panel Explorer-style window:

| Step 1 | *Double-click* | the Control Panel icon |
| Step 2 | *Observe* | that the Address bar displays the Control Panel icon and name, and the content area displays the Control Panel icons for accessing computer system resources |

A.c Using Menu Commands and Toolbar Buttons

You can click a menu command or toolbar button to perform
specific tasks in a window. The **menu bar** is a special toolbar located
below the window title bar that contains the File, Edit, View, Favorites,
Tools, and Help menus. The **Standard Buttons toolbar**, located below
the menu bar, contains shortcut "buttons" you click with the mouse
pointer to execute a variety of commands. You can use the Back and
Forward buttons on the Standard Buttons toolbar to switch between
My Computer and the Control Panel. To view My Computer:

Step 1	*Click*	the Back button 🔙 on the Standard Buttons toolbar to view My Computer
Step 2	*Click*	the Forward button 🔜 on the Standard Buttons toolbar to view the Control Panel
Step 3	*Click*	View on the menu bar
Step 4	*Point to*	Go To
Step 5	*Click*	the My Computer command to view My Computer

| Step 6 | *Click* | the Close button ⊠ on the My Computer window title bar |

A.d Using the Start Menu

The **Start button** on the taskbar opens the Start menu. You use this menu to access several Windows 2000 features and to open software applications, such as Word or Excel. To open the Start menu:

| Step 1 | *Click* | the Start button 🏁Start on the taskbar to open the Start menu, as shown in Figure A-4 |

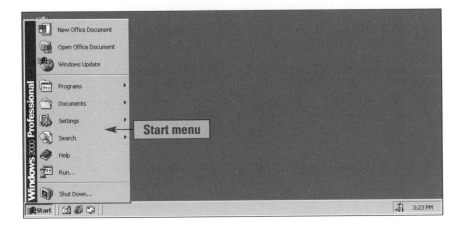

FIGURE A-4
Start Menu

| Step 2 | *Point to* | Programs to view the software applications installed on your computer |
| Step 3 | *Click* | the desktop outside the Start menu and Programs menu to close them |

A.e Reviewing Dialog Box Options

A **dialog box** is a window that contains options you can select, turn on, or turn off to perform a task. To view a dialog box:

| Step 1 | *Right-click* | the desktop |
| Step 2 | *Point to* | Active Desktop |

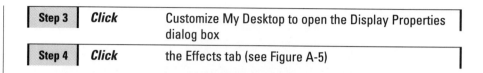

| Step 3 | *Click* | Customize My Desktop to open the Display Properties dialog box |
| Step 4 | *Click* | the Effects tab (see Figure A-5) |

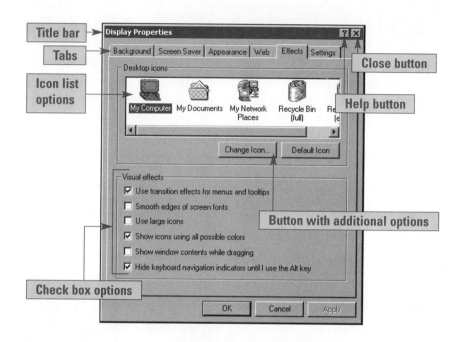

FIGURE A-5
Effects Tab in the Display Properties Dialog Box

Step 5	*Click*	each tab and observe the different options available *(do not change any options unless directed by your instructor)*
Step 6	*Right-click*	each option on each tab and then click What's This? to view its ScreenTip
Step 7	*Click*	Cancel to close the dialog box without changing any options

A.f Using Windows 2000 Shortcuts

You can use the drag-and-drop method to reposition or remove Start menu commands. You can also right-drag a Start menu command to the desktop to create a desktop shortcut. To reposition the Windows Update item on the Start menu:

Step 1	*Click*	the Start button [Start] on the taskbar
Step 2	*Point to*	the Windows Update item
Step 3	*Drag*	the Windows Update item to the top of the Start menu

To remove the Windows Update shortcut from the Start menu and create a desktop shortcut:

Step 1	*Drag*	the Windows Update item to the desktop
Step 2	*Observe*	that the desktop shortcut appears after a few seconds
Step 3	*Verify*	that the Windows Update item no longer appears on the Start menu

To add a Windows Update shortcut back to the Start menu and delete the desktop shortcut:

Step 1	*Drag*	the Windows Update shortcut to the Start button ![Start] on the taskbar and then back to its original position when the Start menu appears
Step 2	*Close*	the Start menu
Step 3	*Drag*	the Windows Update shortcut on the desktop to the Recycle Bin

You can close multiple application windows at one time from the taskbar using the CTRL key and a shortcut menu. To open two applications and then use the taskbar to close them:

Step 1	*Open*	the Word and Excel applications (in this order) from the Programs menu on the Start menu
Step 2	*Observe*	the Word and Excel buttons on the taskbar (Excel is the selected, active button)
Step 3	*Press & hold*	the CTRL key
Step 4	*Click*	the Word application taskbar button (the Excel application taskbar button is already selected)
Step 5	*Release*	the CTRL key
Step 6	*Right-click*	the Word or Excel taskbar button
Step 7	*Click*	Close to close both applications

You can use the drag-and-drop method to add a shortcut to the Quick Launch toolbar for folders and documents you have created. To create a new subfolder in the My Documents folder:

| Step 1 | *Double-click* | the My Documents icon on the desktop to open the window |
| Step 2 | *Right-click* | the contents area (but not a file or folder) |

CAUTION TIP

Selecting items in a single-click environment requires some practice. To **select** (or highlight) one item, simply point to the item. *Be careful not to click the item; clicking the item opens it.*
You can use the SHIFT + Click and CTRL + Click commands in the single-click environment. Simply *point to* the first item. Then press and hold the SHIFT or CTRL key and *point to* the last item or the next item to be selected.

MENU TIP

In the Windows environment, clicking the right mouse button displays a **shortcut menu** of the most commonly used commands for the item you right-clicked. For example, you can use a shortcut menu to open applications from the Programs submenu. You can right-drag to move, copy, or create desktop shortcuts from Start menu commands.

appendix
A

Step 3	*Point to*	New
Step 4	*Click*	Folder
Step 5	*Key*	Example
Step 6	*Press*	the ENTER key to name the folder
Step 7	*Drag*	the Example folder to the end of the Quick Launch toolbar (a black vertical line indicates the drop position)
Step 8	*Observe*	the new icon on the toolbar
Step 9	*Close*	the My Documents window
Step 10	*Position*	the mouse pointer on the Example folder shortcut on the Quick Launch toolbar and observe the ScreenTip

You remove a shortcut from the Quick Launch toolbar by dragging it to the desktop and deleting it, or dragging it directly to the Recycle Bin. To remove the Example folder shortcut and then delete the folder:

Step 1	*Drag*	the Example folder icon to the Recycle Bin
Step 2	*Open*	the My Documents window
Step 3	*Delete*	the Example folder icon using the shortcut menu
Step 4	*Click*	Yes
Step 5	*Close*	the My Documents window

A.g Understanding the Recycle Bin

The **Recycle Bin** is an object that temporarily stores folders, files, and shortcuts you delete from your hard drive. If you accidentally delete an item, you can restore it to its original location on your hard drive if it is still in the Recycle Bin. Because the Recycle Bin takes up disk space you should review and empty it regularly. When you empty the Recycle Bin, its contents are removed from your hard drive and can no longer be restored.

MENU TIP

You can open the Recycle Bin by right-clicking the Recycle Bin icon on the desktop and clicking Open. To restore an item to your hard drive after opening the Recycle Bin, click the item to select it and then click the Restore command on the File menu. You can also restore an item by opening the Recycle Bin, right-clicking an item, and clicking Restore.

To empty the Recycle Bin, right-click the Recycle Bin icon and then click Empty Recycle Bin.

A.h Shutting Down Windows 2000

It is very important that you follow the proper procedures for shutting down the Windows 2000 operating system when you are finished, to allow the operating system to complete its internal "housekeeping" properly. To shut down Windows 2000 correctly:

| Step 1 | *Click* | the Start button ![Start] on the taskbar |
| Step 2 | *Click* | Shut Down to open the Shut Down Windows dialog box shown in Figure A-6 |

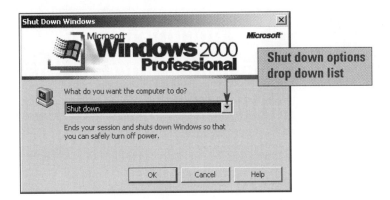

FIGURE A-6
Shut Down Windows
Dialog Box

You can log off, shut down, and restart from this dialog box. You want to shut down completely.

| Step 3 | *Click* | the Shut down option from the drop-down list, if necessary |
| Step 4 | *Click* | OK |

appendix
A

Formatting Tips for Business Documents

Appendix Overview

Most organizations follow specific formatting guidelines when preparing letters, envelopes, memorandums, and other documents to ensure the documents present a professional appearance. In this appendix you learn how to format different size letters, interoffice memos, envelopes, and formal outlines. You also review a list of style guides and learn how to use proofreader's marks.

LEARNING OBJECTIVES

- ▶ Format letters
- ▶ Insert mailing notations
- ▶ Format envelopes
- ▶ Format interoffice memorandums
- ▶ Format formal outlines
- ▶ Use style guides
- ▶ Use proofreader's marks

B.a Formatting Letters

Most companies use special letter paper with the company name and address (and sometimes a company logo or picture) preprinted on the paper. The preprinted portion is called a **letterhead** and the paper is called **letterhead paper**. When you create a letter, the margins vary depending on the style of your letterhead and the length of your letter. Most letterheads use between 1 inch and 2 inches of the page from the top of the sheet. There are two basic business correspondence formats: block format and modified block format. When you create a letter in **block format**, all the text is placed flush against the left margin. This includes the date, the letter address information, the salutation, the body, the complimentary closing, and the signature information. The body of the letter is single spaced with a blank line between paragraphs.[1] Figure B-1 shows a short letter in the block format with standard punctuation.

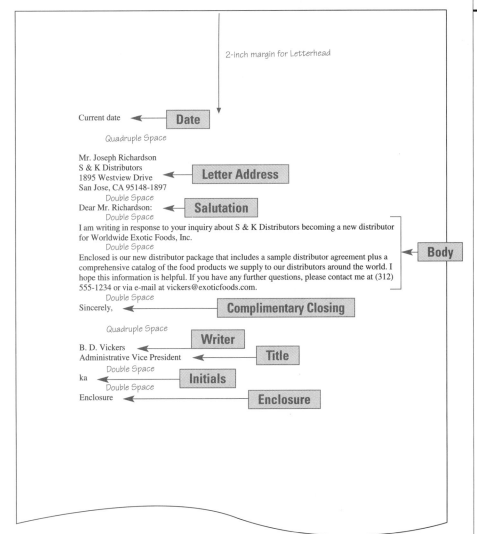

FIGURE B-1
Block Format Letter

appendix
B

In the **modified block format**, the date begins near the center of the page or near the right margin. The closing starts near the center or right margin. Paragraphs can be either flush against the left margin or indented. Figure B-2 shows a short letter in the modified block format with standard punctuation.

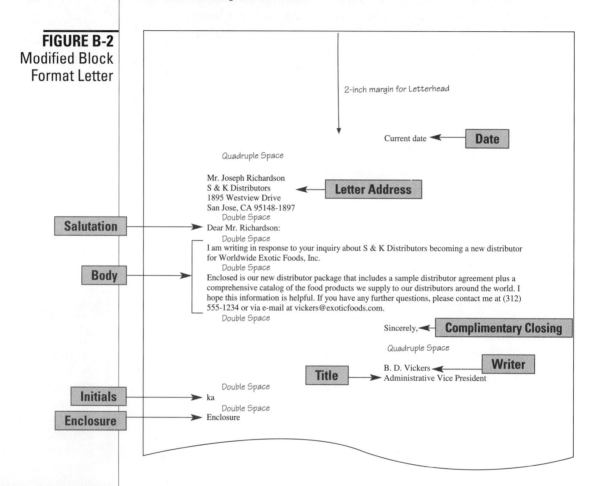

FIGURE B-2
Modified Block
Format Letter

2-inch margin for Letterhead

Current date — **Date**

Quadruple Space

Mr. Joseph Richardson
S & K Distributors — **Letter Address**
1895 Westview Drive
San Jose, CA 95148-1897
Double Space

Salutation → Dear Mr. Richardson:
Double Space
I am writing in response to your inquiry about S & K Distributors becoming a new distributor for Worldwide Exotic Foods, Inc.
Double Space
Body → Enclosed is our new distributor package that includes a sample distributor agreement plus a comprehensive catalog of the food products we supply to our distributors around the world. I hope this information is helpful. If you have any further questions, please contact me at (312) 555-1234 or via e-mail at vickers@exoticfoods.com.
Double Space

Sincerely, — **Complimentary Closing**

Quadruple Space

B. D. Vickers — **Writer**
Title → Administrative Vice President

Double Space
Initials → ka
Double Space
Enclosure → Enclosure

Both the block and modified block styles use the same spacing for the non-body portions. Three blank lines separate the date from the addressee information, one blank line separates the addressee information from the salutation, one blank line separates the salutation from the body of the letter, and one blank line separates the body of the letter from the complimentary closing. There are three blank lines between the complimentary closing and the writer's name. If a typist's initials appear below the name, a blank line separates the writer's name from the initials. If an enclosure is noted, the word "Enclosure" appears below the typist's initials with a blank line separating them. Finally, when keying the return address or addressee information, one space separates the state and the postal code (ZIP+4).

B.b Inserting Mailing Notations

Mailing notations add information to a business letter. For example, the mailing notations CERTIFIED MAIL or SPECIAL DELIVERY indicate how a business letter was sent. The mailing notations CONFIDENTIAL or PERSONAL indicate how the person receiving the letter should handle the letter contents. Mailing notations should be keyed in uppercase characters at the left margin two lines below the date.[2] Figure B-3 shows a mailing notation added to a block format business letter.

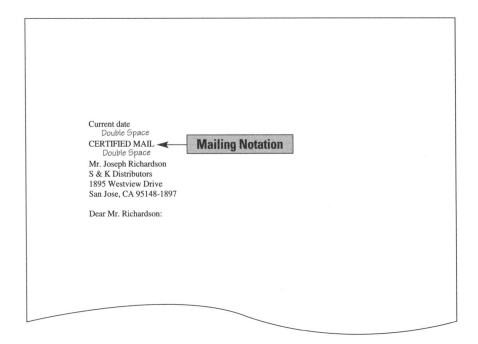

FIGURE B-3
Mailing Notation on Letter

B.c Formatting Envelopes

Two U.S. Postal Service publications, *The Right Way* (Publication 221), and *Postal Addressing Standards* (Publication 28) available from the U.S. Post Office, provide standards for addressing letter envelopes. The U.S. Postal Service uses optical character readers (OCRs) and barcode sorters (BCSs) to increase the speed, efficiency, and accuracy in processing mail. To get a letter delivered more quickly, envelopes should be addressed to take advantage of this automation process.

appendix
B

Table B-1 lists the minimum and maximum size for letters. The post office cannot process letters smaller than the minimum size. Letters larger than the maximum size cannot take advantage of automated processing and must be processed manually.

TABLE B-1
Minimum and Maximum
Letter Dimensions

Dimension	Minimum	Maximum
Height	3½ inches	6⅛ inches
Length	5 inches	11½ inches
Thickness	.007 inch	¼ inch

The delivery address should be placed inside a rectangular area on the envelope that is approximately ⅝ inch from the top and bottom edge of the envelope and ½ inch from the left and right edge of the envelope. This is called the **OCR read area**. All the lines of the delivery address must fit within this area and no lines of the return address should extend into this area. To assure the delivery address is placed in the OCR read area, begin the address approximately ½ inch left of center and on approximately line 14.[3]

The lines of the delivery address should be in this order:

1. any optional nonaddress data, such as advertising or company logos, must be placed above the delivery address
2. any information or attention line
3. the name of the recipient
4. the street address
5. the city, state, and postal code (ZIP+4)

The delivery address should be complete, including apartment or suite numbers and delivery designations, such as RD (road), ST (street), or NW (northwest). Leave the area below and on both sides of the delivery address blank. Use uppercase characters and a sans serif font (such as Arial) for the delivery address. Omit all punctuation except the hyphen in the ZIP+4 code.

Figure B-4 shows a properly formatted business letter envelope.

QUICK TIP

Foreign addresses should include the country name in uppercase characters as the last line of the delivery address. The postal code, if any, should appear on the same line as the city.

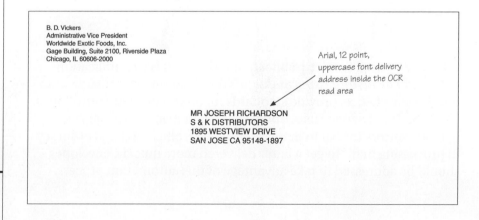

FIGURE B-4
Business Letter Envelope

B.d Formatting Interoffice Memorandums

Business correspondence that is sent within a company is usually prepared as an **interoffice memorandum**, also called a **memo**, rather than a letter. There are many different interoffice memo styles used in offices today, and word processing applications usually provide several memo templates based on different memo styles. Also, just as with business letters that are sent outside the company, many companies set special standards for margins, typeface, and font size for their interoffice memos.

A basic interoffice memo should include lines for "TO:", "FROM:", "DATE:", and "SUBJECT:" followed by the body text. Memos can be prepared on blank paper or on paper that includes a company name and even a logo. The word MEMORANDUM is often included. Figure B-5 shows a basic interoffice memorandum.

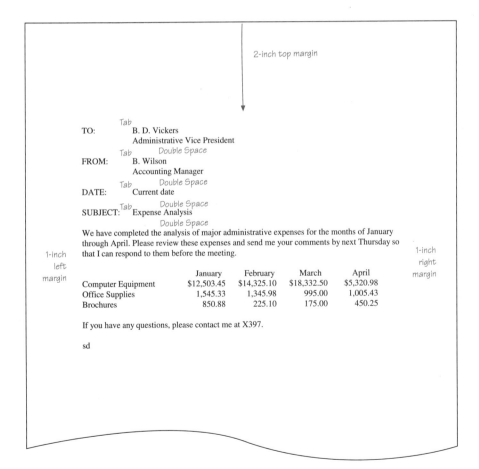

FIGURE B-5
Interoffice Memorandum

appendix
B

B.e Formatting Formal Outlines

Companies use outlines to organize data for a variety of purposes, such as reports, meeting agenda, and presentations. Word processing applications usually offer special features to help you create an outline. If you want to follow a formal outline format, you may need to add formatting to outlines created with these special features.

Margins for a short outline of two or three topics should be set at 1½ inches for the top margin and 2 inches for the left and right margins. For a longer outline, use a 2-inch top margin and 1-inch left and right margins.

The outline level-one text should be in uppercase characters. Second-level text should be treated like a title, with the first letter of the main words capitalized. Capitalize only the first letter of the first word at the third level. Double space before and after level one and single space the remaining levels.

Include at least two parts at each level. For example, you must have two level-one entries in an outline (at least I. and II.). If there is a second level following a level-one entry, it must contain at least two entries (at least A. and B.). All numbers must be aligned at the period and all subsequent levels must begin under the text of the preceding level, not under the number.[4]

Figure B-6 shows a formal outline prepared using the Word Outline Numbered list feature with additional formatting to follow a formal outline.

B.f Using Style Guides

A **style guide** provides a set of rules for punctuating and formatting text. There are a number of style guides used by writers, editors, business document proofreaders, and publishers. You can purchase style guides at a commercial bookstore, an online bookstore, or a college bookstore. Your local library likely has copies of different style guides and your instructor may have copies of several style guides for reference. Some popular style guides are *The Chicago Manual of Style* (The University of Chicago Press), *The Professional Secretary's Handbook* (Barron's), *The Holt Handbook* (Harcourt Brace College Publishers), and the *MLA Style Manual and Guide to Scholarly Publishing* (The Modern Language Association of America).

FIGURE B-6
Formal Outline

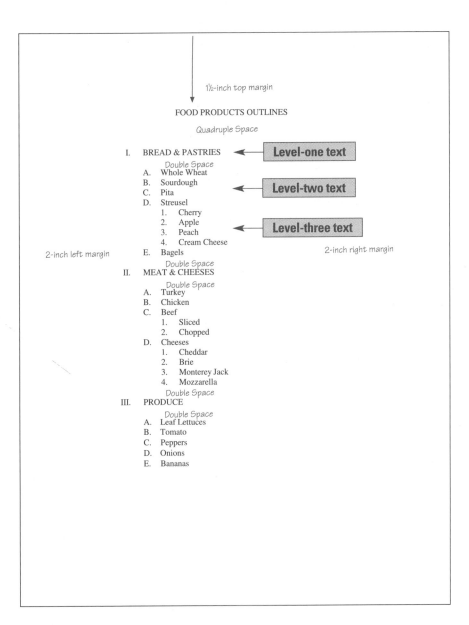

B.g Using Proofreader's Marks

Standard proofreader's marks enable an editor or proofreader to make corrections or change notations in a document that can be recognized by anyone familiar with the marks. The following list illustrates standard proofreader's marks.

appendix
B

Defined		Examples
Paragraph	¶	¶Begin a new paragraph at this
Insert a character	∧	point. Ins̬rt a letter here.
Delete	ℓ	Delete these words.ℓ Disregard
Do not change	stet or . . .	the previous correction. To
Transpose	tr	transpose is to ⁀around turn/
Move to the left	⌐	⌐Move this copy to the left.
Move to the right	¬	M⌐ve this copy to the right.
No paragraph	No ¶	No ¶Do not begin a new paragraph
Delete and close up	(symbol)	here. Delete the hyphen from
		pre‿empt and close up the space.
Set in caps	Caps or ≡	≡a sentence begins with a capital
Set in lower case	ℓc or /	letter. This W̸ord should not
Insert a period	⊙	be capitalized. Insert a period⊙
Quotation marks	ˬˬ ˅	ˬˬQuotation marks and a comma
Comma	∧	should be placed here∧he said.
Insert space	#	Space between these#words. An
Apostrophe	˅	apostrophe is what˅s needed here.
Hyphen	⹀	Add a hyphen to Kilowat⹀hour. Close
Close up	⌒	up the extra spa⌒ce.
Use superior figure	˅	Footnote this sentence.˅ Set
Set in italic	Ital. or —	the words, sine qua non, in italics.
Move up	⌐ ⌐	This word is too ⌐low.⌐ That word is
Move down	⌐ ⌐	too ⌐high.⌐

Endnotes

[1] Jerry W. Robinson et al., *Keyboarding and Information Processing* (Cincinnati: South-Western Educational Publishing, 1997).

[2] Ibid.

[3] Ibid.

[4] Ibid.

Using Office XP Speech Recognition

Appendix Overview

You are familiar with using the keyboard and the mouse to key text and select commands. With Office XP, you also can use your voice to perform these same activities. Speech recognition enables you to use your voice to perform keyboard and mouse actions without ever lifting a hand. In this appendix, you learn how to set up Speech Recognition software and train the software to recognize your voice. You learn how to control menus, navigate dialog boxes, and open, save, and close a document. You then learn how to dictate text, including lines and punctuation, correct errors, and format text. Finally, you learn how to turn off and on Speech Recognition.

LEARNING OBJECTIVES

- ► Train your speech software
- ► Use voice commands
- ► Dictate, edit, and format by voice
- ► Turn Microsoft Speech Recognition on and off

appendix

C.a Training Your Speech Software

Speech recognition is an exciting new technology that Microsoft has integrated into its XP generation of products. Microsoft has been working on speech recognition for well over a decade. The state-of-the-art is advancing. If you haven't tried it before, this is a great time for you to experience this futuristic technology.

Voice recognition has important benefits:

• Microsoft's natural speech technologies can make your computer experience more enjoyable.
• Speech technology can increase your writing productivity.
• Voice recognition software can greatly reduce your risk for keyboard- and mouse-related injuries.

In the following activities, you learn to use your voice like a mouse and to write without the aid of the keyboard.

Connecting and Positioning Your Microphone

Start your speech recognition experience by setting up your microphone. There are several microphone styles used for speech recognition. The most common headset microphone connects to your computer's sound card, as shown in Figure C-1. Connect the microphone end to your computer's microphone audio input port. Connect the speaker end into your speech output port.

FIGURE C-1
Standard Sound Card Headset (Courtesy Plantronics Inc.)

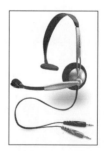

USB speech microphones, such as the one shown in Figure C-2, are becoming very popular because they normally increase performance and accuracy. USB is short for Universal Serial Bus. USB microphones bypass the sound card and input speech with less distortion into your system.

USB microphones are plugged into the USB port found in the back of most computers. Windows automatically installs the necessary USB drivers after you start your computer with the USB microphone plugged into its slot.

FIGURE C-2
A USB Headset (Courtesy Plantronics Inc.)

After your headset has been installed, put on your headset and position it comfortably. Remember these two important tips:

- Place the speaking side of your microphone about a thumb's width away from the side of your mouth, as shown in Figure C-3.
- Keep your microphone in the same position every time you speak. Changing your microphone's position can decrease your accuracy.

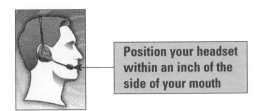

Position your headset within an inch of the side of your mouth

FIGURE C-3
Proper Headset Position

CAUTION TIP

If you see additional buttons on the Language Bar than shown in Figure C-4, click the Microphone button to hide them.

Installing Microsoft Speech Recognition

Open Microsoft Word and see if your speech software has already been installed. As Word opens, you should see either the floating Language Bar, shown in Figure C-4, or the Language Bar icon in the Windows Taskbar tray, as shown in Figure C-5.

Correction   Microphone   Tools   Write   Lined Paper   ?

FIGURE C-4
Floating Language Bar

FIGURE C-5
Language Bar Icon

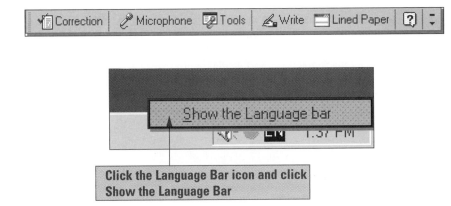

Show the Language bar

Click the Language Bar icon and click Show the Language Bar

appendix C

If you can open and see the Language Bar, jump to Step-by-Step C.2. However, if this essential tool is missing, proceed with Step-by-Step C.1.

Step-by-Step C.1

Step 1	To install Microsoft speech recognition, open Microsoft Word by clicking **Start**, **Programs**, **Microsoft Word**.
Step 2	Click **Tools**, **Speech** from the Word menu bar, as shown in Figure C-6.

FIGURE C-6
Click Speech from the
Tools menu

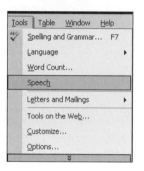

Step 3	You are prompted through the installation procedure. The process is a simple one. Follow the onscreen instructions.

Training Your System

Microsoft speech recognition can accommodate many different voices on the same computer. In order to work properly, your Microsoft Office Speech Recognition software must create a user **profile** for each voice it hears—including your voice.

If you are the first user and have just installed your speech software, chances are the system is already prompting you through the training steps. Skip to Step 3 in Step-by-Step C.2 for hints and help as you continue. However, if you are the second or later user of the system, you need to create a new profile by starting with Step 1.

Step-by-Step C.2

Step 1	To create your own personal speech profile, click the **Tools** button on the Language Bar and click **Options**, as shown in Figure C-7. This opens the Speech Properties dialog box.

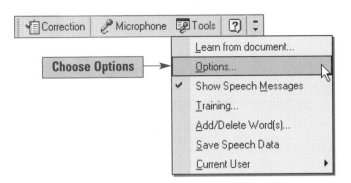

FIGURE C-7
Language Bar's
Tools Menu

Choose Options →

| Step 2 | In the Speech Properties dialog box, click **New**, as indicated in Figure C-8. |

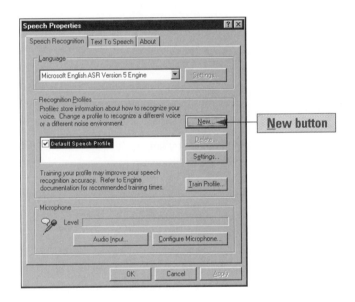

FIGURE C-8
Speech Properties
Dialog Box

New button

| Step 3 | Enter your name in the Profile Wizard, as shown in Figure C-9, and click **Next>** to continue. (*Note:* If you accidently click Finish instead of Next>, you must still train your profile by clicking Train Profile in the Speech Properties dialog box.) |

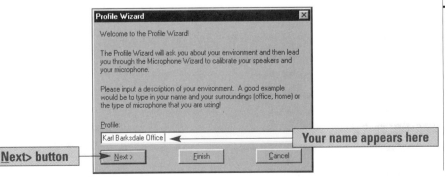

FIGURE C-9
New Profile Dialog Box

Your name appears here

Next> button

appendix
C

Step 4 Adjust your microphone, as explained on the Microphone Wizard Welcome dialog box, as shown in Figure C-10. Click **Next>** to begin adjusting your microphone.

FIGURE C-10
Correctly Position Your Microphone

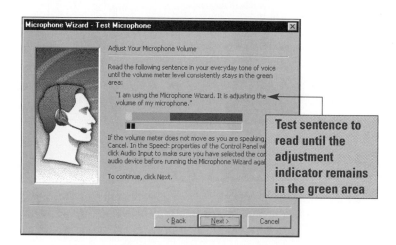

Step 5 Read the test sentence indicated in Figure C-11 until the volume adjustment settings appear consistently in the green portion of the volume adjustment meter. Your volume settings are adjusted automatically as you speak. Click **Next>** to continue.

FIGURE C-11
Read Aloud to Adjust Your Microphone Volume

Test sentence to read until the adjustment indicator remains in the green area

> ### QUICK TIP
>
> Microsoft Office Speech Recognition tells you if your microphone is not adequate for good speech recognition. You may need to try a higher quality microphone, install a compatible sound card, or switch to a USB microphone. Check the Microsoft Windows Help files for assistance with microphone problems.

Step 6 The next audio check tests the output of your speakers. Read the test sentence indicated in Figure C-12 and then listen. If you can hear your voice, your speakers are connected properly. Click **Finish** and continue.

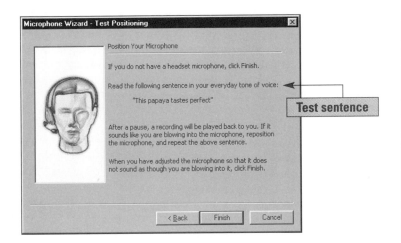

Test sentence

FIGURE C-12
Read Aloud to Test Your
Sound Output

QUICK TIP

Your user file will remember your microphone settings from session to session. However, if others use the system before you, you may need to readjust the audio settings by clicking **Tools**, **Options**, **Configure Microphone**.

Training Your Software

Next, you are asked to train your software. During the training session, you read a training script or story for about 10 to 15 minutes. As you read, your software gathers samples of your speech. These samples help the speech software customize your speech recognition profile to your way of speaking. As you read, remember to:

- Read clearly.
- Use a normal, relaxed reading voice. Don't shout, but don't whisper softly either.
- Read at your normal reading pace. Do not read slowly and do not rush.

CAUTION TIP

Never touch any part of your headset or microphone while speaking. Holding or touching the microphone creates errors.

Step-by-Step C.3

| Step 1 | Microsoft Office Speech Recognition prepares you to read a story or script. Read the instruction screen shown in Figure C-13 and click **Next>** to continue. |

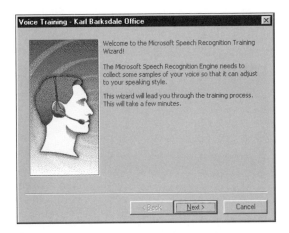

FIGURE C-13
Read the Onscreen
Instructions Carefully

appendix
C

| Step 2 | Enter your gender and age information (see Figure C-14) to help the system calibrate its settings to your voice. Click **Next>** to continue. |

FIGURE C-14
Enter Your Gender and Age
Information

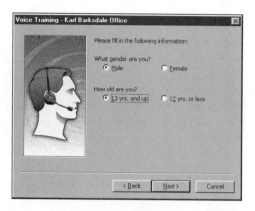

Step 3 | Click **Sample** and listen to a short example of how to speak clearly to a computer. See Figure C-15. After the recording, click **Next>** to review the tips for the training session, and then click **Next>** to continue.

FIGURE C-15
Listen to the Speech
Sample

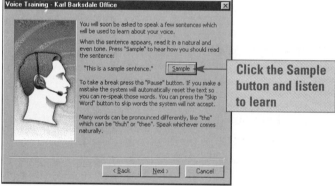

Step 4 | Begin reading the training session paragraphs, as shown in Figure C-16. Text you have read is highlighted. The Training Progress bar lets you know how much reading is left. If you get stuck on a word, click **Skip Word** to move past the problem spot.

FIGURE C-16
Software Tracks
Your Progress

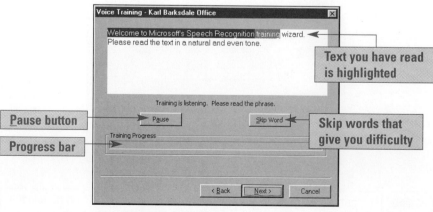

| Step 5 | The screen shown in Figure C-17 appears after you have finished reading the entire first story or training session script. You now have a couple of choices. Click **More Training**, click **Next>**, and continue reading additional scripts as explained in Step 6 (or you can click Finish and quit for the day). |

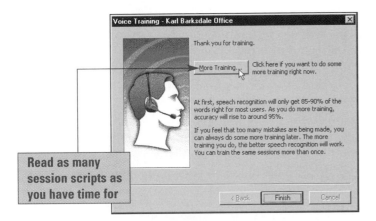

Read as many session scripts as you have time for

FIGURE C-17
First Training Script Completed

| Step 6 | Choose another training session story or script from the list, as shown in Figure C-18, and then click **Next>**. |

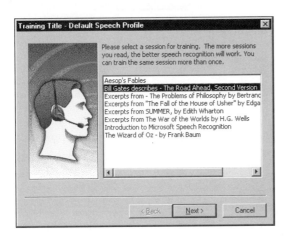

FIGURE C-18
Choose Another Story or Training Script to Read

| Step 7 | At the end of the training process, Microsoft Office Speech Recognition shows you a multimedia training tutorial (you may need to install Macromedia Flash to view the tutorial). Enjoy the tutorial before continuing. |

appendix
C

C.b Using Voice Commands

Microsoft makes it easy to replace mouse clicks with voice commands. The voice commands are very intuitive. In most cases, you simply say what you see. For example, to open the File menu, you can simply say **File**.

Microsoft Office XP voice commands allow you to control dialog boxes and menu bars, and to format documents by speaking. You can give your hands a rest by speaking commands instead of clicking them. This can help reduce your risk for carpal tunnel syndrome and other serious injuries.

Before you begin using voice commands, remember that if more than one person is using speech recognition on the same computer, you must select your user profile from the Current Users list. The list is found by clicking the Language Bar Tools menu, as shown in Figure C-19.

FIGURE C-19
Current Users List

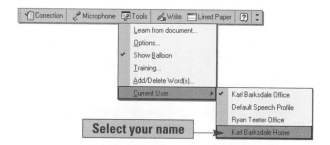

Switching Modes and Moving the Language Bar

Microsoft Office Speech Recognition works in two modes. The first is called **Dictation mode**. The second is called **Voice Command mode**. Voice Command mode allows you to control menus, give commands, and format documents.

When using Voice Command mode, simply *say what you see on the screen or in dialog boxes*. You see how this works in the next few exercises. In Step-by-Step C.4, you learn how to switch between the two modes.

Step-by-Step C.4

Step 1	Open **Microsoft Word** and the **Language Bar**, if necessary.
Step 2	The Language Bar can appear collapsed (see Figure C-20) or expanded (see Figure C-21). You can switch between the two options by clicking the **Microphone** button.

MENU TIP

After you have selected your user profile, you may wish to refresh your audio settings by clicking **Tools**, **Options**, **Configure Microphone**. This will help adjust the audio settings to the noise conditions in your current dictation environment.

Microphone button

FIGURE C-20
Collapsed Language Bar

Clicking the Microphone button with your mouse turns on the microphone and expands the Language Bar.

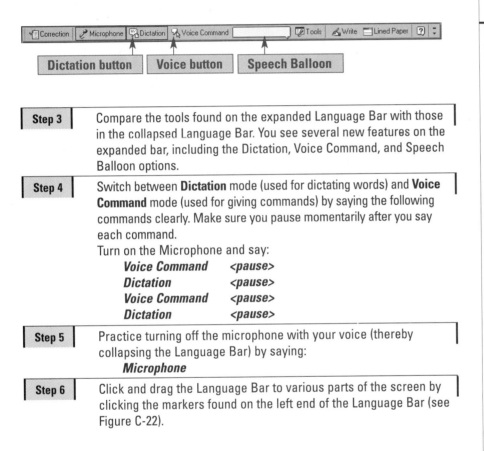

Dictation button   Voice button   Speech Balloon

FIGURE C-21
Expanded Language Bar

Step 3	Compare the tools found on the expanded Language Bar with those in the collapsed Language Bar. You see several new features on the expanded bar, including the Dictation, Voice Command, and Speech Balloon options.
Step 4	Switch between **Dictation** mode (used for dictating words) and **Voice Command** mode (used for giving commands) by saying the following commands clearly. Make sure you pause momentarily after you say each command. Turn on the Microphone and say: *Voice Command* *<pause>* *Dictation* *<pause>* *Voice Command* *<pause>* *Dictation* *<pause>*
Step 5	Practice turning off the microphone with your voice (thereby collapsing the Language Bar) by saying: *Microphone*
Step 6	Click and drag the Language Bar to various parts of the screen by clicking the markers found on the left end of the Language Bar (see Figure C-22).

QUICK TIP

The Language Bar can float anywhere on the screen. Move the Language Bar to a spot that is convenient and out of the way. Most users position the Language Bar in the title bar or status bar when using speech with Microsoft Word.

Click and drag the Language Bar marker

FIGURE C-22
Move the Language Bar to a Convenient Spot

Giving Menu Commands

When you use Microsoft Office Voice Commands, your word will be obeyed. Before you begin issuing commands, take a few seconds and analyze Figure C-23. The toolbars you will be working with in the next few activities are identified in the figure.

appendix
C

FIGURE C-23
Customize Microsoft Word
with Your Voice

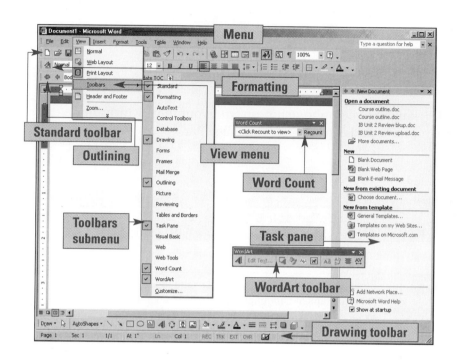

Step-by-Step C.5

Step 1	Switch on the **Microphone** from the Language Bar.

Step 2	Switch to Voice Command mode by saying: ***Voice Command***

Step 3	Open and close several menus by saying: ***File*** *(Pause briefly between commands)* ***Escape*** ***Edit*** ***Cancel*** ***View*** ***Escape***

Step 4	Close or display a few of the popular toolbars found in Microsoft Word by saying the following commands: ***View*** ***Toolbars*** ***Standard*** ***View*** ***Toolbars*** ***Formatting*** ***View*** ***Toolbars*** ***Drawing***

Step 5	Close or redisplay the toolbars by saying the following commands: *View* *Toolbars* *Drawing* *View* *Toolbars* *Formatting* *View* *Toolbars* *Standard*
Step 6	Practice giving voice commands by adding and removing the Task Pane and WordArt toolbar. Try some other options. When you are through experimenting, turn off the microphone and collapse the Language Bar by saying: *Microphone*

Navigating Dialog Boxes

Opening files is one thing you do nearly every time you use Microsoft Office. To open files, you need to manipulate the Open dialog box (Figure C-24). A dialog box allows you to make decisions and execute voice commands. For example, in the Open dialog box you can switch folders and open files by voice.

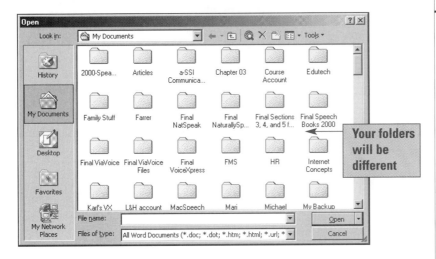

FIGURE C-24
Open Dialog Box

Step-by-Step C.6

Step 1	Turn on the **Microphone**, switch to Voice Command mode, and access the Open dialog box, as shown in Figure C-25, using the following commands: *Voice Command* *File* *Open*

appendix
C

FIGURE C-25
Say File, Open

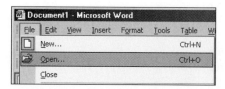

Step 2 Switch between various folder locations with your voice. In this case, you're going to switch between the Desktop, My Documents, and other folders located on the side of the Open dialog box, as shown in Figure C-26. Say the following voice commands to switch between folder locations. Pause slightly after saying each command:
Desktop
My Documents
History
Desktop
Favorites
My Documents

FIGURE C-26
Switch Between Various
Folder Locations

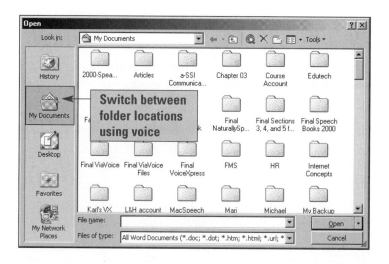

QUICK TIP

Any time a button in a dialog box appears dark around the edges, the button is active. You can access active buttons at any time by saying the name of the button or by saying **Enter**. You can also move around dialog boxes using the **Tab** or **Shift Tab** voice commands, or move between folders and files by saying **Up Arrow**, **Down Arrow**, **Left Arrow**, and **Right Arrow**. When selecting files, you'll probably find it much easier to use your mouse instead of your voice.

Step 3 You can change how your folders and files look in the Open dialog box by manipulating the Views menu, as shown in Figure C-27. Say the following voice commands to change the look of your folders and files:
Views
Small Icons
Views
List
Views
Details
Views
Thumbnails
Views
Large icons
Views
List

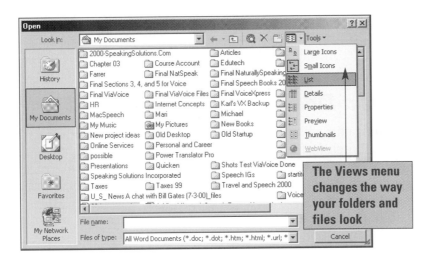

FIGURE C-27
Change the Look of Folders
with the Views Menu

| Step 4 | Close the Open dialog box by using the Cancel command. Say:
Cancel |

Open and Count a Document

In Step-by-Step C.7, you combine your traditional mouse skills with voice skills to accomplish tasks more conveniently. Use your skills to open a file. Then, use your menu selecting technique to open the Word Count toolbar and count the number of words in a document.

Step-by-Step C.7

Step 1	Using your voice, say *File*, *Open* and select the **My Documents** folder (or the location of your Data Disk). View the folders and files in **List** view. (Review Step-by-Step C.6 if you have forgotten how to make these changes in the Open dialog box.)
Step 2	Scroll through the list of files with your mouse until you see the file called *Prevent Injury*. To open the file, select it with your mouse and say: *Open* (or you also may say *Enter*)
Step 3	As the file opens, notice that the document title is PREVENT INJURY WITH SPEECH. Speech recognition can help you avoid serious keyboarding and mouse injuries. Count the words in the article. Open the Word Count toolbar by saying the following: *View* *Toolbars* *Word Count*
Step 4	With the Word Count toolbar open, say the following command to count the words: *Recount*

QUICK TIP

To complete Step-by-Step C.7, the *Prevent Injury* document should be moved from the Data Disk to the My Documents folder on your computer.

appendix
C

Step 5	How many words are contained in the article?

Step 6	Leave the *Prevent Injury* document open for the next activity.

Save a Document and Exit Word

Saving a file will give you a chance to practice manipulating dialog boxes. Switching from the keyboard and mouse to your voice has several benefits. For example, have you heard of carpal tunnel syndrome and other computer keyboard-related injuries caused by repetitive typing and clicking? By using your speech software even part of the time, you can reduce your risk for these long-term and debilitating nerve injuries.

In Step-by-Step C.8, you change the filename *Prevent Injury* to *My prevent injury file* using the Save As dialog box.

Step-by-Step C.8

Step 1	Make sure the ***Prevent Injury*** document appears on your screen. If you closed the document, repeat Step-by-Step C.7.

Step 2	Open the **Save As** dialog box. Notice that it is a lot like the Open dialog box. Try the following commands: *Voice Command (if necessary)* *File* *Save as*

Step 3	Switch to the **My Documents** folder and display the folder in **List** view as you learned to do in Step-by-Step C.7.

Step 4	Click your mouse in the **File name:** text box and type the filename or switch to Dictation mode and name the file with your voice by saying: *Dictation* *My prevent injury file*

Step 5	Save your document and close the Save As the box by saying: *Voice Command* *Save*

Step 6	Close the **Word Count** toolbar using the steps you learned earlier.

Step 7	Close Microsoft Word and collapse the Language Bar with the following commands: (When asked whether to save other open documents, say *No*.) *File* *Close* *Microphone*

C.c Dictating, Editing, and Formatting by Voice

If you have always dreamed of the day when you could sit back, relax, and write the next great American novel by speaking into a microphone, well, that day has arrived. It is possible to write that novel, a report, or even a simple e-mail message at speeds of 130–160 words per minute. However, it takes practice to achieve an acceptable level of accuracy. This section is designed to help you build accuracy.

Microsoft Office Speech Recognition is not made for complete handsfree use. You still need to use your keyboard and mouse much of the time. But, if you're willing to put in some effort, you can improve your speaking accuracy to the point that you can dramatically improve your output.

Dictating

Microsoft Speech Recognition allows you to work in **Dictation** mode when voice writing words into your documents. Switching from Voice Command mode to Dictation mode is as easy as saying ***Dictation***.

In Dictation mode, don't stop speaking in the middle of a sentence—even if your words don't appear immediately. The software needs a few seconds to process what you're saying. Microsoft Office Speech Recognition lets you know it is working by placing a highlighted bar with dots in your document, as shown in Figure C-28. A few seconds later, your words appear.

QUICK TIP

The best way to improve dictation accuracy is to read additional training session stories to your computer. You should read at least three to five stories. Do this by clicking **Tools**, **Current User**, and double-checking to see if your user profile name has a check mark by it. Then, click **Tools**, **Training** from the Language Bar and follow the onscreen instructions.

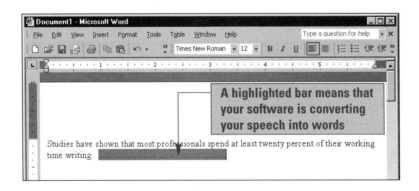

A highlighted bar means that your software is converting your speech into words

Studies have shown that most professionals spend at least twenty percent of their working time writing.

FIGURE C-28
Continue Talking Even If Your Words Don't Appear Instantly

appendix
C

During the next steps, don't be overly concerned about making mistakes. You learn some powerful ways to correct mistakes in the next few exercises. For now, experiment and see what happens.

Step-by-Step C.9

Step 1	Open **Microsoft Word** and the **Language Bar**, if necessary. Don't forget to select your user profile.
Step 2	Turn on the **Microphone**, switch to **Dictation mode**, and read this short selection into Microsoft Word. ***Dictation*** ***Studies have shown that most professionals spend at least twenty percent of their working time writing <period> You can use speech recognition software to help you in any career you choose <period> Microsoft speech can be used in the medical <comma> legal <comma> financial <comma> and educational professions <period>*** ***Microphone***
Step 3	Examine your paragraph. How well did you do? Count the mistakes or word errors. How many errors did you make?
Step 4	Now delete all the text on your screen. Start by turning on the **Microphone** and then switching to **Voice Command** mode by saying (remember to pause briefly after each command): ***Voice Command*** ***Edit*** ***Select All*** ***Backspace***
Step 5	Repeat the selection from Step 2. This time, say any word that gave you difficulty a little more clearly. See if your computer understands more of what you say this time around.
Step 6	Did you improve? Yes/No
Step 7	Delete all the text on your screen again before you continue, using the ***Voice Command, Edit, Select All, Backspace*** commands.

Using the New Line and New Paragraph Commands

In this next set of exercises, you have a chance to use the New Line and New Paragraph commands to organize text. These essential commands allow you to control the look and feel of your documents. (See Figure C-29.) It helps to pause briefly before and after you say each command.

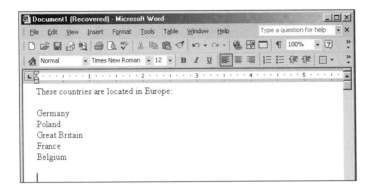

FIGURE C-29
New Line and New
Paragraph Commands
Organize Text

Step-by-Step C.10

Step 1	The New Line and New Paragraph commands help organize lists of information. Dictate the following list of European countries. Turn on the **Microphone**, if necessary, and say: ***Dictation*** ***These countries are located in Europe <colon> <New Paragraph>*** ***Germany <New Line>*** ***Poland <New Line>*** ***Great Britain <New Line>*** ***France <New Line>*** ***Belgium <New Paragraph>***
Step 2	Save the file in the Save As dialog box with the ***Voice Command, File, Save As*** commands.
Step 3	Click your mouse in the **File name:** text box and enter ***Countries of Europe*** as the filename. (*Note:* If you speak the filename, remember to switch to Dictation mode.)
Step 4	Close the Save As dialog box with the ***Voice Command, Save*** commands, and then clear your screen by saying ***Edit, Select All, Backspace.***

Using Undo

Microsoft Office Speech Recognition offers powerful ways to make corrections and train the software to recognize difficult words, so they appear correctly when you say them again. For example, erasing mistakes is easy with the Undo command. That's the first trick you learn in this section.

The Undo command works like pressing the Undo button or clicking Edit, Undo with your mouse. You can quickly erase the problem when you misspeak. All you need to do is switch to Voice Command mode and say ***Undo.***

Q U I C K   T I P

Say the word *Colon* to create a (:).

Q U I C K   T I P

When dictating words in a list, it helps to pause slightly before and after saying the commands, as in *<pause> New Line <pause>* and *<pause> New Paragraph <pause>*.

appendix
C

Step-by-Step C.11

| Step 1 | In this step, say the name of the academic subject, then erase it immediately with the Undo command and replace it with the next subject in the list. Erase the subject regardless of whether it is correct. Switch to Voice Command mode before saying Undo. |

Dictation

Biology	*Voice Command*	*Undo*	*Dictation*
French	*Voice Command*	*Undo*	*Dictation*
American history	*Voice Command*	*Undo*	*Dictation*

| Step 2 | The Undo command deletes the last continuous phrase you have spoken. Say each of the following phrases, then use Undo to erase them. |

To infinity and beyond	*Voice Command*	*Undo*	*Dictation*
The check is in the mail	*Voice Command*	*Undo*	*Dictation*
Money isn't everything	*Voice Command*	*Undo*	
Microphone			

Correcting Errors

Correcting mistakes is obviously important. There are several ways to make corrections effectively.

Because speech recognition software recognizes phrases better than individual words, one of the best ways to correct a mistake is to use your mouse to select the phrase where the mistake occurs and then repeat the phrase. For example, in the sentence below the software has keyed the word *share* instead of the word *sure*. Select the phrase (like the boldface example) with your mouse, then say the phrase again:

What you should select: You sound **very share of yourself**.
What you would repeat: **very sure of yourself**

If you still make a mistake, select the misspoken word with your mouse and take advantage of the power of the **Correction** button on the Language Bar. Carefully read through these steps and then practice what you learned in Step 5.

Step-by-Step C.12

Step 1	If you make an error, select the mistake, as shown in Figure C-30.
Step 2	With your microphone on, say *Correction* or click the Correction button with your mouse.
Step 3	If the correct alternative appears in the correction list, click the correct alternative with your mouse.

CAUTION TIP

A common speech mistake occurs when speakers break words into syllables. For example, they may say **speak keen clear lee** instead of **speaking clearly**.

QUICK TIP

A key to great accuracy in speech recognition is to speak in complete phrases and sentences. Complete sentences and phrases make it easier for the software to understand what you're trying to say. The software makes adjustments based on the context of the words that commonly appear together. The more words you say as a group or phrase, the more information your software has to work with.

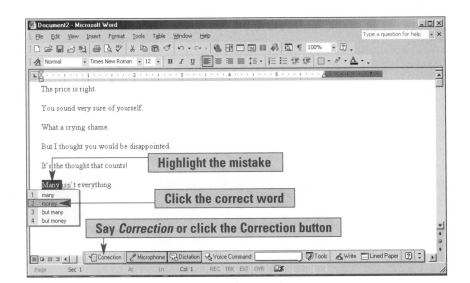

FIGURE C-30
Select the Mistake and
Say *Correction*

Step 4 | If the correct word does not appear, as in Figure C-31, key the
correct response with your keyboard.

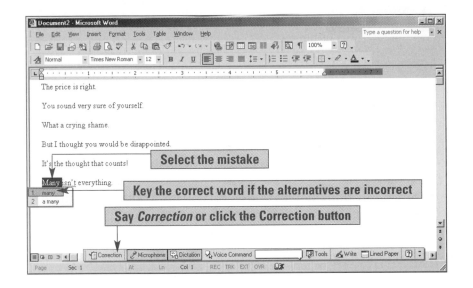

FIGURE C-31
If the Correct Word Doesn't
Appear, Key the Word

Step 5 | Now give it a try. Speak the following sentences. (*Hint:* Say the
complete sentence before you make any corrections.) Try to correct
the error first by repeating the phrase. Then, select individual word
errors and use the Correction button to help you fix any remaining
mistakes:
The price is right.
You sound very sure of yourself.
What a crying shame.
But, I thought you would be disappointed.
It's the thought that counts!
Money isn't everything.

appendix
C

Formatting Sentences

After you dictate text, you can format it, copy it, paste it, and manipulate it just like you would with a mouse. In this exercise, you dictate a few sentences, and then you change the font styles and make a copy of the sentences. That is a lot to remember, so take a look at what you are about to accomplish. Review Figure C-32 to get a sneak preview of this activity.

FIGURE C-32
Dictate, Format, and Copy
and Paste These Lines

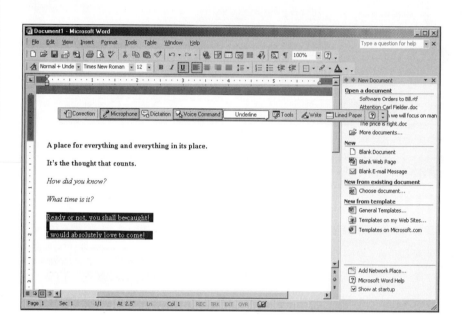

MOUSE TIP

When you correct a mistake using the Correction button, Microsoft Office Speech Recognition plays back what you said and remembers any corrections that you make. This helps to ensure that the software won't make the same mistake the next time you say the same word or phrase. Use the Correction button as often as you can. This helps to improve your speech recognition accuracy.

A few quick reminders before you begin:

- Use your mouse and voice together to bold, italicize, and underline text.
- Say the basic punctuation marks, exclamation point/mark (!), period (.), comma (,), question mark (?), semicolon (;), colon (:).
- Start a new line with the New Paragraph command.

Step-by-Step C.13

Step 1	Speak the following sentences, using the New Paragraph command to space between each. Do not pause in the middle of any sentence. If you make mistakes, correct them using the Correction button, as explained in Step-by-Step C.12.

Dictation
A place for everything and everything in its place.
It's the thought that counts.
How did you know?
What time is it?
Ready or not, you shall be caught!
I would absolutely love to come!

| Step 2 | With your mouse, select the first two sentences and make them bold with the following commands:
Voice Command
Bold |

| Step 3 | Select the two questions and italicize them by saying:
Italic |

| Step 4 | Select the final two exclamatory sentences and underline them by saying:
Underline |

| Step 5 | Copy all the text on your screen and paste a copy at the bottom of your document by saying:
Edit
Select All
Copy
Down Arrow
Paste |

| Step 6 | Print your document with the following commands:
File
Print
OK |

| Step 7 | Close your document without saving using the ***File***, ***Close*** command and then say ***No*** when you are asked to save. |

| Step 8 | Open a new document with your voice with the ***File***, ***New***, ***Blank Document*** commands and turn off your ***Microphone*** before you continue. |

Adding and Training Names

Your speech software can remember what you teach it as long as you follow these simple steps. When you click Add/Delete Word(s) from the Tools menu, the Add/Delete Word(s) dialog box opens. This is a very powerful tool. It allows you to enter a name or any other word or phrase, click the **Record pronunciation** button, and record your pronunciation of the word or phrase.

Step-by-Step C.14

| Step 1 | Click **Tools**, **Add/Delete Word(s)** from the Language Bar, as shown in Figure C-33. |

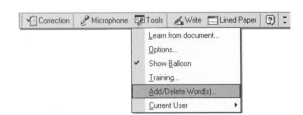

FIGURE C-33
Click the Add/Delete Word(s) Option

appendix
C

| Step 2 | Enter your name into the **Word** text box as shown in Figure C-34. |

FIGURE C-34
Enter Your Name in the
Word Text Box

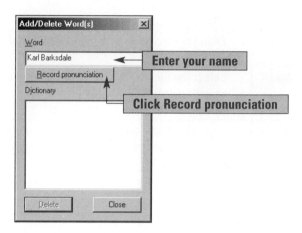

QUICK TIP

If your speech recognition software doesn't hear you properly, your name does not appear in the Dictionary. If this happens, try again. When the system has accepted your pronunciation of the word, the name appears in the Dictionary.

| Step 3 | Click the **Record pronunciation** button and say your name aloud. |
| Step 4 | Your name appears in the Dictionary list. Double-click your name to hear a digitized voice repeat your name. (See Figure C-35.) |

FIGURE C-35
Add/Delete Word(s)
Dialog Box

CAUTION TIP

If your name doesn't appear properly when you say it, return to the Add/Delete Word(s) dialog box, select your name, then click the **Record pronunciation** button and re-record the correct pronunciation of your name.

Step 5	Close the Add/Delete Word(s) dialog box by clicking the **Close** button.
Step 6	Return to Microsoft Word, turn on your **Microphone**, switch to **Dictation** mode. Say your name several times and see if it appears correctly.
Step 7	To improve your accuracy, it's important to add troublesome words to your dictionary. Pick five words that have given you difficulty in the past. Train the software to recognize these words as explained in Steps 1 through 6. As you add and train for the pronunciation of those words, your accuracy improves bit by bit.

C.d Turning Microsoft Speech Recognition On and Off

Microsoft Office Speech Recognition isn't for everybody—at least not in its present form. It requires a powerful CPU and a lot of RAM. It also takes a quality headset. If you don't have the necessary hardware, chances are speech recognition isn't working very well for you.

Perhaps you are simply uncomfortable using speech software. You may be an expert typist with no sign of carpal tunnel syndrome or any other repetitive stress injury. Whatever your reason for choosing not to use Microsoft speech software, it is important to know how to disable the feature.

There are two ways to turn off your speech software. You can minimize the toolbar and place it aside temporarily, or you can turn it off entirely. If you decide you want to use speech recognition at a later time, you can always turn it back on again.

Turning Off Speech Recognition

Microsoft Speech Recognition allows you to minimize the Language Bar, putting it aside temporarily. Minimizing places the Language Bar in the taskbar tray in the form of the Language Bar icon. After the Language Bar has been minimized, it is then possible to turn the system off altogether. To see how this is accomplished, follow Step-by-Step C.15.

Step-by-Step C.15

Step 1	Open **Microsoft Word** and the **Language Bar**, if necessary.
Step 2	Click the **Minimize** button on the Language Bar, as shown in Figure C-36.

Minimize

FIGURE C-36
Click the Minimize Button on the Language Bar

appendix
C

Step 3 When you minimize for the first time, a dialog box explains what is going to happen to your Language Bar, as shown in Figure C-37. Read this dialog box carefully, then click **OK**.

FIGURE C-37
Read This
Information Carefully

Step 4 Right-click the **Language Bar** icon in the taskbar. Several options appear, as shown in Figure C-38. Click **Close the Language Bar**.

FIGURE C-38
Right-Click the Language
Bar Icon

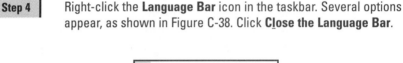

Step 5 Another dialog box opens to explain a process you can follow for restoring your speech operating system after you have turned it off. Click **OK**. The system is turned off and your language tools disappear, as shown in Figure C-39. Close Word. (*Note:* If you click **Cancel**, you return to normal and can continue using the speech recognition system by opening the Language Bar.)

FIGURE C-39
Click OK to Turn Off
Speech Recognition

Turning On Speech Recognition

There are several ways to turn your speech recognition system back on. Follow Step-by-Step C.16.

Step-by-Step C.16

| Step 1 | Open **Microsoft Word** and click **Speech** on the **Tools** menu, as shown in Figure C-40. Your speech recognition software is restored and you can begin using it again. |

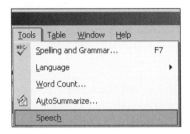

FIGURE C-40
Click Speech on the Tools Menu

If your speech software did not restore itself after Step 1, continue with Steps 2 through 5.

| Step 2 | Click the **Start** button, **Settings**, **Control Panel**. Then double-click the **Text Services** icon to open the Text Services dialog box, as shown in Figure C-41. |

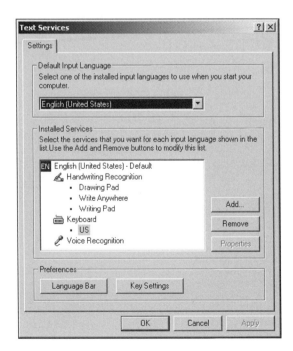

FIGURE C-41
Click Language Bar in the Text Input Settings Dialog Box

appendix
C

| Step 3 | Click **Language Bar** in the Text Services dialog box. |

| Step 4 | In the Language Bar Settings dialog box, click the **Show the Language bar on the desktop** check box to insert a check mark, as shown in Figure C-42. |

FIGURE C-42
Language Bar Settings
Dialog Box

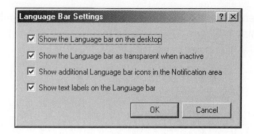

| Step 5 | Click **OK**, then exit and restart your computer. The speech software should be restored and you can begin speaking again. (*Note:* If the Language Bar is still missing after you launch Word, try selecting Tools, Speech one more time.) |

Mastering and Using Excel 2002

APPROVED COURSEWARE

Core MOUS Objectives

Standardized Coding Number	Skill Sets and Skills Being Measured	Chapter Number	Chapter Pages	Exercise Pages	Exercises
Ex2002-1	**Working with Cells and Cell Data**				
Ex2002-1-1	Insert, delete, and move cells	3 4	EI 46–49 EI 68, 84	EI 66 EI 91–96	Skills Review 8 Skills Review 1, 2, 4, 6, 7 Case Projects 1, 3–7
Ex2002-1-2	Enter and edit cell data including text, numbers, and formulas	2 3 4	EI 28–32 EI 43–44, 50, 52, 53–57 EI 72–75	EI 38–41 EI 62–66 EI 91–96	Skills Review 1, 2, 4–8 Case Projects 1–8 Skills Review 1–4, 6, 7 Case Projects 1, 2, 5, 6, 8 Skills Review 1–4, 6, 7 Case Projects 1, 3–7
Ex2002-1-3	Check spelling	5	EI 99–101	EI 117	Skills Review 3
Ex2002-1-4	Find and replace cell data and formats	5 6	EI 98–99 EI 136–137	EI 117 EI 141–142	Skills Review 3 Skills Review 1, 3
Ex2002-1-5	Work with a subset of data by filtering lists	4	EI 86–87	EI 91, 96	Skills Review 1 Case Project 6
Ex2002-2	**Managing Workbooks**				
Ex2002-2-1	Manage workbook files and folders	1	EI 6–7, 13	EI 23–25	Skills Review 1, 2, 4–8 Case Project 2
Ex2002-2-2	Create workbooks using templates	1	EI 17–19	EI 23, 25	Skills Review 3 Case Project 4
Ex2002-2-3	Save workbooks using different names and file formats	1	EI 14–15, 17	EI 23–25	Skills Review 1–8 Case Project 4

Standardized Coding Number	Skill Sets and Skills Being Measured	Chapter Number	Chapter Pages	Exercise Pages	Exercises
Ex2002-3	*Formatting and Printing Worksheets*				
Ex2002-3-1	Apply and modify cell formats	4	EI 70–79	EI 91–96	Skills Review 1–8 Case Projects 1–7
Ex2002-3-2	Modify row and column settings	4	EI 82, 84–86	EI 92, 94–96	Skills Review 2, 7 Case Projects 3, 4, 6
Ex2002-3-3	Modify row and column formats	4	EI 72, 82–84	EI 91–96	Skills Review 1, 2, 4–8 Case Projects 1–7
Ex2002-3-4	Apply styles	4	EI 80–82	EI 94–95	Skills Review 8
Ex2002-3-5	Use automated tools to format worksheets	4	EI 70–71	EI 92	Skills Review 3
Ex2002-3-6	Modify Page Setup options for worksheets	5	EI 102–112	EI 116–119	Skills Review 1–4, 6–8 Case Projects 2–4, 6–8
Ex2002-3-7	Preview and print worksheets and workbooks	1 5	EI 16–17 EI 102, 108–113	EI 23–24 EI 116–119	Skills Review 1–5, 8 Skills Review 1–4 Case Projects 2–4, 6–8
Ex2002-4	*Modifying Workbooks*				
Ex2002-4-1	Insert and delete worksheets	1	EI 11, 13	EI 23–24	Skills Review 4, 5, 6
Ex2002-4-2	Modify worksheet names and positions	1 2	EI 11–13 EI 34–35	EI 23–24 EI 39–41	Skills Review 2, 6 Skills Review 3, 6, 7 Case Projects 3, 4, 8
Ex2002-4-3	Use 3-D references	3	EI 58–59	EI 64–65	Skills Review 7, 8
Ex2002-5	*Creating and Revising Formulas*				
Ex2002-5-1	Create and revise formulas	3	EI 43–44, 49–51	EI 62–66	Skills Review 1, 4, 7 Case Projects 1, 8
Ex2002-5-2	Use statistical, date and time, financial, and logical functions in formulas	3	EI 50–59	EI 62–66	Skills Review 1, 7 Case Projects 1, 2, 6
Ex2002-6	*Creating and Modifying Graphics*				
Ex2002-6-1	Create, modify, position, and print charts	6	EI 121–127, 129–132	EI 141–144	Skills Review 1, 3–8 Case Projects 1, 3–8
Ex2002-6-2	Create, modify, and position graphics	6	EI 127–128	EI 141–144	Skills Review 3 Case Project 3
Ex2002-7	*Workgroup Collaboration*				
Ex2002-7-1	Convert worksheets into Web pages	6	EI 135–136	EI 142, 144	Skills Review 6 Case Project 7
Ex2002-7-2	Create hyperlinks	6	EI 133–134	EI 143, 144	Skills Review 8 Case Project 4
Ex2002-7-3	View and edit comments	6	EI 132–133, 134–135	EI 143–144	Skills Review 7 Case Projects 1, 8

Index

F

F1 (Help) shortcut key, OF 12, OF 15

Favorites
  dialog box, OF 42
  folder, OF 41
  menu, OF 42
  shortcuts, OF 40, OF 41, OF 42

file management, EI 13–14

filename, EI 14
  extension, EI 7

files, managing with voice commands, AP 33

fill handle, EI 45–46

filler list, EI 86–87

Financial function
  Fv, EI 56
  npr, EI 56
  PMT, EI 55–56
  rate, EI 56
  type, EI 56

find, EI 98–99

Find and Replace dialog box, EI 98

folder management, EI 13–14

folders, managing with voice commands, AP 33, AP 35

font, EI 71–72
  chart, EI 125

font style, EI 71–72

footer, EI 106–107
  button, EI 107
  dialog box, EI 107

footnotes. *See* endnotes.

formal outlines, formatting, AP 17

format
  alignment of cell content, EI 72
  AutoFormats, EI 70–71
  axes, EI 125–126
  business documents, AP 12–20
  cell borders and shading, EI 76–77, EI 78
  chart, EI 124
  clear, EI 78–79
  decimal place, EI 75
  fonts and font style, EI 71–72
  formal outlines, AP 18
  Format Painter, EI 78
  indent, rotate, and wrap text, EI 75–76
  letters, AP 13–14
  number format, EI 72–74
  toolbar, EI 4, EI 5, EI 6, OF 5, OF 7,
    OF 22–25, OF 32

Format Cells dialog box, EI 74

Format Painter, EI 78

formula
  3-D references in, EI 58
  bar, EI 5, EI 31–32, EI 44
  copy, EI 45
    AutoSum function, EI 52–53
    basic functions, EI 50–51
    copy and paste, EI 45
    fill handle, EI 45–46
    SUM function, EI 51–52
    with relative, absolute, and mixed cell
      references EI 49–50
  create and revise, EI 43
    edit, EI 44
    enter, EI 43–44
    syntax and rules of precedence, EI 43
  link, EI 58

S

Save As command, EI 14–15

save
   Web page, EI 135–136
   workbook, EI 13–16

Save command, EI 15–16

scaling, EI 104–105

ScreenTip, OF 7, OF 13

scroll, OF 8

scroll bar, EI 4
   resize, EI 13

search
   engines, OF 42
   options, OF 28

Search button, OF 42

Search task pane, OF 27, OF 28

selected value, EI 31

selecting, AP 8

sentences, formatting with speech
   recognition, AP 42

serial numbers, EI 53

server, OF 38

shading, EI 76–77

sheet tab, EI 4
   change color, EI 35
   in Page Setup dialog box, EI 108
   move, EI 12
   rename EI 34–35

SHIFT + F1 shortcut, OF 12, OF 13, OF 15

shortcuts
   ALT + F4 (close application), OF 14
   F1 (help), OF 12, OF 15
   Favorites, OF 40, OF 41, OF 42
   for Toolbars menu, OF 25, OF 26
   hyperlinks, OF 28
   keyboard, OF 8, OF 12, OF 21
   menu, AP 8
   menu, OF 25
   SHIFT + F1 (What's This?), OF 12, OF 13,
      OF 15
   task pane, OF 7, OF 10
   to Web page, OF 42

Show Smart Tag Actions button, OF 31

single-click environment, AP 8

Size command, OF 6

sizing handle, EI 128

slide, OF 3, OF 10

Smart Tags, OF 20, OF 32
   adding, OF 31
   removing, OF 31
   reviewing, OF 30–31, OF 32

software suite, OF 3

speech recognition, OF 4, AP 21–48
   adding and training names in,
      AP 43–44
   adjust audio settings for, AP 30
   correcting errors in, AP 40–41, AP 42
   Dictionary, AP 44
   formatting sentences in, AP 42
   highlighted bar in, AP 37
   installing, AP 23–29
   microphone quality check, AP 26
   restoring software in, AP 47

training software for, AP 27–29

training your system for, AP 24–26

turning on and off, AP 45–48

use of context in, AP 40

user profile for, AP 24

using New Line command in, AP 38–39

using New Paragraph command in, AP 38–39

using Undo in, AP 39

spell check, EI 99

  AutoCorrect, EI 99–100

  spell checker, EI 101

spell checker, EI 101

  dialog box, EI 101

spider, OF 42

spreadsheet, EI 3, OF 3

Standard toolbar, AP 6, EI 4, EI 5, EI 6, OF 5, OF 7, OF 22–25, OF 31, OF 40

Start button/menu, AP 2, AP 3, AP 7, OF 5, OF 7, OF 8, OF 15

start page, OF 39

status bar, EI 4, EI 6, OF 40

style guides, using, AP 18

styles, EI 80

  copy, EI 81

  define and apply, EI 80–82

  dialog box, EI 81

  remove, EI 82

  See also font styles.

SUM function, EI 51–52

syntax, EI 43

system resources, accessing, AP 4–6

T

table, EI 126–127

tab scrolling buttons, EI 4, EI 6

tabs, AP 8

task pane, EI 4, OF 3, OF 5, OF 7, OF 10, OF 26

  closing, OF 30

  docking, OF 20

  floating, OF 29

  list of available, OF 27–30, OF 32

  resizing, OF 29

  shortcuts on, OF 7, OF 10

  working with, OF 27–30, OF 32

Task Pane command, OF 10

taskbar, OF 5, OF 7

template, EI 17–19

Temporary Internet Files folder, OF 41

text

  copying and pasting with speech recognition, AP 42–44

  formatting with speech recognition, AP 42–44

tick mark, EI 124

title

  bar, AP 4, AP 8, EI 5, OF 5, OF 40

  print, EI 111

to do list, OF 3

toolbar

  Formatting, EI 4, EI 5, EI 6

  Options, EI 6

  Print Preview, EI 16

  Standard, EI 4, EI 5, EI 6

toolbar buttons, adding, AP 6

exit, EI 19

locate, EI 6–7

open, EI 6–7

preview, EI 97–119

print, EI 112, EI 113

save, EI 13–16

   manage file and folder, EI 13–14

   Save As command, EI 14–15

   Save command, EI 15–16

Web page, EI 135–136

workgroup collaboration, EI 132

worksheet, EI 3, EI 4–5, OF 3

active worksheet, EI 4

add, EI 11

AutoFormats, EI 70–71

build, EI 42–66

copy, EI 11–13

create from template, EI 17–19

delete, EI 11–13

enhance, EI 67–96

enter and edit data, EI 26–41

move, EI 11–13

navigate, EI 8–9

preview, EI 16–17, EI 97–119

print, EI 16–17, EI 102–112

reposition, EI 11–13

select cell, column, and row, EI 9–11

title, create, EI 68–69

Web page, EI 135–136

wrap text, EI 75–76

World Wide Web (WWW), OF 37, OF 44

WWW. *See* World Wide Web.

X

x86 computer, OF 4

XP. *See* Microsoft Office XP.

Y

Yahoo, OF 43

Z

zoom, EI 34